Establishing Boundaries

Christian-Jewish Relations in Early Council Texts and the Writings of Church Fathers

By

F.J.E. Boddens Hosang

BRILL

LEIDEN • BOSTON
2010

BM
535
.B585
2010

 Bar-Ilan University, Israel

 University of Tilburg: Faculty of Catholic Theology,
The Netherlands

PThU Protestant Theological University, Kampen, The Netherlands

Schechter Institute of Jewish Studies, Israel

Ingeborg Rennert Center for Jerusalem Studies, Israel

The editors gratefully acknowledge the financial support of the Ingeborg Rennert Center for Jerusalem Studies.

This book is printed on acid-free paper.

Library of Congress Cataloging-in-Publication Data

Boddens Hosang, F.J.E.
   Establishing boundaries : Christian-Jewish relations in early council texts and the writings of Church Fathers / by F.J.E. Boddens Hosang.
      p. cm. — (Jewish and Christian perspectives series, ISSN 1388-2074 ; v. 19)
   Includes bibliographical references and index.
   ISBN 978-90-04-18255-4 (hardback : alk. paper) 1. Christianity and other religions—Judaism. 2. Judaism—Relations—Christianity. 3. Theology, Doctrinal—History—Early church, ca. 30–600. 4. Christian literature, Early—History and criticism. I. Title. II. Series.

   BM535.B585 2010
   261.2'609015—dc22

                                                                    2009050332

ISSN   1388-2074
ISBN   978 90 04 18255 4

Establishing Boundaries

Jewish and Christian Perspectives Series

VOLUME 19

CONTENTS

EDITORIAL STATEMENT

Judaism and Christianity share much of a heritage. There has been a good deal of interest in this phenomenon lately, examining both the common heritage, as well as the elements unique to each religion. There has, however, been no systematic attempt to present findings relative to both Jewish and Christian tradition to a broad audience of scholars. It is the purpose of the Jewish and Christian Perspectives Series to do just that.

Jewish and Christian Perspectives publishes studies that are relevant to both Christianity and Judaism. The series will include works relating to the Hebrew Bible and New Testament, the Second Temple period, the Judaeo-Christian polemic (from Ancient until Modern times), Rabbinical literature relevant to Christianity, Patristics, Medieval Studies and the Modern period. Special interest will be paid to the interaction between the religions throughout the ages. Historical, exegetical, philosophical and theological studies are welcomed as well as studies focusing on sociological and anthropological issues common to both religions including archaeology.

The series is published in co-operation with the Bar-Ilan University and the Schechter Institute in Israel, and the Faculty of Catholic Theology of the Tilburg University in the Netherlands. It includes monographs and congress volumes in the English language, and is intended for international distribution on a scholarly level.

Detailed information on forthcoming congresses, calls for papers, and the possibility of organizing a JCP conference at your own institution, can be obtained at: *www.jcperspectives.com.*

ACKNOWLEDGEMENTS

This book initially saw the light as a PhD thesis, defended in Tilburg, the Netherlands, in September 2008. When starting the research as part of the requirements for attaining an MA in Theology, it was not yet clear that the investigation would develop into a doctoral thesis. Obviously, there were times, over the past year or so, when I wished it had not!

The initial idea was launched by Dr. Marcel Poorthuis, of the Research Institute for Jewish-Christian Relations at the Faculty of Catholic Theology in Utrecht. His enthusiasm only stimulated my own tentative steps in the field of Christian-Jewish relations. Several people who had shown an interest in the project encouraged me to continue. Firstly, I would like to thank Professor Gerard Rouwhorst without whose unfailing support this project would never have materialized. His kind encouragement, interest in the results I carefully put before him, and precise analysis of the difficulties I encountered, turned my incoherence into a presentable discussion. Needless to say, the failings and shortcomings in the following pages are mine alone and may indicate how incomplete the understanding of early Christian relations with Judaism still is. It was Professor Paul van Geest who guided me through the minefield of patristic sources and how to deal with the seemingly irreconcilable difficulties in comparing the writings of church fathers and council texts. His advice and unfailing belief in this project and in me meant I could continue where many would have given up.

The financial basis for the years of research was provided for by LJM Stichting, for which I am deeply grateful. Much practical help was given through the kindness of the librarians of the Koninklijke Bibliotheek (Royal Library) in The Hague. My constant badgering for books they never realized they had must have been frustrating yet it was in their reading rooms that this project came into being. Mrs. Isobel Wallace has read the manuscript and patiently corrected the English. I am deeply indebted to her precise work. Similarly, many thanks for the suggestions and corrections made by my brother, J.F.R. Boddens Hosang MA, Deputy Director of Legal Affairs of the Netherlands Ministry of Defence.

Kind recognition should also be given to my bishop, Mgr. A.H. van Luyn sdb, whose personal interest in the project, further supported by financial help from the diocese, encouraged me to investigate the relevance of the topic for Christian-Jewish relations today. It is promising to see that simple contacts between the youth of the synagogue and the youngsters of our local parish can only mean that these young people may grow up without the usual lack of understanding of the other. That this misunderstanding can lead to prejudice, and even worse, we know only too well. The conclusion of one of the parish youth only underlines this when he said: "they really are very much like us, aren't they?"

Finally, I would like to thank my parents whose unfailing interest in this project encouraged me to continue, if not for myself or the topic at hand, then at least for them. I would like to dedicate this to my mother and father who unfortunately never saw the finalization of this work, yet whose discussions and questions over the years pointed me forward where I could only look back.

Elizabeth Boddens Hosang
October 2009

ABBREVIATIONS

AJA   American Journal of Archaeology (Archaeological Institute of America Norwood, 1897).

CAH   Cambridge Ancient History (Cambridge University Press, 1923).

CCH   La Colección Canónica Hispana (Ed. Martínez Díez, G. and Rodríguez, F.; Monumenta Hispaniae Sacra Ser. Canónica Madrid, 1966–1984) 4 vols.

CCSG   Corpus Christianorum Series Graeca (Brepols Turnhout, 1977–).

CCSL   Corpus Christianorum Series Latina (Brepols Turnhout, 1953–).

CIJ   Corpus Inscriptionum Iudaicarum (Ed. Frey, J.-B.; Pontif. Istit. di Archeologia Cristiana Vaticano, 1936–1952) 2 vols.

CPG   Clavis Patrum Graecorum (volume of CCSG; Gerard, M., 1983–1998).

CPL   Clavis Patrum Latinorum (volume of CCSL; Dekkers, E., 1995).

CSEL   Corpus Scriptorum Ecclesiasticorum Latinorum (Hölder-Pichler-Tempsky Vienna, 1866–).

DDC   Dictionnaire de Droit Canonique (Letouzey et Ané Paris, 1935–1965).

DHGE   Dictionnaire d'Histoire et de Géographie Ecclésiastiques (Letouzey et Ané Paris, 1963).

DTC   Dictionnaire de Théologie Catholique (Letouzey et Ané Paris, 1920).

EncEC Encyclopedia of the Early Church 2 volumes (Ed. Di Berardino, A.; James Clarke and Co. Cambridge, 1992).

EJ   Encyclopedia Judaica (Ed. Skolnik, F.; 2nd ed., Macmillan Reference USA, 2007).

JBL   Journal of Biblical Literature (Society of Biblical Literature Middletown/Philadelphia, 1887).

JECS   Journal of Early Christian Studies (Johns Hopkins University Press, 1993–).

JQR   Jewish Quarterly Review (Dropsie University for Hebrew Philadelphia, 1888, NS 1910).

JRS Journal of Roman Studies (Society for the Promotion of Roman Studies London, 1911).

JTS Journal of Theological Studies (Clarendon Press London, 1899).

LCL Loeb Classical Library (Heinemann London, 1912).

LMitt. Lexikon des Mittelalters (Ed. Auty, A.; Artemis-Verlag München, 1980–1999).

LThK Lexikon für Theologie und Kirche (Herder Freiburg/Basel/ Rome/Vienna, 1993–2001).

MAMA Monumenta Asiae Minoris Antiqua (Manchester University Press/London Society for the Promotion of Roman Studies, 1928–) 10 vols.

ODCC Oxford Dictionary of the Christian Church (Ed. Cross, F.L.; Oxford University Press, 2005).

PG Patrologiae cursus completus Series Graeca (Ed. Migne, J.-P.; Garnier Paris, 1857–).

PL Patrologiae cursus completus Series Latina (Ed. Migne, J.-P.; Garnier Paris, 1857–).

RAC Reallexikon für Antike und Christentum (Hiersemann Stuttgart, 1970).

REJ Revue des Etudes Juives (Sorbonne VI Paris, 1880).

SC Sources Chrétiennes (Ed. Du Cerf Paris, 1941).

TRE Theologische Realenzyklopädie (De Gruyter Berlin 1977– 2004).

VC Vigiliae Christianae (Ed. Mohrmann, C.A.E.M.; Brill Leiden, 1947–).

Rabbinic Texts

(M) Mishnah
(BT) Babylonian Talmud
(PT) Jerusalem Talmud
(T) Tosefta
(Midr) Midrash

INTRODUCTION

1 *Fourth Century Developments*

'(…) between 311 and 325, the short period separating Galerius' Edict of Toleration and the Council of Nicea, the age-old protectors of the Roman Empire had been dismissed and replaced by the God of the Christians espoused by Constantine. Traditions that had governed ideas and actions of rulers and subjects alike for hundreds if not thousands of years were yielding to new values hitherto regarded as dangerous to the state.'[1]

The eminent scholar of early church history, Frend, wrote this in 1984. It would however be oversimplifying the issue by stating that everything changed in the fourth century.

Although the emperor Constantine showed a clear preference for Christianity, there was no formal break with paganism in his policy either. It is clear that Constantine's 'conversion' in 312 did not result in the immediate Christianization of the Roman Empire.[2]

In general one may note that from the fourth century onwards the Christianization of society was a slow but steady process. After all, when persecutions ended the Church was favored in many ways. The clergy, for instance, were exempt from jury duty. There seems to have been no great outcry from the pagan population, which included high-ranking officials such as senators. The emperor showed his interest in church issues in other ways. He became involved through church councils.[3] These dealt with issues concerning the identity of the church and its relations to those considered to be outsiders.

The question is then what was the effect of the rise of Christianity on its relations to other religious groups, and especially the religion it had sprung from—Judaism. Did the fact that the Empire became increasingly Christianised have an effect on relations with the Jews—at the official level of state and church? What was the effect at the level of

---

[1] Frend (1984) p. 474.
[2] Millar (1992) p. 103.
[3] E.g. the council of Nicea which was summoned by Constantine in 325: Cameron (2005) p. 98.

the ordinary faithful—now that Christians were less and less a minority? Would the increasing awareness of their identity make Christians more or less tolerant towards the Jews in comparison, for example, to their attitude towards pagans? At the official level, we see that legislation turned against non-(orthodox) believers. Paganism became a direct target in the missionary zeal of the church. However, by the sixth century state and church legislation had turned against Jews in particular.[4]

What was the situation like for relations between the Christian and Jewish faithful—on all levels? The question concerning the rise of Christianity and its relations to Judaism is closely connected to the larger issue of the relations between the two faith groups in the first centuries.

2   Jews and Christians in the Scholarly Debate

The subject of relations between Jews and Christians has been the issue of heated debates amongst scholars.[5] Several questions have been posed concerning the relationship between Christianity and Judaism.[6] Discussions have focused on various themes; two major issues will be discussed here. These two major issues encompass most of the topics addressed by scholars on the subject of Jewish-Christian relations.

2.1   Judaism in Decline?

The first concerns the supposed decline in vitality of Judaism in the first centuries when Christianity grew and spread throughout the Mediterranean world. Adolf von Harnack in the early twentieth century was a major proponent of the idea that with Constantine Christianity not only reached its spiritual but also its political fulfilment.[7] Based mostly on Christian literature from the first centuries he came to the conclusion that Judaism after the fall of the Temple in Jerusalem in 70 CE was no longer a vital force. This is called the 'lachrymose theory'—a point

---

[4] Cf. *CTh* esp. ch. 16 and council rulings from the sixth century onwards; also: Brown (1998).

[5] Cf. Harnack (1906) vol. I; Safrai (1976) p. 349; Parkes (1979) ch. 5, pp. 151–196; id. (1964) pp. 69–79; Neusner (1987); Becker/Reed (2003) pp. 1–32 for a discussion of the publications on the subject.

[6] Cf. Becker/Reed (2003) pp. 1–32.

[7] Harnack (1906) vol. 1, pp. 220–239.

of view that Jewish history is centred on a series of persecutions and tribulations, with little or no positive developments to note. According to Harnack, a vital and universal Christianity no longer needed to deal with a religion as weak as Judaism had become—the Jews as mentioned in the Christian polemical texts were merely exemplary.[8]

It was especially Marcel Simon who attempted to move away from this 'lachrymose theory' by stating that after the years 70 and 135 CE, the Jews felt abandoned, but were they ready to sit among the ruins and cry? His answer was no.[9] To the contrary, Judaism was still a vital force to be reckoned with, actively seeking sympathizers and converts.[10] His point of view developed after the Second World War and was no doubt influenced by the tide of the times. His groundbreaking work attempted to dispel not only the so-called 'lachrymose theory' but also Harnack's supersessionist view, i.e. Christianity had replaced Judaism. Simon's pleas against these views were based on the theory of Jewish vitality. According to Simon, this vitality led to a conflict situation between Christianity and Judaism as both competed for converts.

Louis Feldman in his *Jew and Gentile in the Ancient World* focuses his attention on the relations between Jews and their *pagan* neighbors; however his tome includes implications for the relations between Jews and Christians as well.[11] In a train of thought similar to Simon's, Feldman argues that Judaism was a force to be reckoned with in late antiquity as it grew in strength and was a great attraction to many. Within the land of Israel, Feldman claims, the 'superficial Hellenization' of Jews meant the preservation of Judaism but also negative feelings against them, as they were considered anti-social. Judaism was strong and self confident, as seen in the diversity of existent groups (e.g. Pharisaism and many sects), and could thus withstand challenges such as Hellenism and Christianity, even converting non-Jews (p. 44). As examples of a strong Judaism outside the land of Israel, Feldman mostly depends on evidence from Egypt (ch. 2). His conclusion is that Jews in the Diaspora (i.e. Egypt) maintained their identity but created a certain bond with their surroundings, thus making it easier for outsiders to enter the faith (p. 83). In a later chapter (4) Feldman boldly states that due to its inherent strength and resistance to assimilation

---

[8] Harnack (1906) vol. 1, pp. 5–23; 48–79.
[9] Simon (1948) pp. 19 ff, 167–175.
[10] Simon (1948) pp. 316–355.
[11] Feldman (1993) *passim*.

with Hellenism, Judaism was hated by the masses. The Jews were aware of this but due to their privileges under Roman law knew that they would always be protected (p. 122). Despite the supposed hatred of Jews, the antiquity of their faith was greatly admired. Since pagans were interested in Judaism's supposed antiquity, Christianity sought to emphasize its continuity from Judaism, despite their differences in belief in Jesus of Nazareth. Jews were also admired for their wisdom (interpretation of dreams and knowledge of magic), courage, temperance, justice and piety, and Moses was considered an ideal leader. Judging from the aforementioned, it is therefore not surprising that outsiders would have been interested in Judaism. However, Feldman argues that it is not only outsiders' interest in Judaism, but also Jewish missionary activities which led to conversions. The supposed tremendous growth of the Jewish population in the first century, according to Feldman (ch. 9) can only be due to active missionary activities.[12] To further advance his cause, Feldman quotes a few ancient sources and uses a few Roman sources as evidence for resentment against Jewish proselytism.[13] According to this author, they were even expelled from Rome due to their proselytizing activities. In a word, according to Feldman no further argument is needed to show that the Jewish population grew due to their missionary work. Feldman provides a final example of this success by introducing the topic of the 'God-fearers' (ch. 10). As elsewhere, the author provides a long list of source material. These people were non-Jews who were attracted to Judaism and adopted many Jewish practices yet never really converted. They are also often described as 'sympathizers'.[14] Using pagan, Jewish, Christian, epigraphic and papyrological evidence, with special reference to the discoveries from Aphrodisias, arguments are brought forward for the existence of supposedly large numbers of sympathizers.[15]

---

[12] Feldman's demographic explanations are based on Baron in the *Encyclopaedia Judaica*, yet it is exactly Baron himself who cautions against relying too much on this, that one must be careful with numbers and even that decline is possible after 135 CE: Baron (2nd Ed., 2007) "Population" in the *Encyclopaedia Judaica*, p. 385. See also Rutgers (1995) esp. pp. 363–368.

[13] Ch. 9.4: the Letter of Aristeas, the Sibylline Oracles, 2 Macc. 9:17, 2 pseudepigraphic studies, Philo (whom he uses repeatedly), Josephus *Contra Apion*. 2 (LCL 186).

[14] Feldman (1993) p. 342 ff. See especially note 1 to chapter 10 for an extensive bibliography on the subject.

[15] Cf. Cohen (1999) who even argues that these 'God-fearers' may have existed only in some areas from which the evidence hails. Yet, it is necessary to emphasize that this

According to Feldman, proselytism continued in the third, fourth, and fifth centuries.[16] Evidence provided includes the references to non-Jews following Jewish practices as seen in Christian council texts, the Theodosian Code, and other secular laws (ch. 11). That Judaism was still strong after 425 CE, attracting followers, can be seen in the laws of Theodosius and Justinian. Discussions in the Talmud concerning conversions only underline this line of thought. Due to the strict rulings against conversions, it is possible that in late antiquity there were more sympathizers than actual converts (pp. 413–415).

Feldman offers an interesting new perspective on the relations between Jews and their neighbors in late antiquity. Judaism was still a force to deal with, even after 425 CE (Simon). Feldman shows that the so-called lachrymose theory is not applicable for the periods studied. It naturally follows that other groups would react to a strong Judaism—especially the Christian community.

Miriam Taylor published a review of Marcel Simon's 'conflict theory' based on a critical study of his arguments.[17] According to Taylor, the central argument of adherents to the conflict theory is that Jewish proselytism existed in the early centuries of the Common Era. Christianity would have been angered at continuing Jewish conversions. The adherents to this theory would even argue that the idea of using conversion by the Jesus movement came from Judaism and that proselytising is a natural religious instinct. Taylor argued against this by stating that active converting only happened in early Christianity and that Simon's argument that a religion is only strong when active in missionary activities is not true. There is very little information for Jewish proselytising activities (pp. 10–11).

According to Taylor, Simon and others[18] suggest that Judaism was either isolationist or aggressively proselytizing. She rightly asks whether there is nothing in between (p. 13). The author asks herself,

---

terminology may have been used by gentiles more easily than Jews themselves would have done—i.e., someone copying certain practices from Jews may have been called a 'God-fearer/sympathizer' but certainly not seen as such by the Jewish community itself (p. 170 ff). He also emphasizes that someone described as a "Judaizer" is usually so described by those outside the Jewish community. It depends on where you stand whether someone can be so labelled. It is, therefore, an internal (Christian) problem, according to Cohen, not due to external Jewish pressure, through active missionary activity (p. 195).

[16] Feldman (1993) pp. 342–416.
[17] Taylor (1995) p. 10 ff.
[18] Kraabel, Rokeah, Goodman, McKnight: cf. Taylor (1995) pp. 11–13.

who are these proselytes, and do Christians who take on Jewish practices actively fit the definition of proselyte (p. 14) and is then the existence of proselytes proof of Jewish missionary activity?

Taylor argues against the idea of Jewish missionary activity by stating that Christian texts do refer to conversions (Justin, Tertullian),
however, according to her these texts say more about the gentiles converting than about Jewish missionary activities (p. 15). Jewish views on
proselytism are more ambiguous, according to Taylor. Where Christianity would encourage people to join the faith in order to be saved,
Judaism believed that large-scale conversions would take place on the
'last day', not necessarily in the present time (pp. 17–19). Taylor's conclusion is that ancient Judaism was not isolationist, but certainly not
an active missionary religion either. In the second and third centuries,
a few rabbis encouraged followers to win converts, but these were few
(p. 20). Dividing it into several typologies, Taylor then continues her
analysis of Simon's conflict theory by examining early Christian texts
on Judaism.[19] In her conclusion, Taylor states that in the period following the Second World War it was necessary to reconsider Christian
anti-Judaism. In his re-evaluation of the statements made especially
by Harnack, Simon made a valuable attempt at setting certain ideas
straight. However, the flaw in his argument was that he saw post-70
CE Judaism as a missionary religion, only to succumb to the inherently more successful Christianity. This was contrary to Harnack's
view that the demise was much later and only after a genuine struggle.
Based mostly on early Christian writings, Taylor concludes that the
statements in the various texts were not related to a historical reality
but were based on a view the church had of itself. Its view on Judaism

---

[19] Typology I.1 polemical and apologetic anti-Judaism (how to explain that Christians accepted Jesus and Jews did not); I.2 defensive anti-Judaism (if Christians juda-
ized, the Jewish community must have been powerful); I.3 embittered anti-Judaism (a
reaction of the church to its failure to convert the Jews); II.2 reactive anti-Judaism (the
church was overawed by the powerful synagogue); II.2 strategic anti-Judaism (Christianity used anti-Judaism as a strategy in its rise to power); II.3 recriminatory anti-Judaism (church was oppressed by Jews); III.1 environmental anti-Judaism (Christianity
inherited pagan anti-Judaism); III.2 traditional anti-Judaism (Christian fathers' anti-
Judaism was based on exegesis, supersessionism a logical result); IV.1 theological anti-
Judaism (there is a theological basis for the anti-Jewish writings; this is the core of
Taylor's arguments against Simon and others); IV.2 re-affirmative anti-Judaism (in
its arguments against Marcion the Church actually used pre-Jewish arguments); IV.3
illustrative anti-Judaism (the corpus of anti-Jewish statements became an officially
sanctioned system of interpretation of the church over the centuries).

was based on its struggle towards supremacy where in the argument Judaism was considered 'evil and dark' while Christianity represented the good and light. If Christian anti-Judaism was part of the social and political situation, it would be time-bound. Yet, as we know, Christian anti-Judaism is unfortunately of all times. It is therefore, according to Taylor, part of the church's theological vision, part of its self-definition, intrinsic to its teachings, and thus remains relevant for re-evaluation in all periods (pp. 189–196).

Where Taylor opposes the view of a strongly missionary Judaism, Simon and Feldman actually propose that Jews *were* actively seeking converts. All, however, support the theory of a rather vibrant Judaism—even after the first century. It is in the period of growth of Christianity that Judaism needed to reconsider its own identity.[20]

Where most scholars discussed up to now would mainly use literary sources, Rutgers applies evidence from archeology to provide fresh new insight into the difficult issue of the relationship between Jews and their neighbors.[21]

Rutgers questions Feldman's arguments concerning the growth of Judaism in antiquity (ch. IX). He cautions against using numbers to provide evidence for this growth.[22] Should the numbers be correct, though, we still do not know what the cause was. An increase in the population could also be due to better living conditions, or the fact that Jews in antiquity were opposed to abortion, infanticide and contraception, for example (p. 203).

Another issue used by Feldman to underline his argument for active Jewish proselytism, is the expulsions of the Jews from Rome. That Jews were evicted from the city is known; yet, as Rutgers points out, the *reason* for the expulsions is not clear (p. 206). He concludes that there is evidence for conversion to Judaism in late antiquity, yet the actual examples are few and only incidental. Conversion probably only happened occasionally and incidentally (pp. 208–209). Feldman found further evidence for proselytism in the Theodosian Code where it is stated that measures should be taken against proselytizers. In reply to this theory, Rutgers rather sees these laws as a continuation from

---

[20] bYeb 47a on proselytes; cf. also Boyarin (2004); id. 'Semantic Differences; or, "Judaism"/"Christianity"' in: Becker/Reed (2003) pp. 65–85, esp. p. 71 ff; Schwartz (2001) *passim*.

[21] Rutgers (1998) *passim*.

[22] See note 12.

the age-old edict against Jews, mostly directed against the practice of circumcision more than anything else (pp. 209–219). In the Roman mind, all those who circumcised were Jews—whether genuinely so or not. Rutgers argues that the laws were more against circumcision than against the Jews as such. The Theodosian Code therefore attempts to protect slaves owned by Jews for fear they as well might be circumcised while in a Jewish household.

Based on textual evidence, Goodman concludes that proselytes were welcomed into Judaism, but that this is different from active missionary activity.[23] In the first century there was no incentive, no theological reason for Jews to attract proselytes. The situation seems to have changed somewhat in later centuries at the same time when the church started to seek converts.[24] At the least, various texts seem to suggest that conversion to Judaism continued in later periods, and rabbinic texts reacted to these conversions by offering solutions to deal with these proselytes.[25] By the third century the successful missionary activities of the church encouraged rabbis to re-establish the position of Judaism towards conversions. According to Goodman this did not mean that Jews suddenly developed extensive missionary activities but it seems likely that by this time they were more open to the possibility of gaining converts rather than actively seeking them out.[26]

Harnack's suggestion of a Judaism in decline is questioned by Simon. However, more importantly, the arguments are focussed on the question whether Judaism was an aggressively missionary religion (Simon, Feldman). This is denied by Taylor and Rutgers. Both Taylor and Rutgers rightly state that it is difficult to come to these conclusions based on the evidence provided. Taylor, however, suggests that it was not so much a question of Judaism developing in an aggressively missionary way, but more a question of Christianity developing its own identity. While developing its own identity, in the theological discussions it held Christianity turned against the faith it had sprung from, which was of course Judaism. Rutgers, using archeological material, also downplays Feldman's theory of a strongly missionary Judaism.

The question therefore remains—what was the situation which Christianity faced in the fourth century? Did Christians face a vital

---

[23] Goodman (2007) pp. 92–93.
[24] Goodman (2007) pp. 113–114.
[25] Goodman (1994) pp. 135–138.
[26] Goodman (1994) pp. 129–153.

and missionary Judaism which was attractive to Christians and which they felt they needed to compete with, as is suggested by certain church father texts? Did this image of an aggressive Judaism develop because of a genuine concern by church leaders? Or was it rather a reflection of a literary image of Judaism? Or was Judaism an introverted faith, only concerned with its own issues? As Christianity grew and found more political support, its relations towards Judaism necessarily needed to be reconsidered. The question is also whether the attitude of Christians towards Jews was different from that of pagan Romans before the Christianization of the Roman Empire.

2.2 *Parting of the Ways?*

The second issue is related and refers to the question of the 'parting of the ways' of Christianity and Judaism. Several questions arise. When did the parting of Christianity from Judaism take place? At what level? The classical view of a clear parting divided the rift between Christianity and Judaism into different, rather well-demarcated periods.[27]

The earliest period saw no division, Judaism and Christianity were one. The second period saw the development of Christian theology— Jesus as Son of God and the substitution theory of church replacing synagogue—leading to genuine, or supposed, tensions between Christians and Jews. This period is followed by Christianity developing into a separate sect, yet still remaining a minority group in the Roman Empire. Finally, the church becomes legal and eventually gains a dominant status. Harnack proposed as a date for the definite rift between Christianity and Judaism around 140 CE.[28] Various factors caused the final rift between Christianity and Judaism. These factors, according to Evans, include Christianity's aggressive gentile mission and its lenient entrance requirements, when compared to Judaism; the divinity of Jesus; and the nationalistic views of Judaism which, after 135 CE caused more discontent between gentile and Jewish Christianity.[29]

According to these views, the separation between Christianity and Judaism originated in the first or second centuries (70 or 135 CE).

---

[27] For example, see Porter/Pearson (2000) pp. 36–51 where the authors quote Paul's letter to the Galatians and Ignatius' Letter to the Magnesians in order to underline this idea.

[28] Harnack (1906) vol. I, p. 77.

[29] Evans (2000) pp. 203–235.

This classical view has more recently been discussed anew by those who would favor the fourth century as the moment of the parting of the ways.[30] This line of thought states that when Christianity became the religion of the majority, Judaism reconsidered its own position and became more aware of its identity. The question is whether either theory still holds true. It is quite possible that in the theories developed by church leaders in the first centuries a separation was deemed necessary or even mandatory, but what, realistically speaking, was the actual situation "on the ground" like? Was the situation the same for all regions—eastern and western Mediterranean? At what point is it possible to speak of a parting of the ways between Christianity and Judaism—and on what level?

Articles written by several authors and published in one volume by Becker and Reed provide an even more recent discussion on the issue of Christians and Jews in late antiquity.[31] Rather than arguing that Jews and Christians developed separately and that interaction from the second century was mostly polemical, these authors assert that there may not have been any parting as such until a much later date, perhaps even early Medieval times (p. 1 ff). The attempts by some leaders throughout late antiquity and early medieval times in trying to keep the groups separate show that a parting had not yet happened at all levels—that there still was some form of interaction between the two religious groups.[32] Statements made by church leaders show that until very late antiquity, even early Medieval times, there was no clear division between Christianity and Judaism.[33]

The question then arises of when the rupture happened, and what the situation was like when the Christianization of the Roman Empire, from the fourth century onwards, was established. What effect did this have on the relations between Christians and Jews, and at what level did the parting eventually take place?

When discussing the possible parting of the ways Leonard Rutgers makes an important distinction between 'culture' and 'religion'. His argument is whether the rupture is to be considered merely a religious

---

[30] Neusner (1987) *passim*; Stemberger (2000) *passim*; Boyarin (2004) *passim*.
[31] Becker/Reed (2003) *passim*.
[32] Becker/Reed (2003) pp. 22–24. For examples of this interaction see for example the article by Stökl Ben Ezra in this volume on fasting practices in late antiquity, pp. 259–282.
[33] Cf. the introduction, written by the editors.

issue, or also a cultural one—as far as any such division is at all possible. Rutgers notes that when referring to Judaism scholars usually do
not distinguish between Jewish culture and religion.[34] What probably
happened in antiquity was that people easily borrowed from others
what they wished to use, without a genuine desire to closely connect
to that religious group. This also happened in Judaism: Jews were
involved in many aspects of non-Jewish daily life (theatre, jobs etc.)
around them without wishing to appropriate the religion. He shows
that Jews were well integrated into late antique society. They used the
same workshops as pagans for their sarcophagi, their synagogues were
in accessible parts of the cities, and they held many different positions
in society (ch. III, IV, V). Archeological evidence shows that Jews were
buried in the same cemeteries as their gentile neighbors, spoke Greek,
had Greek names, yet would adhere to their Jewish religious practices
(ch. VI). For example, they could go to the theatre without paying
homage to the gods that usually accompanied such a visit. Jews were
found in different layers of society, they purchased from workshops
of mixed religious backgrounds just as non-Jews would appreciate
Jewish articles.[35] As Rutgers states: "in antiquity, fascination with the
accoutrements of another culture did not mean that one automatically
longed to become identical to the representations of that culture".[36]
One can therefore assume that this occurred for all peoples in antiquity no matter what their religious affinity or social background was.
It is impossible to assume that religion and culture can in any way be
seen as two different entities—they are entwined and must be seen as
such.

Both Boyarin[37] and Fredriksen[38] agree with the point of view that
religion and culture cannot be seen as separate from each other. However, both focus on religion and ethnicity.

Fredriksen states that ancient society presupposed that all peoples
had their own gods. Pagans, when describing Judaism, either extolled
its virtues or abhorred its practices, just as they did with other peoples
such as the Britons or Germanic tribes. Loyalty to one's own god was
of the utmost importance. What was especially abhorrent was when

---

[34] Rutgers (1998) pp. 15–44.
[35] Rutgers (1998) pp. 226–227.
[36] Rutgers (1998) p. 227.
[37] Boyarin (2003) pp. 65–85.
[38] Fredriksen (2003) pp. 35–63.

one gave up the allegiance to one's god and transferred the loyalty elsewhere (i.e. conversion). This was the concern one had for the God-fearers or sympathizers. Loyalty to one's gods meant loyalty to ones tribe/region/area. Transferring this loyalty elsewhere meant being a traitor to one's land. All ancient peoples were polytheists: they kept their own god, yet admitted the existence of other gods as well. All religions in the ancient city were accessible, to a certain extent. The idea that the 'explosion in numbers of Jews' in late antiquity was due to proselytism remains highly speculative. Jewish culture was accessible to all; they did not need to set up 'missionary' activities. What one sees is that people from all walks of life copied practices they could use themselves. There were for instance magicians who happily used Hebrew names in their incantations. Those who copied Jewish practices could be called "God-fearers". One can therefore state, as Fredriksen posits, that pagans remained pagans when they visited the synagogue. They did nothing different from many others: borrow what you think you can use, discard what you do not.[39] It does seem likely that there may have been Jews who wished to make converts, and they were consequently attacked as such. Most did not do so: they knew that gentiles had their own (G)god, they could borrow from Judaism, yet not give up their own allegiance. That was kept for Jews themselves, and the few who did actually convert. Thus, there were many different forms of Judaism, according to the area one inhabited. Just as there were many Judaisms, there were also many Christianities: the faithful borrowed from others and developed their own interpretation of their faith.[40]

Boyarin as well states that in antiquity religion was not seen as separate from one's ethnicity.[41] Judaism meant that originally a person came from Judea. One was a member of a nation and thus its religion. Thus conversion meant naturalisation, changing one's 'nationality'.

This was the case until the onset of Christianity. Both Boyarin and Fredriksen emphasize that with the rise of Christianity things changed. According to Boyarin, Christianity brought a change to this view as it was universal. He suggests that Christianity developed a different con-

---

[39] Fredriksen, *op. cit.*, p. 52.
[40] Kraft (2003) pp. 87–94.
[41] Cf. Boyarin (2003) pp. 65–85.

cept of religion.[42] The coming of Christianity again, and especially its rise to 'power', gave the impetus for Judaism to become more aware of its own identity and religion became an issue separate from culture.[43] The 'Christian concept' of religion—which saw religion separate from ethnicity and culture—as it emerged, undoubtedly had its effect on how the citizens of the Roman Empire, Christians as well as Jews, viewed themselves. Fredriksen in principle seems to agree with this thought. Christian anti-Judaism differed in essence from pagan anti-Judaism.[44] Pagan anti-Judaism was a subspecies of a more general contempt for unfamiliar foreign customs, yet Christian anti-Judaism was a deeper feeling that Christians should not even socialize with Jews. Near the end of her article, Fredriksen concedes that even though Christian anti-Judaism was radical and principled, it also knew a literary variant. This literary anti-Judaism existed after the fourth century as well but was never as influential as is suggested. The rhetoric developed in the second century and became the model for how one should not behave. The notion that Jews and Judaism were especially bad developed into negative remarks and standard comments to be found in many texts. It is a more useful exercise to research to what extent literary rhetoric agreed with social reality. Most theories discussed above are based on theological textual evidence. Even Boyarin's arguments of the Christian concept of religion are mostly based on literary sources. Yet, what was the social reality: was the partition of religion and culture, and thus the partition of Judaism and Christianity, as rapid as the literary anti-Judaism texts would have us believe? Taylor opposes Simon's 'conflict theory', suggesting a rather more literary struggle, a battle against an image of Judaism as found in Christian theological writings. Is there any information suggesting other types of contact rather than bellicose and literary? Purported theological divisions do not imply that there was separation at the cultural level, as Rutgers implies. It is interesting to note that Taylor, using literary material, comes to a conclusion of a theological nature, while Rutgers suggests the possibility of interaction—using material remains. A similar question, following Fredriksen, may be asked of Boyarin—whether his idea of the 'Christian concept of religion' is not also too much based on literary

---

[42] Boyarin (2003) pp. 65–85.
[43] Boyarin, *op. cit.*, pp. 67–74.
[44] Fredriksen in Becker/Reed (2003) pp. 47–48.

sources. In both cases, one may wonder what the social reality was like.

In the fourth century the church had more means of spreading the idea of Christianity separate from Judaism. However, to what extent were the church leaders successful in keeping the groups separate from each other? Different sources need to be used in order to answer this question.

If Judaism was supposedly no longer an active faith after the first century (Harnack) there would no longer be any significant contacts with other groups, one would assume. Yet, these contacts did take place. So, what were these contacts, and when, how and why did they end?

The question remains as to what one can understand to be meant by a 'parting of the ways'. Is it a parting at the official church level, as emphasized in the writings of church fathers? It is unlikely that a complete rupture occurred at the level of the ordinary faithful—who, as we have seen, were at all times borrowing, using what was needed. One can again repeat the question—what parting of the ways—in what respect can one assume that there was any rupture at all? Further-more, what happens in the fourth century and later—when Christi-anity grows? Were relations between Christians and Jews from the fourth century onwards mainly a theological argument? In developing its own identity, its theological definition, a negative view of Judaism played an important part in early Christianity. Yet, what was the situa-tion 'in reality' like? Literary argumentation does not necessarily mean that therefore day to day contacts did not exist, or when they did, they were antagonistic. Several authors have clearly indicated that one can-not separate religion from society, that there were no clear boundaries between pagan and other practices. Yet, where does the relationship between Jews and others fit in? What was the situation like? In order to answer this question a different type of source material from the usual will need to be studied.

3   A Different Type of Source Material: Council Texts

Until now, most studies by historians on late antique Christian-Jewish relations were mainly based on the writings of church fathers (cf. Harnack, Simon, Taylor).

Broadly speaking, we may categorize the texts written by church fathers into three large groups.[45] Each group of texts was written for a specific purpose and this is relevant to the issue at hand.

Historical texts, such as 'histories', historical poems, and letters, one assumes, may refer to a specific situation. However, this must be judged when discussed in the following pages.

As soon as theological arguments combined with Scriptural references are included, the specificity of the situation becomes less clear. This is also the case in homilies and theological treatises.

Homilies, our second category, may address a specific situation or else, at least, were delivered due to a situation which the preacher felt the need to address. Yet, it may not always be clear whether the occasion calling for a response was a specific situation only, or whether the homilist also used the opportunity to voice his theological vision. In short, are the Jews referred to in the homily a genuine entity or not?

With *theological treatises* (third category) this is even less clear. The closeness of Christianity to Judaism, from which it issued, meant that during the period of extracting itself from its roots, Christianity emphasized its status as a legitimate religion and consequently the decrease in relevance of Judaism. It is therefore not surprising that Christianity used the same sources as Judaism but used them to claim why Judaism had ceased in relevance: Scripture (Old Testament versus the New) and Messianism (Jesus as the Messiah) to show that Christianity was the only authentic religion. Thus, anti-Jewish polemics were born, gradually also using the charge of deicide in the debate.[46] The result is the development of the theory of a lack of understanding by Jews, the accusation of deicide, the belief that the historical situation shows that God is punishing the Jews for their mistakes. These are the central themes of Christian anti-Jewish writings.[47] These thoughts mostly developed from the second century onwards, after 135 CE. The idea of deicide developed after John wrote his gospel in the late first century as it gradually became clear that the Jews would not follow Jesus.[48] The anti-Jewish writings existed after the first century in

---

[45] I realize of course that this is only a general categorization which does not claim to be definitive.

[46] Cf. Jiménez Patón (1998) pp. 24–27.

[47] Cf. Langmuir (1990) p. 285.

[48] Langmuir (1990) p. 288.

patristic polemics, now well known.[49] Occasionally, the works were collected as testimonies or more complete monographs on a certain theme related to Jews.[50] Also used as a way of transmitting the message is the dialogue with a (possibly fictive) opponent. Occasionally, homilies were used.[51] All these writings start with Old Testament exegesis in order to instruct the listeners and readers about Judaism. Therefore, the majority of the anti-Jewish writings of this type (theological treatises) were to teach the Christian community that the church had replaced the synagogue, using all possible examples from Abraham onwards. The themes were repetitive: Mosaic Law was no longer valid and subsequent argument on the inferiority of Jewish law and cult to Christianity, Christianity as the true Israel, the new covenant, Messianism completed in Jesus, and all this is seen through the historical events showing that God was punishing the people.[52]

Some scholars have indicated before that church father texts on the whole provide little concrete evidence for the actual contacts between Christians and Jews and that therefore other source material must be used. Any source material by itself provides only part of the story. Church father texts were written with a specific purpose in mind: to convince their audience of a certain issue.

Archeological material—from a specific region and period—may provide what seems to be 'neutral' additional information to the evidence gleaned from patristic sources. However, a sarcophagus, oil lamp, mosaic fragment or inscription says little by itself. Even when information on the location where the object was found is provided, additional explanation as to the background of the archeological evidence is needed—finds from the surrounding area, date, and motivations of the archaeologist, for example.

Added to patristic sources, archeological material can provide useful additional information but this may not be enough to reach any conclusions specific to our topic: Christian-Jewish relations.

---

[49] Justin's *Dialogue with Trypho* (appr. 150) (PG 6, 471 f), Melito of Sardis on the Easter date (late second century), the second to third century Tertullian and his *Adversus Iudaeos* (PL 2, 633 f) and *Adv. Marcion.* (PL 2, 1107 f), to Eusebius of Caesarea's *Demonstr. Evang.* (PG 22, 9 f).

[50] See for example Albl (1999) *passim*.

[51] For example: Tertullian *Adv. Iud.*; Justin *Dialogue with Trypho*; John Chrysostom *Adv. Iud.*

[52] Cf. also Jiménez Patón (1998) pp. 24–27.

Besides the church father texts and archeological evidence there are two different types of written source material which provide additional information on Christian-Jewish relations.

One is Roman imperial legislation. Religion and religious practices were part of public life—for the good of all people. A person's civic and religious identity were one. Laws addressed issues concerning all public affairs, including religious practices. Private affairs, including private religious rituals, ultimately also concerned the individual and his clan, and were thereby also subject to jurisdiction. The modern concept of religion as relegated to the private domain is therefore not applicable to (late) antiquity.[53] All aspects of religion and various religious cults could therefore be addressed.

From the fourth century, Christian legal texts were gradually incorporated into imperial legislation as Christianity gained legal status within the empire. Eventually, laws since the time of Constantine were codified under the Theodosian Code, to be adapted by the Visigothic kings, and Justinian's Code and Digest. The Theodosian Code went into effect in 439 and was then the only source of law. Book 16 of the Code deals with the church and other religions and was accepted by the church as an authoritative source of canon law.[54]

The Theodosian Code is a collection of laws. Through this collection, one sees how Roman emperors viewed Christian religion develop. Paganism and Judaism had a protected legal status under Roman law into the fourth century. As the emperors gradually chose Christianity as the preferred religion, they wished to adapt the laws to also include privileges for the Christian religion and its adherents—clergy and faithful. A short interlude in this process is, of course, the brief reign of emperor Julian. Where, under Constantine, the laws still provided benefits and protection for pagan cults, gradually this would change. Orthodox Christianity became the norm, so legislation increasingly turned against those who were not: pagans, heretics and also Jews. This occurred especially from Theodosius onwards: paganism was now no longer an officially recognized religion, and was to be replaced by Christianity—a choice 'revealed to him by divine inspiration': all citizens of the empire were to practice 'the religion transmitted by the apostle Peter' (CTh XVI.1.2). Laws gradually turned against

---

[53] Ando/Rüpke (2006) pp. 8–13.
[54] Linder (1987) p. 33.

those not adhering to the orthodox faith: heretics and pagans. It was a first attempt by an emperor to seek harmony in church and state. The emperor was the 'secular arm' of the church, wishing to establish peace and unity in cult and state.[55] Jews were still protected by law and could practice their faith, however, conversion to Judaism was not allowed (CTh XVI 8.7). Jews who had 'converted' to Christianity were to be protected (CTh XVI.8.1, 5). Gradually, however, the Jews were restricted in their public activities (CTh XVI.8.16; 8.24) and eventually even called a 'perversion'(CTh XVI.8.19) awaiting their conversion to Christianity or the complete disappearance of their religion.

The Breviarium was the code of law of the Visigoths and was promulgated in 506. It replaced the Theodosian Code and had incorporated most of it.[56] A revised Code initiated by Justinian went into effect in 534. It as well relied heavily on the previous codes.[57]

Another—also legislative—source to be used is one hitherto used only sparingly: council texts. The texts date to the fourth century and later. In this study, fourth to sixth century council documents will be looked at where clear indications are given on the mixing of Christianity with other beliefs and especially Christianity's relations with Judaism.[58]

Councils are meetings attended by representatives of a number of individual churches to resolve problems in common, often on doctrinal or disciplinary issues.

In the fourth century, the emperor would often call together a council, which had wide-ranging effects on the position of the bishops in their own region. Bishops, after all, held not only spiritual but also temporal power. They were advisors to the emperor and representatives of the people. Councils were intended to enhance security and unity in the empire, and thus were of religious and political significance. Unity in beliefs was a necessity.

---

[55] Noethlichs, K.L. 'Revolution from the top? Orthodoxy and the persecution of heretics in imperial legislation from Constantine to Justinian' in: Ando/Rüpke (2006) pp. 115–125.

[56] Linder (1987) pp. 32–53.

[57] Linder (1987) pp. 46–50; Liebs (2000) in CAH XIV 'Roman law' esp.: 'Codification' pp. 244–252.

[58] Councils and laws discussed below will be those with specific references to Jews, contacts between Jews and Christians and Christians accused of 'judaizing practices'. Where general reference is made to a combined group of 'Jews, heretics and pagans', i.e. not a specific reference to Jews or judaizing as such, these are left out: cf. e.g. Carthage (419), c. 129 and Hippo (427) c. 6.

In the period before Constantine, church leaders would meet and discuss doctrinal issues, e.g. the dating of Easter or the effects of Montanism.[59] The third century Tertullian, in his *Liber de Jejuniis*, indicates in what high esteem these meetings were held.[60] Cyprian of Carthage indicates in his letters that there was no fixed time between these meetings. They could be called together when necessary, e.g. when there were problems concerning heresy.[61] Councils often began as congregational meetings of clergy and laity, but would be expanded, as needed, to include other clergy from a wider area. The geographical layout of the region and the severity of the issues decided the size of the meeting. The numbers also depended on the distance, the safety of travel and the age of the participants. It is unclear to what extent the council gatherings were required attendance for regular priests. Council texts can give a good insight into the life of the Church at the time.[62]

In the early church there is no distinction between 'council' and 'synod'. One is the Latin word, the other is Greek.[63] From the fourth century, the councils were held more frequently and the gatherings were larger. After all, gradually it became safer to travel in this period

---

[59] Gaudemet (1994) p. 115. On the conciliar movement see also Hess (2002) pp. 24–26.

[60] *De Jejuniis* 13,6 (PL 2, 972): "throughout the provinces of Greece there are held in definite localities those councils gathered out of the universal churches, by whose means not only all the deeper questions are handled for the common benefit, but the actual representation of the whole Christian name is celebrated with great veneration" (per Graecis illa certis in locis concilia ex universes ecclesiis per quae et altiora quaeque in commune tractantur, et ipsa repraesentatio totius nominis christiani magna celebratur).

[61] E.g., *Ep.* LXXI, 4 (PL IV, 408–411). The council of Elvira was probably called together because of lapsed Christians after the last great persecutions.

[62] That council texts do not only refer to theoretical cases can be seen in the fact that the situations discussed are also found in similar descriptions in church father texts and for example Theophanes' *Chronographia* (PG 108) which mentions (Novatian) Christians celebrating Easter with Jews: one of the issues mentioned in council documents especially in the East. See also, on the issue of recreating society from ancient legal texts: Aubert/Sirks (2005) esp. from p. 169. Rutgers (1998) pp. 209–219, on the problems of using the Theodosian Code as a historical source. The Theodosian Code is a Roman legal code and consists, as is usual in Roman law, of a compilation of older and newer legislation. That it is difficult to discern the actual situation from this text is obvious, yet the fact that the various legislation against, for example, proselytism continues shows that at least the faith was still attractive to non-Jews. This can only be enhanced by the archeological evidence put forward by the author.

[63] Cf. Ammianus Marcellinus, *Rerum Gestarum* XXI, 16, 18 (LCL 315): '…throngs of bishops hastened hither and thither on the public post-horses to the various synods, as they call them…' (…ut catervis antistitum iumentis publicis ultro citroque discurrentibus per synodos (quas appellant)…).

following the last great persecutions. Even if Nicea did ask for regular local meetings, this was rarely possible: at Carthage, for example, meetings were held often, yet not on a regular basis.[64]

In this period, we cannot yet speak of "ecumenical councils" as we know them. The fourth and fifth century 'ecumenical' councils (Nicea, Constantinople, Ephesus) were mostly an Eastern affair with little attendance from the West.[65]

As stated above, the issues were primarily concerned with what were considered to be 'wrong' teachings and beliefs (heresies).[66] However, synods would also serve to end quarrels amongst bishops and clergy and to improve pastoral care and organization of the priesthood.[67]

Many of the issues discussed in the councils form the basis not only for church law but also for several provisions in secular law.[68] Church law was initially, in general, not universal but regional, and dealt with local problems. Secular law was always necessarily universal in nature. The topics obviously also differed: imperial secular law was more general, and covered every aspect of life, contrary to church rulings. Eventually, where there is an overlap in topics, one sees a closer relation between church and state.[69] For example, it is known that the *Novellae* used council rulings and inserted these into Roman law.[70] Emperors, from the moment they had converted to Christianity, or a form of Christianity, acknowledged the 'power' of the bishops. That is to say bishops alone had jurisdiction over matters of faith and church issues.

The expanding role of the church and its relation to the imperial government meant that many issues discussed in church councils also found their way into imperial legislation, and vice versa. Also, bishops

---

[64] Nicea canon 5: 'each province to hold a council twice a year, composing of all bishops of the province [...] The first to be held before Lent [...], and the second in the autumn' (ἑκάστου ενιαυτου χαν ἑκάστην επαρχίαν δις του ετους συνόδους γίνεσθαι ἵνα κοινη πάντων των επισκόπων της επαρχίας επι το αυτο συναγομένων) Hefele/Leclercq (1907) I.1, pp. 548–9.

[65] Gaudemet (1994) p. 117.

[66] Cf. Eusebius on Paul of Samosata (*Hist. Eccl.* 7) (SC 31), or the question of the celebration of Easter and the Quartodecimans (*HE* ch. 5,23) (SC 31).

[67] Gahbauer (2001) p. 561.

[68] Such as the Codex Theodosianus, Lex Rom. Visigothorum, Breviarum Alarici, Edictum Theoderici, Justinian's Code, Digest, and Novellae.

[69] Especially between the council rulings and the Novellae, the Codex Theodosianus and Justinian's Code.

[70] Wiel (1991) *passim*.

gained more independence in enforcing church law, but were equally present at the palace thus influencing state affairs.[71]

Church council rulings had little judicial control over Jews. Church rulings on Judaism were directed against the Christian faithful when they were in contact with Jews or were accused of judaizing practices. Rulings against Jews occur mostly where they were in touch with Christians.[72] Eventually, the church leaders felt this contact was too close in all areas and started issuing rulings against Jews alone. This happened mostly from the sixth century onwards, when political and religious relations were close.[73] For many ordinary people and rulers, especially in the unstable years of the waning power of the Roman Empire, barbarian invasions and failing legal systems, church law seemed most reliable and was thus appealed to regularly.[74]

Documents of meetings earlier than the council texts studied here do exist.[75] Yet from the fourth century onwards actual canons of council meetings have survived. It is therefore this period which will be the focus of our study.

Using the evidence presented by the council texts and archeological material, an attempt will be made to look at the writings of relevant church fathers as well, from each region and period studied. Patristic sources are obviously a different type of text than council texts. Jewish sources will be used where relevant to our discussion of individual situations as described in the canons. What I propose to do is to extract

---

[71] Hunt (1998) in *CAH* XIII 'The church as a public institution' esp.: 'Bishops and the law' pp. 272–276.

[72] Pakter (1988) pp. 43–56; 64–68.

[73] Cf. from the sixth century onwards: the council rulings against the Jews, e.g. at Toledo and in Gaul.

[74] Cf. also Honoré (1998) pp. 3–5; 24–25; 156; 159; Harries (2001) pp. 68–92, esp. 76–77; id. (1999) chapters 3 and 10. And of course the many works by the eminent scholar on church law, Jean Gaudemet—e.g. his *La Formation du Droit Séculier et du Droit de l'Eglise au IVe et Ve Siècles*, esp. part III; pp. 178–212.

[75] To name but a few: the *Didache* (late 1st c., eastern Mediterranean): with prescriptions on baptism, fasting, the Eucharist, the organisation of the Christian community, ministers and the faithful, liturgy and the election of bishops to deacons. The *Didascalia* (appr. 230, east. Mediterranean): on similar issues as found in the Didache, also statements on heretics and Jews (ch. 13 and 21). The *Apostolic Tradition* (3rd c.? probably from the west) more elaborate yet on similar issues; it is obvious now that there are more liturgical tasks, so more advice to give! The *Constitutio Apostolica Ecclesiastica* (appr. 300, in the east): on moral prescriptions and the organisation of the church. And the *Apostolic Canons* which will be discussed further on, after the section on Laodicea. See also: Wiel (1991) *passim*.

enough information from the council text of a certain region in order
to gauge the situation of Christian-Jewish relations in that region and
period. To this, archeological material is added in order to complete
the picture. This information is then used to 're-read' the patristic texts
from that region and period in order to attempt to recreate the situation which the patristic text may refer to. When the church father
appears to be discussing an actual situation, this will be noted, as well
as where it appears to be 'theological discourse'. To this will be added,
where relevant, a look at imperial legislation—there where it may elu-
cidate or provide further information on the topic at hand. In the end,
what we hope to do is to attempt to recreate Jewish-Christian relations
in late antiquity.

The texts studied come from the eastern and western parts of
the Mediterranean and reach into the middle to late sixth century. The
first text to be studied comes from early fourth century Spain—the
last from 6th century Gaul. We will now turn to the earliest document—that of the council of Elvira in early fourth century Spain.

CHAPTER ONE

THE COUNCIL OF ELVIRA

The first text of a council which has been delivered to the present day is that which was held in the Spanish town of Elvira, a suburb of modern-day Granada.[1] The council took place around 305 CE and was the first known gathering of bishops and church representatives from any one nation. The list of bishops attending indicates how far Christianity had spread in Spain at this time. The canons describe people of many different walks of life, thus painting a vivid picture of the inhabitants of the early fourth century Iberian peninsula: from landowners (c. 49), charioteers and actors (c. 62), freedmen (c. 80), to slaves (c. 41). Other canons show that Christians still found solace in 'magical practices', but were also converts from the pagan priesthood ('*flamines*').[2] The council brought forth eighty-one canons, several of which refer to contacts between Christians and Jews, and 'judaizing' activities by the Christian faithful.

1 Pre-Fourth Century Archeological and Literary Evidence for Jews and Christians in Spain

1.1 The Jewish Evidence

Jewish presence in Spain, in the period preceding the fourth century, is attested through material evidence. Even though the dating in several cases may be somewhat debated, at least some evidence shows a Jewish presence in Spain in early times.[3]

An amphora was found in Ibiza with Hebrew inscription and probably dates to the first century.[4] Two letters are indicated on the

---

[1] Most relevant publications on the council are: Dale (1882), Laeuchli (1972), Reichert (1990), and more recently Sotomayor/Ubiña (2005).

[2] Magic: for example sorcery and idolatry c. 6, 20, 29, 34 etc.; pagan practices: e.g. canon 2, 3, 39, 41 etc.

[3] Niquet (2004) pp. 159–166; Bradbury (2006) 'The Jews of Spain'.

[4] Solá Solé (1960) pp. 291–294; Noy (1993) n. 178.

amphora: a *resh* and a *daleth*. These letters possibly indicate part of a name.[5] The presence of this amphora is interesting due to its date, and as it is found in a maritime area (the island of Ibiza) trade links may also account for its presence.

Not much Jewish literary evidence exists for the period preceding the fourth century.

An interesting Latin funerary inscription dates to the third century and was found in Abdera.[6] The place is the modern Adra, on the coast south of Granada. The inscription reads as follows:…NIA SALO… NVLA AN I MENS IIII DIE I IVDAEA: '[An]nia Salo[mo]nula one year 4 months one day, Jewess'. This Jewish child may have lived in this area, to have died at an early age.

Josephus, in his "Wars of the Jews",[7] claims that Herod Antipas was banished to Spain by the emperor Gaius. However, in the "Jewish Antiquities"[8] he states that Herod Antipas was sent in perpetual banishment to Gaul, specifically to Lyon, by Gaius. A suggested solution to this apparent contradiction is that Herod might have been sent to a place named "Lugdunum Convenarum", a town in the modern day border region of Spain and Gaul.[9]

Other Jewish texts are more vague, and are mostly dated to a somewhat later period. In the Midrash Rabbah Leviticus (XXIX,2), R. Meir calls for the return of the Diaspora from, i.e., Gaul and Spain.[10] This approximately fifth century text probably mentions these areas, amongst many others, as an example of (from) "everywhere", rather than indicating a specific region. The Targum Jonathan on Obadiah verse 20 (probably dated after the fourth century[11]) mentions exiles who are in "Spain".[12]

---

[5] Cf. Solá Solé (1960) pp. 291–294.

[6] CIJ n. 665; Cantera (1956) nr. 283. Noy (1993) n. 179; possibly also n. 188: an epitaph inscription followed by '*iudeus*'.

[7] *Bellum Iudaicum* II, 183 (LCL 203).

[8] *Antiq.* XVIII, 252 (LCL 433).

[9] Hoehner (1972) p. 262 n. 1. See for further discussion on this town, chapter IV on Gaul, section 1.2 Christian evidence.

[10] "From Gaul and Spain, and from her neighbors, and Babylon, Media, Greece, Edom…of all the nations I have scattered thee". Translation in English by Israelstam and Slotki (1971) p. 371.

[11] The earlier rabbis tend to see "Sepharad", the place mentioned in the text as Sardis in Asia Minor. Later rabbis prefer Spain. Cf. 'Sepharad' in: *EJ* vol. 18, p. 292.

[12] "Exiles of this people of the Israelites (shall possess) what is in the land of Canaan as far as Zarephath, while the exiles of Jerusalem who are in *Spain* (my italics) shall possess the cities of the land of the south". English translation by Cathcart (1989) p. 102.

In a Christian text, a commentary, Saint Jerome (345–420) states a list of countries. He indicates that in Messianic times Jews are expected to return from many areas, including Spain, Gaul and Britain.[13] One can assume that he means "all reaches of the world".

There seems to be little reason to assume that there were large Jewish settlements in the area before the year 70: the Ibiza amphora can be due to trade, and the evidence on Herod Antipas is too vague and marginal (*if* Josephus even referred to Spain at all). It would be possible to assume that Jews arrived in the region between the year 70 and the second to third centuries.

In a more recent publication, it is suggested that Jews came to the Iberian Peninsula after the fall of Jerusalem, in 70 CE.[14] The majority of the Jews who came had been slaves, according to Blázquez, quoting others, and did not travel for commercial interests.[15] In any case, Jews were already in Spain before the arrival of Christianity.[16] According to García Moreno, Christian missionaries used the Jewish communities to spread the good news.[17] This, he says, is proven by placing a map of ancient Christian religious structures on that of the earliest synagogues: the result is that both are found in the same areas. This is an interesting suggestion; however, the evidence for early Christian buildings is so sparse that this conclusion seems to exaggerate the little material evidence there is.[18]

1.2   *The Christian Evidence*

The earliest Christian material remains are of a funerary nature.[19] The early sarcophagi are mostly from Roman workshops, and were found in the region along the coast and along the large rivers of the Ebro and Guadalquivir.[20]

---

[13] *In Isaiam* XVIII, LXVI, 20 (CCSL LXXIII A).

[14] Blázquez (2002) p. 409.

[15] Blázquez (2002) p. 411.

[16] Dale (1882) p. 254; García Moreno (2005b) pp. 35–42.

[17] García Moreno (2005) p. 181; id. (2005b) p. 55.

[18] See, for example, the map in Cantera Burgos (1984) and the maps provided by Schlunk/Hauschild (1978) or Palol (1969). However, one does need to note that in all cities where there are remains of early Christian religious buildings there are also remains of (early) synagogues (except at Merida, Badajoz and Jaen).

[19] Schlunk (1978), p. 19; Palol (1969), p. 52.

[20] At Zaragoza, Toledo, and Córdoba, and at Gérona on the coast, supposedly of the martyr Felix: Schlunk, p. 19 f.

The earliest literary reference to the possible existence of Christians in Spain is in the New Testament. In the letter to the Christians of Rome, Saint Paul mentions his intention to visit Spain.[21] It has been assumed that the apostle brought Christianity to the country.[22] The suggestion is that Paul, traveling from the east, went via Rome to Spain, thereby covering the northern half of the Mediterranean.[23] Edwards, in his commentary on Paul's letter to the Romans, sees Clement of Rome as a testimony to this argument. The first century bishop of Rome, Clement, states that Paul "…having taught righteousness to the whole world, even reaching the *bounds of the West* [my italics]".[24] Some scholars have interpreted 'the bounds of the west' as referring to Spain.[25]

The so-called 'Muratorian Canon'—the oldest list of canonical New Testament writings with varied dating[26]—also affirms that Paul had reached the peninsula via Rome. The fragmentary 'catalogue' suggests that Luke, the author of the last part of the New Testament book of Acts, omitted to recount that Paul left the City [i.e., Rome] for Spain (lines 34–39).[27] The authenticity of the text is doubtful, and it is also difficult to say whether Paul actually reached Spain even if his intent was obvious.[28]

Further early Christian literary references date to the period when Christians were already clearly present in the Iberian Peninsula.

Irenaeus (approx. 180) in his *Adversus haereses* (I, 10) mentions that the 'same beliefs exist everywhere: in the German, Iberian, and Celtic regions'. It seems likely that by naming all these regions, he means to say that 'the entire world' believes in one truth.[29]

The second century Tertullian affirms that there were more Christians in Spain than in Mauretania.[30] His treatise *Adversus Judaeos* was

---

[21] Romans 15: 24, 28.
[22] E.g., Leclercq (1906) pp. 26–27.
[23] Edwards (1992) p. 350.
[24] Clement 1st Letter to the Corinthians, 5,7; translated and published in: Bettenson/Maunder (1999) p. 9.
[25] Leclercq (1906) p. 27; Edwards (1992) p. 350.
[26] Varying from late second to fourth centuries. Hahneman (1992) pp. 27–30.
[27] Hahneman (1992) pp. 192, 195; Latin text appears on pp. 6–7. Text is based on Milan Library *Codex Ambrosianus* I.101 sup. For a discussion on the text see: Metzger (1997) pp. 196, 306.
[28] Sotomayor (1979) pp. 159–165.
[29] Irenaeus *Adv. Haer.* I, 10 (SC 263). My translation.
[30] 'Hispaniorum omnes termini': *Adv. Jud.* VII, 4 (CCSL II, 1354–1355).

written to emphasize that the Christ had been born and that all should believe in Him. Tertullian then continues by naming regions all over the then known world where believers lived.[31]

In about 255, bishop Cyprian of Carthage writes to Stephen, bishop of Rome, about the Christian communities of León, Astorga, Mérida and Saragossa.[32] It emerges from the epistle that by the middle of the third century large parts of Christian Spain were already organized with bishops, deacons and priests as a certain priest Felix is named, but also a deacon Aelius.[33] Cyprian complains of apostasy in Spain under the persecutions of Decius. The places mentioned in the letter are communities which, according to legend, were converted by 'seven messengers' ('*Siete Varónes*') sent by Saint Peter.[34] Later manuscripts such as the sixteenth century Roman Martyrology mention seven men sent by the "holy apostles" to bring the faith to Spain. They apparently baptized pagans, and then left the group to settle elsewhere. One, named Cecilius, came to Illiberi. The original document containing these stories may date to the seventh century and may be from the Baetica region. According to Sotomayor, most authors agree that there is very little to say about this story, and treat it as a legend.[35] Unfortunately, there is no archeological or more trustworthy literary evidence for their existence.[36]

2   *Fourth Century Evidence for Jews and Christians in Spain*

From the fourth century onwards, evidence appears to become not only more abundant but also more trustworthy.

---

[31] For the reference also mentioning Spain: *Adv. Jud.* VII (CCSL II, 1339–1396).

[32] *Ep.* 67 (CCSL IIIc, 447 f). Opening of the letter mentions León (Legionem), Astorga (Asturica), Mérida (Emerita); in ch. VI, 1 Saragossa (Caesaraugusta) is mentioned.

[33] The letter is concerned with the presbyter Felix and the faithful of León and Astorga, and the deacon Aelius and the faithful of Mérida (*Ep.* 67: I, 1).

[34] Sotomayor (1979c) pp. 156–159. To be found in the ninth century martyrology of Adon of Vienna: under 'May 15' (PL 123, 266–7). Published in Latin by Dubois/ Renaud (1984). For information on the martyrology of Adon: Dubois (1990) pp. 43–48.

[35] E.g., Sotomayor (1979c) p. 159.

[36] Sotomayor (1979) pp. 150–156; Fontaine (1973); Palol (1969) pp. 42–44.

2.1   *Jewish Evidence*[37]

On the coast, south of modern day Barcelona, lies Tarragona from
where we have a bilingual inscription, in Latin and Greek, dating to
the fourth century.[38] The Latin inscription on the slab reads as follows: 'In the name of the Lord, rests in this tomb Rab Lasies, related
to the master. May he rest in peace'. In Greek it says: 'Here rests Rab
Latues, in the name of the Merciful, *archisynagogos*. He came from
Kyzikos,[39] he is just; (freed) without doubt (from) Gehenna, he died
in the Lord'.[40] It is possible that the 'master' indicated in the Latin
inscription is the *archisynagogos* of the Greek inscription. At least in
this case, a synagogue leader is mentioned, i.e., indicating strong evidence for a Jewish settlement.

Evidence for a synagogue itself probably comes from Elche ('Illici',
or Alcudia, in nearby coastal Alicante).[41] The rectangular building is a
hall and apse, with entrance area. On the mosaic floor Greek writing is
found. The building has been indicated as a Christian cult center[42] or,
more likely, a synagogue,[43] dating to the fourth century. The inscription has led to much discussion. The text, in Greek, runs as follows:
πρ[οσ]ευχὴ λα(ῦ)... That is to say: 'the place of prayer of the people
of...'. On the north end the inscription reads: ...χης (?) ἀχόντων κ(αὶ)
πρε(σ)βυτ(έ)ρων. This could be read as: 'the *archontes* (?) and pres-
byters'.[44] The third inscription, on the southern side, contains fifteen
letters: εὐπλοίας υσυ.....υχα. Indicating:

'......happy navigation...',

[37] See also García Moreno (2005b) p. 35 ff; Niquet (2004) pp. 166–177, including
possible new evidence of an inscription from Tarragona (pp. 169–171).
[38] Vallicrosa (1957) pp. 3–10, whose dating is based on the inscription. The translation in Spanish is his, English translation mine. More recently: Niquet (2004) p. 169
who corrects the work by Vallicrosa and Noy (1993) n. 186.
[39] For place name, cf. Vallicrosa (1957) p. 9.
[40] The latter part reads: ΚΥΖΗΚΕ[ΝΟΣ] ΔΗΚΕΩ[Σ] ΓΗΑΝΗ[Α]ΝΕΥ ΑΩ [ΒΗΣ]
ΚΥΡΗΕ ΤΕΘΝΕ.
[41] CIJ 662–664; Noy (1993) n. 180, 181.
[42] E.g.: Schlunk (1978) p. 9.
[43] E.g.: Bowers (1975) p. 397; Cantera Burgos (1984) n. 42.
[44] CIJ 663.

a thanks for a safe maritime passage.[45] According to Bellido, and quoted by Cantera,[46] the inscriptions show that this was originally a synagogue as *proseuche* is rarely used for churches.[47] It is likely that the building was later turned into a church.

From the fourth to fifth centuries date several pieces of lead with inscription in Hebrew,[48] from the island of Mallorca. The pieces were found on a grave of one person, near other Jewish graves. All three pieces of lead bear the same inscription in Hebrew, reading: 'Samuel son of R Haggai'.

A Jewish inscription was found at Pallaresos (Tarragona),[49] and may date to the fourth century.[50] The text is preceded by a palm tree and menorah. The writing is in Latin, and says: 'this is the tomb of Isidora—of good memory, daughter of Iona and Axia—of good memory, may her soul rest in peace with all Israel, amen amen amen'.

A trilingual inscription from Tarragona probably dates to the sixth century.[51] On one side of the marble "box" are two birds facing a tree and menorah, probably a tree of life. In front of one of the birds is what looks like a *shofar*. The text above reads in Hebrew: 'peace to Israel, us and our sons'. Above the other side it says, in Latin: '*pax fides*'. Several Greek letters are seen above.

Another trilingual inscription dating between the second and sixth centuries[52] comes from Tortosa, near Tarragona. The slab has an inscription in Greek, Latin and Hebrew. At the top of the inscription is a 'Star of David', preceding the Hebrew text which reads: 'Peace upon Israel. This tomb belongs to Meliosa, daughter of Juda and the

---

[45] CIJ 664.

[46] Cantera Burgos (1984) p. 213.

[47] Cantera Burgos (1984) p. 213. For *proseuche* as 'prayer house of Diaspora Judaism' see also McKay (2001) p. 64. Noy (1993) n. 182; Niquet (2004) pp. 174–175.

[48] Vallicrosa (1958) pp. 3–9, with his (Spanish) translation. Noy (1993) n. 177, Niquet (2004) p. 173.

[49] Cantera, (1956) nr. 290. Translation in Spanish is his, English version mine. Latin: '*memoria bone recordationis Isidora filia bene memorii Ionati et Axiaes pauset anima eius in pace cum omne Israel [am]en amen amen*'. See also Noy (1993) n. 187; Niquet (2004) p. 167.

[50] Bowers (1975) dates the inscription to the fourth century: p. 397.

[51] Cantera (1956) n. 243 dates the inscription to the sixth century. Beinart quoted by Bowers (1975) dates it to the second century, but appears to wish to date most objects to a very early period: pp. 396–397. Noy (1993) n. 185; Niquet (2004) pp. 168–169.

[52] CIJ 661; Noy (1993) n. 183; Niquet (2004) p. 173.

lady Maryam. May her memory be a blessing, May her spirit have eternal life. May her soul be in the bonds of the living. Amen. Peace'. Similar texts follow in Latin and Greek, adding that the deceased was 24 years old.

An epitaph, possibly from the fourth to eighth centuries,[53] hails from Mérida. The Latin text reads: 'the Lord's name be blessed, who gives life and brings death. In the tomb rests...son of Rebbi Se[muel], prayer leader of the community. Bound in the bonds of eternal life.[54] Open the doors of paradise, enter in peace. Died at the age of 63, full of wisdom. Knowledgeable in the art (of...?). I, Simeon, son of Rebbi Ja[cob], peace'.

It seems likely that the name mentioned last is the one who had the stone made.

2.2   *Christian Evidence*[55]

Fourth century Christian remains are mausoleums which were built near settlements mentioned in texts: Tarragona,[56] Murcia,[57] and Badajoz.[58] The villa Centcelles near Tarragona, for example, has a mausoleum consisting of a crypt underneath a large round hall. The hall is decorated with mosaics with representations of the Good Shepherd, and biblical scenes such as the story of Jonah. The representations closely resemble the representations as found in the catacombs at Rome.[59] Many Christian sarcophagi date to this period, often showing various representations from different backgrounds, pagan or Christian.[60] By the late fourth century local workshops developed.[61]

There are chapels found near (large) mansions dating to the late fourth century, as at Torre de Palma, Fraga and La Cocosa.[62] A large church has been found at Marialba (León) dating to the fourth cen-

---

[53] Cantera/Millás (1956) n. 289: eighth century. My translation.

[54] Literally: 'Ligatus in ligatorium vitae'.

[55] See Sotomayor (1979c) ch. IV, pp. 120–165; and Schlunk (1978) ch. I, pp. 5–28.

[56] E.g., the villa Centcelles: Palol (1967) p. 72; Schlunk (1978) p. 15 ff.

[57] E.g. the martyrium La Alberca: Schlunk (1978) p. 10 ff.

[58] E.g., the villa La Cocosa, with a chapel: Schlunk (1978) p. 11 ff.

[59] E.g.: Petrus and Marcellinus, Callixtus, and Domitilla: Palol (1967) p. 72.

[60] Sotomayor (1979c) 136–140. For sepulchral decorations see Sotomayor (1979c) pp. 140–142.

[61] As at Tarragona: Schlunk (1978) p. 19 ff.

[62] Palol (1967) p. 52 ff.

tury, and a smaller one at Elche, where we also know of the existence of a synagogue.[63] From the fifth century onwards there is more evidence of Christian religious structures.[64]

One of the literary sources most informative for the fourth century is the Spanish Christian poet Aurelius Prudentius Clemens (b. 348 in Tarragona). His literary works include the *Liber Peristephanon*, a collection of hymns on the lives of martyrs.[65] These hymns mention various Christian communities in Spain: Barcelona (Peristephanon hymn IV, 33), Calahorra (hymn I and VIII), Cataluña (hymn IV, 43), and Cordova (hymn IV, 19). In Tarragona, for example, the bishop Fructuosus and his deacons Augurius and Eulogius were martyred in 259, under the persecutions of Valerius (Peristeph. hymn VI).[66] Fourth century Christian tractates on various subjects attest to the growth of the church in Spain.[67]

2.3   *Jews in Christian Texts*

Fourth and fifth century Spain provides us with church fathers who mention Jews and Judaism in their texts: Gregory of Elvira and Prudentius for the fourth century and Severus of Minorca for the fifth century.

We know little of Gregory except through Jerome in his *De Viris Illustribus*.[68] According to him, Gregory of Elvira died at an 'advanced age', which was in approximately 392.

In Gregory's homilies called the *Tractatus Origenis*,[69] he discusses issues related to various Old and New Testament passages. Several of these passages refer to Jews and Judaism and discuss topics well known from other church fathers' exegeses: the issue of the 'true Israel', the

---

[63] Sotomayor (1979c) pp. 144–145.

[64] See Schlunk (1978) map on p. 7.

[65] Text in Latin and French: Lavarenne (1951).

[66] Early Christian archeological remains in Spain often corroborate the literary evidence: cf. the Roman amphitheatre in Tarragona: the place of the martyrdom of Fructus, Augurius and Eulogius: Fontaine (1973); the Christian necropolis under the basilica at Tarragona: Schlunk (1978) p. 14.

[67] E.g. Gregory of Elvira, Ossius of Córdoba, Potamius, or Priscillian for example: Sotomayor (1979c) ch. V and VI.

[68] *De Viris Illustribus* 105; Richardson (1896). Quasten vol. 4, pp. 84–89, esp. p. 88.

[69] *Tract. Orig.* (CCSL LXIX, 5–146).

'true Easter', the replacing of the synagogue by the church, circumcision and the Sabbath.[70]

Aurelius Prudentius Clemens was born in 348, presumably in Calahorra in Tarraconensis, and lived until approximately 410. He was not a theologian but was a barrister and received high honors from the emperor. Later in life, Prudentius retired to be able to write. All of Prudentius' literary works can be dated to between 395 and 405. His text '*Apotheosis*' was written in approximately 400. It is a didactic and polemic poem which exposes the wrongs of others and defends Christian doctrine on the mystery of God and the divinity of Christ. Most of the poem is directed towards other groups, only part of the work is against the Jews.

The verses 321–551 are directed towards the Jews.[71] In these verses, he attacks the Jews for denying the divinity of Christ (lines 330–340), their blindness in not understanding the prophets of old (l. 355 ff), the acceptance of the Christian message by the pagans and not the Jews (l. 402 ff), a section on the emperor Julian (l. 450 ff), and the eternity of the Christian temple as opposed to the Jewish Temple (l. 500 ff). He claims that, since the destruction of the Temple in Jerusalem in the year 70, Judaism is obsolete. Jews deserve to wander and be punished for their 'crimes'. Prudentius emphasizes historical and theological arguments. Most of his work in general is against pagans and heretics; only a small part is against Judaism, and this is mostly based on explaining historical facts (i.e., the fall of the Temple). It often happens that Jews are mentioned in the same treatise as other, often termed 'heretical' groups.[72] The theological arguments against these groups are usually Christological-based.

Prudentius' arguments seem less vitriolic than those of others, e.g. Commodian.[73] According to Schreckenberg, this is because the reality was that the Jews in the region where he wrote were less strong now, and he therefore writes against a less forceful Judaism.[74] As the pagan and heretic rhetoric in his work is more forceful and lengthy, Fabian concludes, it must have been closer in his surroundings. One wonders,

---

[70] Cf. also similar discussions in Ambrose of Milan, Prudentius, Augustine, Paulinus of Nola etc. Cf. González Salinero (2000) pp. 37–44. See also Muñoz (1998) pp. 45–62; Morin (1900) pp. 267–273.

[71] LCL 387, 398.

[72] Cf. Hilary *De Trinit.*, Ephrem the Syrian. See Shepardson (2002).

[73] Fabian (1988) pp. 31–40; González Salinero (2000) p. 44.

[74] Schreckenberg (1973) p. 104; Fabian (1988) p. 40.

could it not also be that he came from a pagan background[75] and that due to his conversion to Christianity he was more vehement towards his former co-religionists. It is also possible that the good contacts he saw between Christians and Jews led him to downplay his arguments somewhat. Seeing what Prudentius' reaction to paganism was like and knowing what the situation was like in late antique Spain, it seems realistic to assume that his anti-Jewish writings as well were inspired by the local (Spanish) situation.

The situation of the Jews in Minorca is also relevant.[76] The letter of bishop Severus of Minorca is dated to 418 CE and states that many Jews on the island lived in the town of Magona. Christian-Jewish relations were fine on the island until the arrival of the relics of Saint Stephen. Stephen was one of the early Christian martyrs who had died at the hands of Jews. When the relics of Saint Stephen were brought to Magona to be placed in the cathedral, the relations between Jews and Christians became tense, due to growing religious zeal amongst the Christian inhabitants of the town. Many Christians, led by their bishop, wished to go on pilgrimage to the relics at Magona. At this time, both bishop Severus and the leader of the Jewish community of the city had a dream. As a result, the leader of the Jewish community converted to Christianity. Of course, the Jewish population of the town was suspicious! Through misunderstandings and rising tension, riots amongst the two faith groups broke out during which the synagogue was burnt. However, Severus stated triumphantly that a large group of Jews asked for baptism (ch. 17).[77] The emphasis on this particular fact by bishop Severus led to Christian rioting against the Jews. A Jewish man on Minorca had converted, yet after the rioting and burning of the synagogue others were inclined to follow suit. It seems that the role of the religious leader, and especially his homilies, is crucial in Christian-Jewish relations.

The works by both Gregory of Elvira and Prudentius would appear to fit into the category of 'theological treatises'. Their arguments are not new: the use of Scripture to emphasize Christianity's superiority (considered to be the 'true Israel') over the Jewish cult (especially the feast of Passover and circumcision) and historical facts to reiterate

---

[75] Jiménez Patón (1998) p. 32.
[76] *Ep. Sev.*: Bradbury (1996). Niquet (2004) pp. 175–177.
[77] Text in Latin and English: Bradbury (1996) pp. 100–101.

why Judaism was now obsolete (the fall of the Temple in the year 70). The letter of Severus appears to contain a different type of information: less theological reflection.

The evidence from the fourth and fifth centuries appears to be more trustworthy for evidence of Jewish settlements in Spain: cf. the Tarragona and Elche synagogue inscriptions, the testimony of Jerome and the letter of Severus of Minorca. The archeological and literary evidence for Christians is also more complete for the period from the fourth century onwards.

Then there is the text of the council of Elvira. The council uses at least four canons to describe Jewish-Christian relations. This must indicate the presence of Jews in this region. The text shows that the church had spread, that Christians were present in many parts of the country, that Jews were also present, and that these groups, according to the church leaders, had very close connections. Let us now turn to the text of this council of Elvira.

3   The Council of Elvira

The council held at Elvira is of interest because it produced one of the first written legal documents of canon law. The council text shows problems typical for that time, and that region, and actions that would need to be taken.

The text appears in the so-called "*Hispana*" document, a collection of canonical texts, so called because it includes many Spanish council texts.[78] Versions of the *Hispana* collection can be found in more than fourteen manuscripts.[79] Of these manuscripts, the oldest is in Vienna[80] (d. 633). This manuscript lists councils up to Toledo IV (approx. 633). Martínez Díez calls this manuscript the 'Isidoriana'[81] as it is suggested it was created under the inspiration of bishop Isidorus of Sevilla (approx. 560–636).[82]

---

[78] Martínez Díez (1966); Maassen (1956) *passim*. The text of the Hispana can be found in PL 84, 1–848. For clarification of the following discussion, see the chart in Martínez Díez (1966) CCH, vol. I, p. 205.

[79] Cf. Maassen (1956) I.

[80] Codex Vienna *Nat.Bibl. lat.* 411.

[81] Martínez Díez (1966) *CCH*, vol. III.

[82] Gaudemet (1985) p. 156.

Later, more councils were added to the list as found in Vienna. Two versions of these later manuscripts exist:

- the *Iuliana*,[83] named after bishop Julius of Toledo (approx. 680–690) which dates to approximately 681 (adding the councils of Toledo V through XII and Braga (675)). The Iuliana version exists in later manuscripts which come from Gaul (Gálica, according to Martínez Díez)[84] and the Toledo region (Toledana).[85]
- the *Vulgata*, dating to approximately 694.[86] Again, this exists in different, later, manuscripts. One is named 'Saint Amand' (d. approx. 8th–10th c.).[87] The Saint Amand text is a systematic list of fourth to seventh century Gallic council texts, augmented by the Spanish councils from Elvira to Toledo VIII (653). At the end of the manuscript is the document known as the 'Statuta Ecclesiae Antiqua'. This Vulgata version in particular, as delivered to us in the Saint Amand text, is used by most scholars who study Spanish council texts, in particular that of Elvira.[88]

The council of Elvira issued 81 canons. The majority of the larger slightly later synods usually issued approximately 20 statements.[89] In addition, the unorganized fashion in which the Elvira decrees appear to have been assembled gives rise to the assumption that here we are dealing with a collection of different original manuscripts.[90] In

---

[83] The text of the Iuliana can be found in PL 84, 302–310; Martinez Diez *CCH* vol. IV, pp. 233–268.

[84] Found in: Codex Vatic. Pal. 575 (120r–123v; dating to the tenth century); Codex Vienna 411 (dating to the ninth century); and Codex Vallicellano Roma D.18 (dating to the tenth century). Cf. Martínez Díez (1966) *CCH*, IV, pp. 233–268.

[85] In the Codex Escurial D-I-2 (tenth century); Codex Escurial D-I-1 (: 119v–210v: tenth century); Codex Escurial E-I-12 (tenth/eleventh century). Martínez Díez, *CCH* IV, p. 233.

[86] Gaudemet (1985) pp. 156–158.

[87] Maassen (1956) I, p. 780; Gaudemet (1985) p. 149.

[88] Text found in Hefele/Leclercq (1907) I.1, pp. 221–264; Martinez Diez *CCH* vol. IV, pp. 233–268. The council is mentioned in the Vulgata text in Codex Angelica Roma Ms 1.091 (9/10th c.); Codex Urgel. *folio* 88r (10/11th c.); Codex Tolet. XV.16: *f* 115 v (11th c.); Codex Tolet. XV.17 (11th c.); Codex Gerund. (11th c.): Martínez Díez, *CCH* IV, pp. 233–268.

[89] The general council at Arles (314): 22, the ecumenical council at Nicea: 20, and Serdica (343): 20 canons.

[90] Meigne (1975) pp. 364–366. Against its textual unity: cf. Molkenbuhr, in: Hefele/ Leclercq (1907) I.1, p. 214, n. 4. Since the early twentieth century, most scholars are in favor of the original unity of the text, despite it having been found in many different

comparison with the documents of other large councils, Meigne argues that where elsewhere the grouping of the statements seems to have been done in a logical fashion, this is not the case in the Elvira text.[91] Other Spanish council texts offer no positive help for reconstructing the Elvira text.[92] Meigne would prefer to divide the Elvira text into three groups: A (decrees 1–21), B (13 decrees, from canon 63 through 75) and C (the 47 remaining decrees: 22 to 62 and 76 to 81).[93] Due to their subject matter, two canons are left out: c. 33 and 80. He continues with an extensive comparison between 'Elvira' and other council texts in the use of language: the word 'sacerdos', for example, and the language of the punishments that follow each decree.[94] As a result, he argued that the groups A and B into which he had divided the Elvira document are relatively similar in language and would be dated to an early period (303–5).[95] Based on style and content, he compared group C to other council texts and came to the conclusion that it could be dated to a later period, after the council of Nicea (325).[96]

Despite the feeling that at times the author seems to force the evidence into his theory, his argument would clarify the problem of a seemingly disjointed collection of decrees. It seems likely that the collection known as the text of the council of Elvira is composed of various documents assembled by churches into what was to become one document on canon law. This would therefore explain the jumbled fashion in which the collection appears to us now, and would explain the decrees on subjects that were not an issue until later (e.g., clerical celibacy: c. 33).

The date when the meetings in Elvira were held is controversial. The only date mentioned in the original documents is the 'Ides of May', i.e.

---

manuscripts: see, for example, Hefele/Leclercq (1907) I.1, p. 214; Garcia Villada (1929) pp. 302–3; Meigne (1975) pp. 361–387; Reichert (1990). Cf. a more recent discussion in: Vilella (2002) p. 119 f; Ubiña, (2002) p. 162 ff; Sotomayor/Ubiña (2005) pp. 67–75.

For more recent discussions of the uniformity of the document; following Meigne (that the Elvira text comes from different documents) is Vilella (2002b) p. 545 ff. Less negative is Ramón Teja of the University of Cantabria in Santander, who voiced his general concerns on the unity of the text in a personal communication, for which I am grateful. Also by him, in Teja (2002) p. 15 ff.

[91] Meigne (1975) pp. 366–8.
[92] Saragossa (380) and Toledo (400): pp. 368–9.
[93] Meigne (1975) p. 366.
[94] Meigne (1975) pp. 369–373.
[95] Meigne (1975) pp. 373–374.
[96] Meigne (1975) pp. 374–386.

May 15th.[97] A text at the beginning of the acts of the synod mentions Nicea and the emperor Constantine. A date of 324 was therefore suggested. However, no other date is mentioned. It is now argued that this text was superimposed later. To corroborate this argument evidence has been put forward that one of the bishops attending the council was Ossius of Cordoba and he was certainly not in Spain in 324. Furthermore, several passages in the text refer to violent persecutions during which many Christians abandoned their faith. Therefore, the council must have followed a period of persecutions. Diocletian and Maximian ordered the last large-scale persecutions of Christians in 303–305 CE. In addition, lapsed Christians were dealt with much more strongly at Elvira than elsewhere, for example Nicea. This reaction is normal for a situation closely following upon persecutions. The conclusion is that the council was probably held in 305 or 306. Diocletian and Maximian had abdicated, Constantius Chlorus became ruler over the Spanish region and the persecutions had ended. The bishops met at Elvira to deal with lapsed Christians and with moral corruption.[98]

The list of participants shows how widely Christianity had spread in Spain by this time.[99] The list includes representatives from the complete Spanish region, excluding Mauretania. The reason could be that Mauretania either had no bishop to send, or was not invited or that people considered the trip too far and dangerous. Nineteen bishops attended the meetings, including some well-known names such as Felix of Cadiz, Ossius of Cordoba, Valerius of Caesaraugustana (Saragossa) and Patricius of Malaga. Also on the list were 24 priests, deacons and many lay faithful. Baetica sent most representatives: probably because the meetings were held in its region, but possibly also because it was an intensely Christian area.[100] The deacons were not mentioned by name, possibly because they were "only" assistants to their bishop. Galicia and Tarragona sent one bishop each.[101] Lusitania sent three bishops (Merida, Ossanova, and Evora), and Cartagena eight (of Acci,

---

[97] Mentionend in the opening text after the list of participants: Martinez Diez *CCH* vol. IV, p. 241.

[98] Hefele/Leclercq (1907) I.1, pp. 212–220. The superimposition of the date is adequately discussed in all later publications (see Dale (1882), Laeuchli (1972), Reichert (1990), Sotomayor/Ubiña (2005)).

[99] Bareille *DTC* 2386; Gaudemet (1963) pp. 317–318; Orlandis/Ramos-Lissón (1981) pp. 6–7; Sotomayor/Ubiña (2005) pp. 75–88; 137–155.

[100] Orlandis/Ramos-Lisson (1981) pp. 3–30.

[101] Tarragona (Tarraconensis) sent bishop Valerius of Zaragoza (Caesaraugusta).

Castulo, Mentesa, Urci, Toledo, Salavia, Lorca and Basti). From Baetica came six bishops: Ossius of Cordoba, Sabinus of Sevilla, Flavianus
of Elvira, Patricius of Malaga, and the lesser known bishops of Martos
and Ipagrum.[102]

The presidency of the council is unclear. At the top of the list of participants is the name of Felix of Cadiz. This is presumably so because
he was the president of the synod, or because he was the oldest bishop.
Another possibility is that Cadiz held the oldest bishopric. The role of
Ossius of Cordoba is also important. It has been suggested that he was
the president, but there is no evidence for this assumption.[103] It is said
that Ossius had political plans to replace the crumbling administration of the Empire by that of the Church.[104] Later, he was a participant
at Nicea[105] and at Serdica,[106] and became advisor to Constantine in
312/313.[107] At the later synods, Ossius pleaded for more and better
organized clergy, certain powers for bishops and compulsory attendance at Sunday Mass, issues also discussed at Elvira.[108] De Clercq
suggests that Ossius put forward these issues.[109]

There seem to be inconsistencies in the content and language of the
canons. Many canons have an extremely strict first section, to be followed by a much more moderate second part.[110] This may have been
due to disagreement within the group of council fathers. The canons
may be the result of arguments and discussions. The leaders not only
wished to admonish the faithful; they also needed to establish their
own positions. Another reason could also be the fact that the text was
collected from various documents (see above).

Synods were not homogeneous group meetings. They can be compared to senatorial meetings in ancient Rome. The case would be
presented: called the *relatio*. This would be followed by the proposed
decisions: the *sententiae*. The resulting debate was the *altercatio*, after
which came the voting and decision.

---

[102] Orlandis/Ramos-Lissón (1981) pp. 6–7; Sotomayor (1979c) pp. 89–94.
[103] Fox (1986) p. 664.
[104] Gaudemet (1963) p. 320, using Dale (1882).
[105] Eusebius *Vita Constant.* 3.7 (Cameron/Hall (1999)).
[106] Athanasius *Apologia ad Constantinum* 4 (SC 56b).
[107] Eusebius *Hist. Eccl.* 10.6.1–3 (SC 55).
[108] Clergy: Elvira c. 33 and Nicea: Sozomen *Hist. Eccl.* 1.23 (SC 31); Sunday liturgy:
Elvira c. 21 and Serdica c. 11 (in Hefele/Leclercq (1907) I.2, p. 737 ff).
[109] De Clercq (1954) p. 117.
[110] E.g. canons 9 and 68.

The council dealt with many different subjects. The first twenty canons, as indicated by Meigne, appear to discuss the transgressions committed at this time for which public penance was normal, involving idolatry and pagan practices and (sexual) relations.

The remainder appears to be a jumble of different topics where the organization and tasks of the clergy can be found together with discussions on sexual relations and marital issues, but also on relations with non-Christians. Punishment involved the issue of 'communio'.

The concept of *communio* at Elvira, and elsewhere, was on two levels.[111] The first was obviously receiving communion at the Eucharist. Attendance at Sunday worship was required; punishment for non-attendance could follow (c. 21, 46). Attending the services meant being part of the community. A Christian was defined as someone who belonged to the *communio*. This is the second level of the concept 'communio'. Thus the concept of 'communio' was on the community level as well. The punishment of not receiving communion meant being excluded from the community. When this punishment was inflicted for a longer period, the culprit would feel this deeply.[112]

Issues discussed at the council focus largely on the relation between the Christian faithful and their pagan surroundings through idolatry, marriage and other (sexual) relations. At Elvira, in fourth century Spain, boundaries of the Christian community had to be set, in order to develop the self-identity of the Christian community. In the early church, various issues relating to sin and penance were being discussed. What was considered wrong behavior was decided by the religious community one (wished to) belong to. By establishing what was proper or improper behavior, boundaries were set between the faithful of a religious group and outsiders. Penance for sinful behavior was related to 'communio'—and thus to whether one was part of the community or not. Therefore rules had to be made for the faithful concerning their relations with others outside of the Christian community. Jews and other non-Christians were obviously outside this community and needed to be kept away from (too close) contacts with the Christian faithful. Six out of the eighty-one canons at Elvira deal with contacts between the Christian faithful and Jews. The canons deal

---

[111] Laeuchli (1972) pp. 81–82; Ramos-Lissón (1980) pp. 26–37.

[112] In Greek, the word 'communio' means community, that which is common. This becomes the word for fellowship, or sharing, in communal rituals such as Christian liturgy and the Eucharist: *EEC*: 'Communion'.

with marriage of Christian girls to Jews (c. 16), Christians committing adultery with Jewish women (c. 78), land blessings by Jews (c. 49), and clergy or faithful eating with Jews (c. 50). A discussion of the individual canons just mentioned will now follow. After this, we will look at other canons which scholars consider refer to judaizing practices.

Canon 16

> *Haeretici si se transferre noluerint ad Ecclesiam catholicam, nec ipsis catholicas dandas esse puellas; sed neque Judaeis neque haereticis dare (legari) placuit, eo quod nulla possit esse societas fideli cum infideli: si contra interdictum fecerint parentes, abstineri per quinquennium placet.*

> Heretics, if they are unwilling to change over to the catholic Church, are not to have catholic girls (in marriage); nor shall they [the girls][113] be given to Jews or heretics, since there can be no community for the faithful with unfaithful: if parents act against this prohibition, they shall be kept out for five years.[114]

Several interesting matters arise here. The canon is directed towards the parents, not the marriageable girls. In this canon, the prohibition on intermarriage is directed against Christian girls and not young Christian men. The third point to note is the punishment: five years is a relatively heavy punishment.

In order to try to understand why the canon is directed towards the parents and not the girls themselves, we must first look at the concept of the family and marriages in the (late) ancient world.

In the Roman world, the family, or *familia*, meant the entire household. This included husband, wife, children, relatives and slaves. The family was united through common religious observances and by economic interdependence.[115] It was the parents' responsibility to find suitable husbands and wives for their children. The father played a central role in wedding procedures. The groom received the legal guardianship of his bride at marriage, the wedding was the transfer of the *manus*, the personal legal authority, of the father to the husband. By the time of the late Empire, however, the woman often remained

---

[113] My insertion, for clarification.
[114] All Latin texts are from Hefele/Leclercq (1907) I.1, pp. 221–264. Translations are mine.
[115] Ferguson (1993) p. 65; on marriage in antiquity: Ubiña (2005).

under the father's jurisdiction, even when she was married, until his death.[116]

Christian parents probably followed Roman laws on marriage. This meant that girls could be wed from the age of twelve onwards, boys from the age of fourteen. However, in practice, young men did not marry until much later. The result was that they were often at least ten years older than their wives, thus reemphasizing the central role parents (fathers) played in searching for a good partner for their female offspring who were often very young.

Before a legal marriage occurred (the *iustum matrimonium*) several other steps were taken such as the betrothal. This was a contract between families, and as such no small matter.[117] Marriage was thus a serious business, the result of a contract. It was therefore of great importance to find an appropriate candidate for the children.

Christian writers found (inter-)marriage a fruitful topic. The second century author Tertullian had already written about the dangers of marrying a non-believing husband.[118] He gives a detailed description of where these difficulties might lie.[119] As a result of the difficulties encountered, the wife would have to perform all religious duties by herself without the support of the husband. Tertullian encourages Christian women to marry Christian men even if this means marrying below their social class.[120] He further argues that if a woman were to marry a non-Christian, the danger lies in the fact that she could turn away from the faith if, as an obedient wife, she followed her husband

---

[116] She would then acquire her own legal rights. The result was that the husband in this case would be the *pater familias* but not have the legal powers over his wife. Many women as a result had unusual legal autonomy when their father died. The dowry custom meant that as an independent legal person the woman then often also had economic power over her husband. (Osiek/Balch (1997) p. 61; Ubiña (2005) pp. 275–280; cf. also Arjava (1996) pp. 28–75.

[117] Gifts were exchanged, dowries paid, and the marriage contract set up. A priest's blessing was needed. Nathan (2000) pp. 83–86. For a bishop to bless the marriage contract, see: McLynn (1994) p. 258.

[118] *Ad Uxorem*, esp. II (SC 273, 94–97).

[119] The wife may want to keep a fast, while the husband wishes to hold a banquet (*Ad Uxorem* II, iv.1 (SC 273). The wife may want to visit 'the brothers', thereby going into people's homes which her husband undoubtedly will not allow (II, iv. 2). Similarly, she will want to spend the entire night away from home for the Easter celebrations, something her husband would not look upon favorably either (II, iv.2). A Christian woman will want to visit those in need, or offer hospitality to 'a brother', thus encountering her unbelieving husband's wrath (II, iv.3).

[120] *Ad Uxorem* II, viii.

in all things.[121] A wife obviously became subordinate to her husband and could thus reject her own religion. If two non-Christians were to be married and the wife became a Christian this apparently did not go against Tertullian's beliefs.[122] However, that this situation could also lead to problems can already be seen in the earlier writings of Justin Martyr.[123] Tertullian describes a husband and wife who were pagans; the wife converted to Christianity. However, when the husband failed to follow her example, she chose to divorce him.

These examples refer to mixed marriages between pagans and Christians. It is possible that a similar concern existed where marriage by Christians to Jews was concerned. Christians therefore encouraged endogamy. Families made the faith grow, and were useful units for transmitting and extending Christian worship: not unlike Jewish ideals.[124] The issue was the difficulty a woman encountered when she married into a household of a different religious background. She could then have to adhere to the religious preferences of her husband. The council fathers must have been aware of the possibility of succumbing to judaizing practices when a Christian girl married a Jew.

What is not mentioned in this canon is the marriage between a Christian man and a non-Christian woman. Of the authors discussing this canon, Garcia Iglesias finds exactly this aspect so surprising.[125] His suggestion is that it is possible that because the canon specifically states marriages between Christian women and non-Christian men that this is what happened, not the reverse.[126] Marriages between Christian men and non-Christian women just did not happen very often, and therefore it was not stated in canon law. He also states that there were more women than men in Spain at this time, so the problem was greater concerning Christian women: the focus of this canon.

Another possibility is that, according to Daube, in ancient law not all situations were mentioned.[127] This situation is referred to as the 'self understood'. It could apply to the fact that a certain situation is so much taken for granted that it is not necessary to refer to it in law:

---

[121] *Ad Uxorem* II, iv.1.
[122] *Ad Uxorem* II, vii.
[123] *Apologia Deutera* ch. 2 (SC 507).
[124] Nathan (2000) p. 54.
[125] Garcia Iglesias (1978) p. 71.
[126] However, see also *CTh* 3.7.2; 9.7.5 which do refer to Christian men and Jewish women.
[127] Daube (1973) *passim*.

everyone knows it is simply not done.[128] In this case, it could be self-understood that as Judaism teaches that the faith is passed on through the mother, marriage to Jewish women would necessarily be avoided by Christians. This is a possible explanation for the fact that it was self-understood not to marry a Jewish woman. The canon first focuses on heretics, then Jews. Marriage to either group was simply not done. Heretics for they were considered too close for comfort, Jewish women as they passed on the faith.

Del Valle however suggests that a Jewish woman was *no threat* to her husband's faith, therefore marriage between a Christian man and a Jewish woman was no problem, and thus not stated.[129]

The argument suggested somewhat earlier by Pakter is that it does not seem likely that Jewish women would be married to (Christian) men. According to Pakter, Jewish women were not considered desirable partners since Judaism was no longer a favored religion in the Empire.[130] However, the fact that precisely this issue occurs in other council texts when marriage to Jewish women *is* mentioned goes against this argument.[131]

In conclusion, one sees that the canon is directed towards the parents of Christian girls. This seems clear considering marriage customs in the ancient world. The fact that no mention is made of young men, may be the 'issue of the self-understood' in ancient law as described by Daube. That a canon needed to be issued against the marriage of girls may however be because a girl would usually have to follow the faith of her new *familia*. Tertullian already voiced his concerns about Christian girls marrying pagans. The girl to be wed will be going to anther *familia* and will therefore follow the faith of her new family. Thus, the faith of the new family must be acceptable to the parents.

The concern here is about Jews and heretics marrying Christian girls. The canon preceding this canon is concerned with marriage to *pagan* youths, yet no punishment follows, only a strong warning against marrying Christian girls to pagans. The canon under discussion, however, is followed by punishment. It may be that the idea was that one just

---

[128] E.g., Plutarch's *Moralia*: 'men do not marry women related by blood, including aunts and nieces'. There is no mention of the mother, daughter or sister. This is because this is self-understood; it is a settled taboo.

[129] Del Valle (1998) p. 16.

[130] Pakter (1992) p. 720.

[131] Orléans II (533) c. 19 (Jewish women); Clermont (535) c. 9 (both men and women); Orléans III (538) c. 13 (marriage to all Jews forbidden).

never marries ones daughter to a pagan, it was simply not done—
hence no punishment. Jews and heretics were a different matter. They
were in closer relation to Christianity as far as matters of faith were
concerned. Influence by these groups within the community, when
marrying Christian girls, would be detrimental. Pagan beliefs stood
further away from Christianity than the thoughts of heretics and Jews.
Heretic and Jewish partners were therefore considered more of a problem than pagan youths (canon 15) and were thus considered the least
ideal of all partners available to Christian girls.[132]

The punishment of five years is heavy, but not the heaviest penalty imposed at Elvira. However, it is severe enough to understand
how seriously the council fathers saw the 'threat' of marriage between
(Christian) girls and heretics and Jews. These groups were either close
to the Christian community yet harbored 'wrong' beliefs (heretics) or
happened to be just that group which the Christian community was
attempting to move away from in the search for its own identity too.
Too close for comfort, one might say. Hence the strong punishment
in this canon.

The topic of intermarriage also appears in the Theodosian Code
(3.7.2 and 9.7.5). The law CTh 3.7.2 dates to 388 and states:

> *Ne quis Christianam mulierem in matrimonio Iudaeus accipiat, neque*
> *Iudaeae Christianus coniugium sortiatur. Nam si quis aliquid huiusmodi*
> *admiserit, adulterii vicem commissi huius crimen obtinebit, libertate in*
> *accusandum publicis quoque vocibus relaxata.*

> No Jew shall take a Christian woman in marriage, neither shall a Chris-
> tian marry a Jewess. Indeed, if anyone shall commit something of the
> kind, his crime shall be considered as an adultery, with the right to
> accuse allowed the general public.[133]

This ruling is against mixed marriages, between Jews and Christians
and is directed towards men and women, and not only the parents (of
girls) as in the canon of Elvira. The penalty is equal to that imposed
on adultery. This transgression equals homicide and the punishment
is the death penalty. Not only the accused but also his or her family

---

[132] Laeuchli (1972) p. 37 in discussing these canons (15 and 16) judges the punishment of canon 15 ('end in adultery of the soul') less harsh than canon 16; which in
turn is less harsh than c. 17 prohibiting Christian parents allowing their daughters to
marry pagan priests ('not be given communion, even at the end').

[133] Linder (1987) p. 179, incl. his translation.

is included in the punishment. The issue is apparently interesting enough for the state as well to address it.

Linder claims that this law was copied from canon law, possibly at the initiative of Ambrose who was very much against the marriage of Christians to non—Christians.[134]

The exact same text and date appear in CTh 9.7.5, and is repeated in CJ 1.9.6 and the Breviarium 3.7.2.

The punishment is harsher than in church law, moreover in this case both men and women are addressed and not just the parents of marriageable girls as in canon law.

CANON 49

> *Admoneri placuit possessores, ut non patiantur fructus suos, quos a Deo percipiunt cum gratiarum actione, a judaeis benedici, ne nostram irritam et infirmam faciant benedictionem; si quis post interdictum facere usurpaverit, penitus ab Ecclesia abjiciatur.*

> Landholders are warned not to allow the crops, which they have received from God with an act of thanksgiving, to be blessed by Jews lest they make our blessing ineffectual and weak. If anyone dares to do this after the prohibition, he shall be thrown out of the Church completely.

Various issues are of interest here. Christian landholders receive their crops 'from God with an act of thanksgiving'. Yet, they then have their crops blessed by Jews. It is not clear in what function Jews performed the blessing. Apparently this was not allowed, for the Jewish blessing rendered 'our [Christian] blessing ineffectual and weak'. The punishment is severe—it was obviously considered a grave fault.

It is common in humanity to assume that the fertility of the earth and the produce thereof comes from a god/God. This was so in pagan society as well: the deity must be kept appeased in order to receive from the earth. Agricultural activities, not surprisingly, therefore included prayers and offerings.[135]

In Christianity as well, it is believed that God creates everything, therefore everything comes from God. As a result, one should give Him thanks. Furthermore, objects owned by people can also be blessed by giving thanks to God. For example, land and food and drink can

---

[134] Linder (1987) pp. 86, 178; Ambrose *Ep.* 19.
[135] Franz (1909) p. 1.

serve the Lord.[136] The act is one of praising God for the item present, rather than actually blessing the object itself.[137] Already in the earliest period of the church, formulas for the benediction of fruits existed. The bringing of the first fruits of the land for benediction was connected to showing gratitude to God in remembrance of the 'desert experience' (Deut. 8; 26: 1–11: God will look after His people even in hard times).[138] The so-called Apostolic Tradition mentions the blessing by the bishop of the first fruits of the harvest by giving thanks and praising the Lord (sections 31 and 32). In chapter 31 the text reads, "we give you thanks O God, and offer you the first fruits which you have given to us for our use, (...)".[139] Chapter 32 lists the produce to be blessed, followed by "with all that one takes one gives praise to God, glorifying Him while taking it".[140] While in Deuteronomy the list is limited to certain produce, in later Christian tradition the list was to include all sorts of products of the land.[141] The earliest, 8th/9th century version of the Byzantine *Euchologion*, a collection of liturgical prayers, registers a prayer for the first fruits.[142]

The sprouting of seeds and the growing of produce was of concern to landholders. They would therefore place the seeds and the planting under the protection of God. Requests for prayers over seedlings was not uncommon, especially prayers which were to fend off all dangers. The blessings over the fields were to ensure that the fruits of the earth might multiply, grow and cause those who gather to always bless the Lord.

Yet, these (Christian) landholders had their crops blessed by Jews. Jewish blessings are part of daily life. In Judaism, guidelines concerning

---

[136] See Gen. 27:27 and Ex. 23:25. These are not Christian texts of course, but they are useful for our argument due to the weight they carry in the Christian tradition.

[137] 'Benediktionen', in: *TRE* V (1979/1980). However, man also needed to pray for rain to ensure the fertility of the earth and good produce as a result. (*Constitutiones Apostolorum* VIII, 13, 7: 'let us pray for good weather and the growth of crops'. Vol. III, SC 336.)

[138] The list in Deuteronomy is similar to the list in Hippolytus: cf. Bauer (1952) pp. 71–75.

[139] My translation. "gratias tibi agimus deus, et offerimus tibi primituas fructuum, quos dedisti nobis ad percipiendum (...)". Publ.: Bradshaw (2002).

[140] "In omnibus autem quae percipiuntur sancto deo gratias agant in gloriam eius percipientes".

[141] *Constitutiones Apostolorum* VIII, 40 (SC 336). See, for the limited list: the *Traditio Apostolica* ch. 32 (SC 11b).

[142] Parenti/Velkovska (1995) n. 182, pp. 203–204.

topics of daily life are found in the Mishnah, Tosefta and Talmud.[143] The idea behind much of the Mishnah is that God created many kinds and classes of things. The Mishnah places these in a certain order thus creating an organized and balanced world for those who follow it. One of the 'chapters', or 'divisions', is on agriculture (*Zeraim*). The first tractate (section) is on blessings, called '*berakhot*'. The division discusses how to handle agricultural produce according to Scripture, tithing, and offerings to the poor. All produce comes from God, and this must be acknowledged through observing rules and honoring Him. It is thought that, except for God, holiness is transactional not immanent. That is to say, nothing is inherently sacred yet it can become so when sanctified by man. Produce of the land comes from God and is sanctified by man, acting under God's commandment. The blessing in the Mishnah *Berakhot* 6.1 ff reads as follows: "blessed art Thou O Lord, our God, King of the Universe, Creator of...(the fruit of the tree/the fruit of the vine/the fruit of the ground/who brings forth bread from the ground/ creator of the fruit from the ground)". The blessing of the land and its produce and the blessing of the articles involved is rather a thanksgiving for the produce and a sign of gratitude to the Giver. A question which may be asked is whether the Mishnah provides a complete impression of the use of benedictions in Judaism. The Mishnah gives the impression that the benediction is 'merely' a thanksgiving, glorification. However, one may wonder whether the Jewish faithful considered these benedictions as such, or possibly considered them more ritualistic, magical practices.[144]

Why did Christian landowners have their land blessed by Jews? Who were these Jews: rabbis or lay people? Why were the council fathers so afraid of these blessings and why was this considered such a grave fault, even to be followed by excommunication? The punishment is strict: eviction from the church. To be evicted from the Church means being evicted from the community. This punishment is rarely used in these council texts. Similar cases concern canons 20 (persistent usury), 41 (idolatry) and 62 (working in the performing arts).

The canon mentions the fear that a Jewish blessing would have adverse effects on a Christian land blessing. The impression is that

---

[143] Especially the tractate *Berakhot*: Ber; T: t.Ber 6:1; PT: p.Ber 6.

[144] See for example, reciting the *Shema* before going to sleep; 'Magic' in: *EJ* vol. 13, p. 343.

according to the council fathers the blessing of land by Jews had a negative effect on the Christian blessing. Christians apparently had specific ideas about Jewish blessings.

As all agricultural produce belongs to God, that part which is used by man must be blessed. A *berakha* is a manner in which the produce is redeemed.[145] In Christianity the opposite is true. Blessings create sacredness which renders food into something spiritual, even magical.[146] This is what may be happening here.

Jewish influence on blessings, amulets and many aspects of religious practices was well known in antiquity. In the first place, Jewish wisdom was greatly admired. Origen states that the Jews should be enumerated among the most ancient and wisest of nations.[147] Furthermore, Jewish knowledge of magic continued to be referred to, in all periods.[148] Jews and Christians recognized the powers of miracles, but distinguished between trickery and miracles accomplished with the aid of God. Moses, for example, had knowledge of the divine name which made him 'great' and gave him the possibility to perform miracles.[149] Eventually, his name became part of writings on magic. Jewish names, such as Adam, Abraham, Isaac, Jacob[150] and Solomon,[151] and even the name of God,[152] appear on magical papyri. It even appears that certain oaths, when taken before the Torah scrolls in the synagogue, made the oath more awesome to Christians.[153] Interest in Jewish skills went further. Their skills in astronomy were well known.[154] Jews were known to possess powerful healing spells, amulets and potions.[155] In the fourth century, Julian claimed that the Jewish magical crafts were associated

---

[145] PT: Ber. 6.1: Leonhard (2007) pp. 312–313.

[146] Leonhard (2007) p. 317.

[147] Origen *Contra Celsum* 4.31 (SC 132).

[148] Feldman (1993) pp. 379–181.

[149] Origen *Contra Celsum*, 1.21 (SC 136).

[150] PGM XXII, b 1 (Jacob), PGM XIII, 817; (Abraham, Isaac, Jacob): Betz 1986. PGM XXXV,15 says: "I conjure you all by the god of Abraham, Isaac and Jacob (lit. 'Abram', 'Isaka', 'Iachob'), that you obey my authority completely, each one of you obeying perfectly, and that you stay beside me and give me favor [...] because of the power of Iao (that is, God), the strength of Sabaoth, the clothing of Eloe, the might of Adonai, and the crown of Adonai [...]": Betz (1986).

[151] E.g. fig. 1058 ff, the judgment of Solomon with baby: Goodenough (1953).

[152] PGM I, 311 ('Eloaios'), PGM IV, 1577; VII, 564; XXXVI, 42 ('Eloai'): Betz (1986).

[153] John Chrysostom *Adv. Jud.* I.3 (PG 48, 847).

[154] Feldman (1993) p. 379.

[155] Chrysostom *op. cit.* 8.4 (PG 48,934).

with the fact that they could get a god to do what they wanted.[156] These skills became so popular that Christians would sleep in the synagogue at Daphne, near Antioch, for its presumed healing powers, just as in antiquity one slept at the temple of Asclepius.[157] This is what the council fathers undoubtedly were aware of.

There were always actions taken against magic, such as the burning of books containing spells.[158] Often, the magicians then went underground. The somewhat later Theodosian Code also turned against men using magic (9.16.3). However, it is interesting to note that an exception is mentioned for those who seek these types of remedies in order to protect harvests because 'by their actions no person's safety or reputation is damaged but they (i.e., those using "magic") want to protect divine gifts and labors of men' which could otherwise be damaged by, for example, hail.

The magical papyri as described above were discovered in the nineteenth century by the collector Jean d'Anastasi and a substantial number were purchased by him. Their dates range from the early Hellenistic period to late antiquity, and they are mostly from Greco-Roman Egypt. The papyri show the religious pluralism typical of antiquity. Often much is borrowed from the local traditional religion, in this case, the ancient Egyptian cults. However, much Jewish influence is also evident. The result is a syncretism of Egyptian, Babylonian, Greek, and Jewish religious influence with a little Christianity added. It seems that the magicians turned to the 'famous Jewish God' to strengthen their spells, and then also called on His associates to further their cause.[159] Syncretism can also be seen in amulets combining the names of different religions without strictly adhering to only one. Names such as Adonai, Sabaoth and Moses intermingled with Greek and Egyptian names were very common. There was no preference for any one religion.[160] Even if the issue in the council text refers to 'regular' Jewish

---

[156] Feldman (1993) p. 380.

[157] Feldman (1993) p. 381; Rutgers (1998) p. 118. Chrysostom *Adv, Jud.* 8.6 (PG 48, 852).

[158] Cf. Acts 19: 19; Suetonius *Augustus* 31 (LCL).

[159] Betz (1986) pp. xliv–xlviii; Cohen (1996) p. 255.

[160] Gager (1972) p. 136. Cf. also the charms and amulets shown in: Goodenough (1953) Vol. 2: The Archeological Evidence from the Diaspora. Even though Goodenough carefully places the finds in categories such as "Jewish", "Christian" or "pagan", it does appear to be very difficult to make this distinction as the objects usually combine various religious aspects (see on this also Gager, p. 136).

blessings, the fear as expressed by the council fathers in punishing this so gravely implies that there was more happening here—something related to issues of magical practices which were considered closely related to 'regular' blessings.

Christians were obviously aware of the attraction of certain aspects of the Jewish religion. Jewish blessings apparently held a certain power for Christian landowners and council fathers. It is of course a fact that that which is done by another group, and especially if not acceptable to orthodoxy, will more easily be labeled as 'magic', an epithet not usually applied to oneself. We do not know who these Jews who performed the blessings were, nor whether they were invited to perform these duties or did so of their own accord. This question, stated above, therefore remains unanswered. Nor do we know whether this happened on a regular basis or whether it was occasional. What we can say is that (Christian) landowners felt the need to request Jews to bless their land and that the Christian faithful felt that these blessings were more powerful than the Christian blessings.

The Theodosian Code (16.7.3) speaks out against Christians involved in non-Christian cults—whether they be pagan, Jewish or Manichaean. The law dates to 388 and is a lengthy decree on Christians participating in non-Christian cults. The law appears in a shorter version in Justinian's Code (CJ 1.7.2) and the Breviarium (16.2.1). The part of the text applicable to our discussion reads:

> *Christianorum ad aras et templa migrantium negate testandi licentia vindicamus admissum. Eorum quoque flagitia puniantur, qui Christianae religionis et nominis dignitate neglecta Iudaicis semet polluere contagiis.* [...]

> We punish the crime of Christians passing over to altars and temples by abrogating their power to bequeath in testament. Also those who despise the dignity of the Christian religion and name and polluted themselves with the Jewish contagions shall be punished for their disgraceful acts.[161]

The text is lengthy and unclear both on specifics as on punishment. Linder sees here the state enforcing canon law on syncretistic activities and actually uses the canon of Elvira as the example.[162] The similarities

---

[161] Linder (1987) pp. 170–171; incl. his translation.
[162] Linder (1987) p. 168.

to the canon under discussion are of course few, however the issue is the same: Christians should not be involved in non-Christian religious activities.

CANON 50

Si vero quis clericus vel fidelis cum judaeis cibum sumpserit, placuit eum a communione abstineri, ut debeat emendari.

If any of the clergy or the faithful eats with Jews, he shall be kept from communion in order that he be corrected, as he should.

The canon addresses the issue of communal meals between clergy and Jews, and the faithful and Jews. The punishment is not too harsh: the 'culprit' is kept away until (s)he amends their ways.

The punishment when dining in such company is linked to communion. One may assume that as the issue here is eating, that the *'communione abstineri'* refers to being kept away from receiving communion. The person who makes the mistake of eating with Jews shall not be allowed to receive communion. That is to say, he will therefore not be part of the community, of those receiving communion, at least for a while: until he repents and has received pardon.

The issue of meals where Christian clergy and/or the faithful eat with Jews is a concern which returns at many councils well into the Middle Ages.[163]

The question is whether the problem would lie only in Christians eating with Jews, or also with any other group not part of the Christian community. In order to clarify the issue concerned, it would be useful to diverge slightly and investigate meal customs in the ancient world. Meals are more than just the partaking of food and drink. In order to understand a people, it is necessary to understand their meal practices.[164] Meal practice and social organization are analogous. Having a meal with other people means being accepted into that group for that occasion.

---

[163] Cf. the councils of Laodicea (367) canon 38; Vannes (465) canon 12; Agde (506) c. 40; Epaon (517) c. 15; Orléans III (538) c. 13; Metz (888) c. 7; Coyaca, Spain (1050) c. 6 etc.
[164] Douglas (1973) p. 55.

Graeco-Roman Meals

All meals in the ancient world included a ritual element. Completely secular social life did not exist. There were different types of meals in antiquity: these depended on the occasion, they were meant for socializing and food played an important role.

A banquet, or main meal (*cena*), consisted of two parts: the opening (δεῖπνον) with various courses, followed by the drinking part of the meeting (συμπόσιον). The latter part of the meal in particular could include various types of entertainment,[165] undoubtedly sometimes somewhat excessive in execution. The meal elements created a relationship among the diners. They were a male affair where social relations played an enormous role. That is why it was considered so important to follow a certain set of rules.[166]

After the meal, the tables were removed, the women left and the συμπόσιον, the drinking part, followed. This wine drinking after the meal were bonding meetings between the guests. It gradually became more institutionalized and prayers were important and hymns expected. The symposium started with the mixing of the wine, and libations were poured. Conversation was essential and considered educational for the young people present.[167] Themes for discussion were philosophical topics, or the recitation of poetry or stories.[168] At the end, incense, prayers, libations and hymns closed the evening.[169] Social relations were the focal point of meal practices in the ancient world where not just neutral rituals but religious practices became more institutionalized. It is obvious that being involved in such rituals not only meant that one became part of the group but also that one was present when libations were poured. One became involved with (pagan) offerings as well.[170] This was a concern for Jews as well as Christians.

---

[165] Best known is of course: Plato *Symposion* 176 E (LCL 166). Also: Plutarch *Quaestiones Convivales* (in: *Moralia* vol. VIII LCL 424).

[166] It was thus essential to know when to arrive: one could not be too late or even too early. (Bradley (1998) p. 40). It was best advised to look at your neighbor in order not to make too many mistakes. (Cf. Plutarch, *Moralia*: 42 F, 45 E, 50 D (LCL 197)).

[167] Plato, *Symposion* 176 A (LCL 166).

[168] Plato, *Symposion* 176 E, and following.

[169] Leyerle (1999) p. 39.

[170] McGowan (1999) pp. 60–88; Smith (2003) pp. 28–30.

Jewish Meals

Since ancient times, meals in Judaism as well were a means to reaffirm or establish a relationship. In the Bible, meals were expressions of hospitality and friendship, whether with one's fellow man or the special relationship with God.[171] Jewish meals, especially the Friday evening or Sabbath meal, followed Graeco-Roman norms on etiquette and ethics.[172] There were instructions on reclining, seating procedures, and how and when to eat.[173] The final cup symbolized the communal aspect of table fellowship, not unlike the *symposia* described above.[174]

Christian Meals

The meal practices of early Christians were of course also inspired by religious beliefs. The communal setting was related to the symbolism of an idealized, eschatological, community.[175] This is especially evident in the exclusive nature of those partaking of the food and drink which has been blessed.[176] Especially in early Christianity the communal meal was closely connected to a religious context. The commemoration of Jesus' table fellowship was included in the group's partaking of food and drink. As this specific aspect gradually developed it became a more symbolic meal, the Eucharist, which was then gradually celebrated in a specific cultic area. The communal meal may have continued as an *agape*, or friendship, meal.[177]

Christian ritual communal meals are described in the first century *Didache* and the later *Apostolic Tradition*. The communal part includes an individual blessing over a cup, as is also seen in the Jewish tradition.[178] The situation described in the Apostolic Tradition (ch. 27) suggests two scenarios: either the participants received food to be taken away, or they ate together. One assumes that it was especially in the communal partaking of food that strict rules applied. The situation described shows how much the ritual aspect was intertwined with

---

[171] Cf. Moses: Ex. 24: 1–2; in an eschatological sense: Is. 24:6.
[172] M: Ber 6:5–6; bBer 8. Cf. Plutarch *Quaestiones Conviviales* 614 E (LCL 424).
[173] PT: Ber 4.8.
[174] M: Ber 8.
[175] Smith (2003), p. 279.
[176] *Didache* 9:5 (SC 248); Rouwhorst (2006).
[177] Smith (2003) p. 285.
[178] *Traditio Apostolica* 26 (SC 11b), cf. mBer 6.6. Cf. Bradshaw (2002) p. 142.

the partaking of food. The rituals involved made these gatherings not much different from the Jewish meals and Graeco-Roman banquets, yet the communal aspects in Christian gatherings were more emphasized. Christian ritual meals were replete with exclusivity, except for those within the community.

One may conclude from the above that meals were no ordinary matter. Meals were closely connected to community and its rituals. It is therefore not surprising that the council fathers were so much against joint meals, especially where they concerned Christians and Jews—just the group whose practices the Christian community was attempting to divest itself of. Yet, this proved to be difficult.

Incidentally, Christians and Jews also shared a common concern about the food to be eaten. Christians were careful about eating and drinking with others, as the consumed items could, after all, be associated with idolatry and impurity. Thus it was difficult to participate in meals with others.[179] Jewish dietary restrictions meant difficulties in sharing a meal with non-Jews. It seems possible that Jews in a non-kosher environment adhered to a more 'ascetic diet' than was necessary: after all, bread, water and vegetables are easier to eat if necessary than becoming involved in meat and wine (im-)purity issues.[180] There were Christian groups as well who had an ascetic affinity to bread and water, such as the followers of Priscillian (who lived in Spain).[181] After all, meat and wine were considered 'objects of desire' and 'causes of lust', bread and water were therefore preferred.[182] These views on food not only identified these specific groups but also made it clear who could eat with whom.

Yet here we encounter concerns about communal gatherings, which meals were, rather than specific dietary concerns.

At Dura-Europos it seems that a synagogue, Christian house-church, and pagan temples existed on the same street. There were dining confraternities attached to the temple complexes. These types of confraternities were made possible for various purposes: for religious duties such as burials, but also for social contact through dining and discussion.[183] Archaeological evidence shows that in Roman Judea

---

[179] Cf. Paul's letter to the Corinthians; McGowan (1999) pp. 65–66.
[180] McGowan (1999) pp. 257–258. On meat and wine prohibition, see M: AZ 2:3.
[181] McGowan (1999) p. 214; Chadwick (1976).
[182] McGowan (1999) p. 214.
[183] Bellinger (1956) plate 1; White (1998) p. 189.

synagogues had dining areas where social functions for the congregation could take place. It is of course interesting to speculate as to whether these functions included non-Jews as well.[184] An inscription at Aphrodisias speaks of people involved in dining activities and food distribution.[185] On the inscription, both Jewish and non-Jewish names figure. The dining area connected to the synagogue could thus become the meeting-point for Jews and non-Jews, set apart from the worship area itself.

In the Tannaitic period (approx. 70–200 CE), rabbinic literature described ways in which Jews and non-Jews may interact. All these types of contacts were directed towards peace: a desire to establish 'shalom': order and peace. These pronouncements, called 'takkanot' are contextual, applicable to certain groups in particular situations, and are ethical in nature.

For example, in the Tosephta Peah it speaks of the 'dish for the poor (tamchui: or soup kitchen)[186] is for every day, the funds for the poor (kuppah) are for the day before the sabbath. The dish for the poor was for all the poor and consisted of providing meals, i.e. a soup kitchen.[187]

Communal dining, in the extended household according to Graeco-Roman ideas, occurred within all social groups, whether Jewish, Christian or pagan. These meals could be held in areas close to the buildings for worship, or within the home. After all, meals were part of the complex system of social integration. Thus, it seems likely that guests from different religious backgrounds could meet at these functions, Christians, Jews and pagans alike.

It is obvious that the purely liturgical (Eucharistic) meal increasingly came under ecclesiastical control. Christian and Jewish worship was held in appropriate buildings, in the liturgical setting controlled by the community. However, we see at Elvira that the rules for rituals and meals in whatever setting were not always that clear-cut.

From the above it appears that meals were a communal affair often involving ritual practices, prayers and particular types of entertainment and discussions. It was this ritual aspect which was the result of being part of a communal gathering which was of concern to the council

---

[184] White (1998) p. 188.
[185] Cf. Reynolds/Tannenbaum (1987) passim.
[186] See also M: Peah 8,7; BT: Bab Baha 8b; PT: Peah 8,7.
[187] Scholder (1998) pp. 37, 39, 55.

fathers at Elvira, rather than specific dietary restrictions. Christians joining Jews at table fellowship meant at least temporarily being part of the Jewish communal gathering and participating in Jewish rituals and prayers, which was something to be avoided, the council fathers thought.

CANON 78

> *Si quis fidelis habens uxorem cum Judaea vel gentili fuerit moechatus, a communione arceatur; quod si alius eum detexerit, post quinquennium acta legitima paenitentia poterit dominicae sociari communioni.*

> If one of the faithful who is married commits adultery with a Jewish or pagan woman, he shall be cut off, but if someone else exposes him, he can share Sunday communion after five years, having completed the required penance.

The canon is concerned with adultery between a Christian man and a Jewish or pagan woman. This is considered an unlawful action. Yet, the punishment is related to issues on two levels. If the man commits the fault he is evicted from the community. However, if someone else exposes the 'crime', the punishment is less severe. When someone else exposes him, he may return to the community after five years; not in the first case.

Based on this, the following questions can be asked:

– The canon speaks of adultery with a Jewish or pagan woman. Would adultery with a Christian woman be less of a problem? In other words, is the issue adultery as such or specifically an inter-religious relationship as well as the aforementioned transgression of adultery?
– Why is the punishment so harsh—because of adultery or specifically adultery with a non-Christian woman? And why is it less harsh when the culprit is found out?
– Why is the canon directed only towards men? Were they to be held responsible?

Adultery was seen as an especially grave sin. It is mentioned several times at Elvira.[188] The canons seem to represent a rather rigorist point

---

[188] Canons 18, 30, 31, 47, 64, 65, 69, 70 and 72.

of view. This is also seen where, for example, idolatry is concerned. In most cases no penance is possible any more.[189] However, where adultery is concerned occasionally the transgressor, after penance, may return to the community. For example, if a woman ends the adulterous relationship she may receive communion after ten years (c. 64). For clerics the penance is harsher (c. 18, 30, 65). If a young Christian man sins he is only to be admitted into the fold after marrying and fulfilling the required penance (c. 31). However, anyone committing the sin of adultery twice is denied communion 'even at the end' (of life) (c. 47).

What we see in these examples is that both men and women are addressed and punished, occasionally rather harshly—the guilty person can be cut off from the community all together. This drastic punishment appears rarely at Elvira, except in the following cases: canon 20 speaks of clergy involved in usury: if they persist, they will be cast out; canon 41 speaks of faithful involved in idolatry; canon 62 discusses charioteers and pantomime actors who keep their profession;[190] canon 49, discussed above, speaks of landholders having their land blessed by Jews. In the aforementioned cases, the repeated offender will be "considered outside of the church" (canon 41), or "thrown out of the church completely" (canon 49).

The 'lesser' punishment of being restricted from receiving communion for five years also appears in several canons. In this case, all are concerned with ethics and idolatry: canon 14 concerns girls who have had sexual relations (not with the intended husband) before marriage; canon 16, as discussed above, speaks of catholic girls marrying Jews and heretics; canon 40 is concerned with landholders involved with idolatry; canon 69 also speaks of a man who commits adultery once, although here with a woman whose religion is not specified. However, in canon 69 it is stated that if during the penance of five years he should fall ill, he may receive communion again, and be part of the community. In canon 72, the case describes a woman who has committed adultery but then marries the man. False witnesses, informers and deacons who have committed mortal crimes also receive similar punishment.

---

[189] Canons 3, 41.
[190] See also reference to these professions in the *Traditio Apostolica* 16 (SC 11b).

The period of five years is the period in which the faithful prepare for reception into the church. Canon 11 describes the situation of a (female) catechumen. Should she become ill "during the five-year period" she may be baptized.

By the second century divorce and apostasy were considered grave sins. These sins were considered so grave that the question arose whether the church was capable of pronouncing a penance in order that the penitent be readmitted to the community or whether it should be left to God to judge.[191] Three sins were considered the gravest of faults: divorce and adultery, apostasy and idolatry, and murder. After the Decian persecutions especially, apostasy required a revision of the earlier more rigorist punishment, and a form of penance was provided. Only in those regions where a more rigorist stance was still pursued was the refusal of re-admittance into the community held in place. This we see in several canons at Elvira.[192]

In conclusion, adultery was considered a grave offence. One may assume on the basis of this canon that it was considered even worse when committed with a Jewish or pagan woman since it was a double offence of sexual transgression and inter-religious relations (see canon 16).

Two questions still remain, however:

– The canon speaks only of men. What happens if a Christian woman commits adultery with a pagan or Jewish man? Is this worse or comparable to the canon under discussion?
– The other issue concerns the punishment when found out—the second part of the canon compared to the first part.

As far as the first point is concerned, there is little comparative material. These questions are therefore difficult to answer.

As far as the second issue is concerned, the punishment of not receiving communion for five years is only relevant when the culprit is discovered. Otherwise, i.e. when *not* discovered, the punishment is worse: eviction from the community. This is puzzling. How can one

---

[191] Messner (1992) p. 86. see also Paverd (1981) *passim*.
[192] This canon on adultery, c. 1 and 2 on idolatry, c. 6 on sorcery, c. 7 on 'sexual offenses' etc.

be punished, by eviction from the community, for something without being found out? If discovered the punishment is milder. The thought behind this may be that only God can punish the unseen. This is not unknown in the early Church, in certain rigorist groups, as is seen in, amongst others, Tertullian's *De Pudicitia*. That apostasy, adultery and murder were considered crimes too grave to be punished by the (religious) community, is a thought shared with Judaism. The punishment in Judaism was to be cut off from the community.[193]

The word used to describe these sins is תרכ, *karet*:[194] a sin committed before the eyes of God alone, which he will judge. The word *karet* means 'excommunication', or 'extermination'. It is a divinely imposed punishment for transgressions such as desecration of the sabbath, eating leaven at Passover, incest and adultery (of interest concerning this canon), and eating certain forbidden foods. Whenever the word '*karet*' is used, this indicates the severity of the transgression described. If the transgression is committed deliberately, extirpation follows, if inadvertently, a sin offering suffices. Besides being cut off, *karet* can also mean premature death. This early death is then considered divine punishment for transgressions which only God has seen.[195] The crime is considered a violation of the covenant against God's order, against his will. Thus, the person is doomed to die, as he has become *herem*, one who has broken the sacred relation between God and his people.[196] Repentance annuls *karet*.

In this council ruling, it appears that the crime has been committed without anyone seeing it, for the second half of the ruling applies to "if someone else exposes him". If the transgressor sins and does not confess, punishment is left to God. If found out, and, one assumes, he repents, the required penance of 5 years follows. If he does not confess, he lives in (mortal) sin; in effect cut off from God and communion with his fellow believers.[197]

---

[193] Sellès (1990) pp. 455–464.
[194] Cf. Lev. 17:10; Ezech. 14:8. See also BT: Ket 30a, M Ker 1:1—these texts all refer to extirpation following severe transgressions.
[195] *EJ* vol. 11, 'karet', pp. 806–807.
[196] Stern (1991) pp. 155, 209 f.
[197] Laeuchli (1972) p. 40, considers the 5 year penance more grave than being cut off. He assumes that *arceatur* (cut off) 'did not imply an extreme disciplinary measure'. His reasoning is not clear to me.

This ruling may have been influenced by rigorism; adultery was considered a grave sin.[198] Re-admittance is possible—'if someone else exposes him', and the transgressor repents. The punishment of part of the canon appears to resemble the Jewish *karet*, yet it seems more likely that the canon was influenced by rigorism. The fact that there is a milder option—if discovered—may indicate how divided the points of view were concerning the transgressions discussed at Elvira.[199]

This topic is not discussed in civil law yet the laws on intermarriage which we saw above compare the mixing of religions in matrimony a crime comparable to adultery, and to be punished as such.[200]

There are three further canons which some consider to be judaizing practices by the Christian faithful, or at least close contacts between the two religious communities.

Canon 26

Errorem placuit corrigi, ut omni sabbati die superpositiones celebremus.

The mistake must be corrected that we celebrate (observe) extensions (of the fast) every Saturday.[201]

The word '*superpositiones*' is translated by Blaise as 'extending the fast until the next day'.[202] These 'extensions of the fast', i.e. fasting until the next day, are apparently held every Saturday. That these extensions refer to a fasting practice can also be seen in canon 23 where '*superpositiones*' is preceded by '*jejunii*', that is to say 'fasting'. In that canon the faithful are encouraged to extend the fast (*jejunii superpositiones*) every month, except July and August 'due to some people's weakness'.

So, the issue that the fathers wish to go against is a practice of 'extending the fasting until the next day'. This apparently occurred every Saturday. The question is which extension: from which day until the following?

---

[198] Canons 7, 18, 47, 63, 65, 70, 72 etc.
[199] Laeuchli (1972) ch. 2, pp. 17–55, esp. pp. 37–38.
[200] See Elvira canon 16, and *CTh* 3.7.2 and 9.7.5; *CJ* 1.9.6 and *Breviarium* 3.7.2 and 9.4.4).
[201] The translation has been discussed with a few people, but the above version seems most likely. With many thanks to Prof. Dr. G.A.M. Rouwhorst, Utrecht/Tilburg.
[202] Blaise (1954): 'jusqu'au lendemain'.

In Christianity as well as Judaism, fasting was seen as a ritual of purification, a sign of repentance or preparation for a great religious occasion. Both religious groups knew moments when fasting was common.

In the early church, Wednesday and Friday were normal fasting days.[203] The first century *Didache*, chapter 8, states that Jews fasted on Monday and Thursdays. It further advised that Christians should avoid these days and fast on Wednesdays and Fridays. The third century *Didascalia* also encouraged fasting on Wednesday and Friday.[204] The argument put forward by the *Didache* is also used by the fourth century Apostolic Constitutions:

> that your fasts may not happen at the same time as the hypocrites;[205] they fast the second and the fifth day of the week.[206] You should either fast the five days, or the Wednesday and the day of preparation (παρασκευήν), because it is the Wednesday that the trial to condemn the Lord came to a head and Judas promised to betray him for money; the day of preparation (παρασκευη) because it is the day the Lord suffered the passion on the Cross under Pontius Pilate. But the Sabbath and the Sunday you must celebrate, for the first commemorates the creation of the world, and the second the resurrection. Only one Sabbath in all the year you must observe especially, that of the entombment of the Christ; it is better to fast on that day and not celebrate; for the Creator is under the earth, mourning him supersedes joy of the creation, for by nature and dignity the Creator is worth more than the creatures.[207]

It would therefore seem from this text that Wednesdays and Fridays were normal fasting days for Christians in the fourth century. Holy Saturday was also encouraged as a fasting day as we see above, and in Eusebius.[208] Saturday and Sunday were days for feasting (except for Holy Saturday). However, apparently in some parts of the western Mediterranean Saturday was also seen as a fasting day during the year. The Saturday fast continued from the regular Friday fast, the day

---

[203] 'Fasts and fasting': ODCC (2005) based on the *Didache*. On Wednesday and Friday as fasting days, cf. Tertullian *De Orat.* 19, 1 (PL 1, 1286); *Hermas Past., Sim.* V,1 (SC 53). Fasting days were known as 'stational days'. In the aforementioned texts, *in statione esse* means 'to fast'. Jews fasted on Monday and Thursday, cf. *Didache* 8.1 (SC 248).

[204] Ch. 21: Vööbus (1979); English translation Dunlop Gibson (1903).

[205] I.e. the Jews.

[206] Monday and Thursday.

[207] *Const. Apost.* VII, 23 (SC 336).

[208] Eusebius *HE* V, 23–25 (SC 41).

of Jesus' crucifixion, and was known as '*superponere jejunium*'. Along similar lines, until the fifth century there was also no celebration of the Eucharist on Saturdays.[209]

That a fast occurred on regular Saturdays is mentioned by Augustine and Jerome. They state that, in the west and then especially in Rome and Spain (of particular interest for our discussion), regular Saturday fasting occurs. Augustine, in his letter to Casulanus (*Ep.* 36), states that there is no fasting on Saturday in Milan under Ambrose, but that it did occur in Rome.[210] He seems rather in favor of this practice. It is Jerome who clearly states that in the late fourth century in Rome and Spain fasting takes place on Saturdays, even as daily Eucharist is common.[211] He as well encourages these practices.

By the early fifth century, pope Innocent I in his letter to Decentius of Gubbio recommends Saturday fasting on a weekly basis because Saturday was considered the day when Christ's body lay in the tomb.[212] By the sixth century it appears to have become an even more regular practice, for example in Spain.[213]

What is it then that that the council of Elvira speaks out against? Apparently fasting happened regularly on Wednesday and Friday, yet also on Saturday in the western Mediterranean. The extension of the fast, apparently at Elvira, was observed 'every Saturday'. The question then is: from Friday to Saturday (morning) or from Saturday to Sunday?

The last possibility is shown in a text by the third century Victorinus of Pettau:

> the seventh day the Lord rested from all his labors; he blessed that day and sanctified it (cf. Genesis 2). On that day it is our custom to extend the fast (*hoc die solemus superponere*) so that, on the day of the Lord, we can go forth towards the bread while giving thanks. The day of the preparation (*parasceue*) (which is Friday: cf. Lc. 23:54; Mt. 27: 6) as well, the extension of the fast is done (*parasceue superpositio fiat*) in order not to give the impression that we observe with the Jews that Sabbath which the Christ himself, 'who is master of the Sabbath' (: Mt. 12:8), said by the prophets that 'his soul hates it' (Is. 1: 13–14), this Sabbath which he has abolished in his body.[214]

---

[209] ODCC (2005): 'Saturday'.
[210] Augustine *Ep.* 36, 16 (CCSL XXXI, 140–141).
[211] *Ep.* LXXI.6, *Ad Lucin. Baetic.*, written in approx. 398 (CSEL 61, 1).
[212] Innocent I, from approximately 402 to 417. *Ep.* XXV, 4 (PL 20, 555).
[213] Cf. Isidore of Seville (560–636), *De Eccl. Offic.* I, 43,1 (CCSL CXIII).
[214] *De fabrica mundi* 5 (SC 423).

Based on the evidence provided above, we can conclude that fasting occurred not only on Friday but also on Saturday. The 'extension of the fast' can be celebrated from Friday to Saturday. If, however, the Saturday was a fasting day in Spain (cf. Jerome) the extensions could be observed from Saturday to Sunday (see Victorinus) in order to celebrate the Sunday Eucharist properly. This was a normal occurrence during the Easter weekend (: Eusebius), but could have happened more regularly on other Saturdays as well—see the aforementioned letter of Innocent to Decentius of Gubbio. This would then be what the council of Elvira reacts against.

The contentious claim that this canon is related to Jewish issues is based on a different translation of the text by various authors.

Most modern authors discussing this canon seem to state that the translation of this canon suggests fasting *should* take place on Saturday—that is to say, the opposite of what it actually says in our text. According to García Iglesias, the bishops at Elvira wished to christianize through mortification the day of joy of the Jews.[215] The Saturday fast, according to him, was part of a discussion among ancient authors where those who were opposed to the Saturday fast were accused of judaizing, and those in favor were considered true believers. Flórez also interprets the 'error', i.e. not fasting on Saturday, as a judaizing tendency. The other interpretation he offers is that those who did not fast on Saturday saw this particular fast a practice 'against the tradition of the Apostles'.[216] Dale also sees this canon as anti-Jewish, that is to say against the Jewish practice of feasting rather than fasting on Saturday. However, he also discerns an ascetic trend in the thoughts of the fathers. The more stringent the measures, the better it was for their unruly flock. The Saturday fast would follow the practice of the Easter Triduum: enhance purity in preparation for the great feast on Sunday.[217]

According to García Iglesias, it is possible that due to the strong Jewish influences in Spain, the council fathers wished to reinstate the ancient practice of fasting on Saturday.[218]

---

[215] García Iglesias (1977) p. 67.
[216] Flórez (1904) p. 199.
[217] Dale (1882) p. 194. Dale sees the ascetic tendency of the fathers in various canons, especially for example in the encouragement for virginity as an example of purity.
[218] García Iglesias (1977) *passim*.

According to our translation, the issue here is *extending* the fast every Saturday. Once again, the suggestion is rather that fasting occurred on Saturday and that the council rules against the extension of this Saturday fast.

We can conclude that some people in Spain did fast on Saturday, possibly all day. It is doubtful that the Saturday fast had an anti-Jewish origin. The council fathers did not speak out against this but against extending the Saturday fast. The fathers may have thought of groups such as Montanists and Priscillianists who were known for their diverging views on fasting practices, including Saturday fasts (should the 'day of extension' refer to this day).[219] That the canon refers to anti-judaizing activities is doubtful, as seen above.

One further issue to mention in our argument is that not everyone was convinced that Jews only 'feasted' on Saturdays. Roman authors seemed convinced that some Jews fasted on Saturday.[220] It is often assumed that these authors had made a mistake in their description of Jewish customs, or that they had thought of the fasting practices on Yom Kippur.[221] It seemed to outsiders that some Jews kept to activities on the Sabbath and on high holy days which they interpreted as fasting. However, the Sabbath was considered by Jews to be sacred and therefore one needed to separate oneself from the material world.[222] Due to its sacred nature, the Sabbath was seen as reason enough to abstain from all pleasure. In the Talmud, the Sabbath is seen as referring to Yom Kippur, when no food or drink is consumed during the day.[223] In the blessings of the Babylonian Talmud, a Sabbath fast is mentioned.[224] The fast is then often meant in combination with a day of prayer and study.[225] It is therefore possible that ancient authors interpreted the combination of serious study and prayer on Sabbath as a fast. These Jews occasionally preferred study to feasting on this day. In the Babylonian Talmud, a person is mentioned who fasted

---

[219] Chadwick (1976) which remains a useful source for early Spanish church history; Trevett (1996) *passim*.

[220] Cf. Suetonius *Augustus* 76:2 (Stern n. 303), Pompeius Trogus *apud Iustinus* XXXVI, 2.14 (Stern n. 137): Stern (1974); cf. also: Leon (1960) p. 245; cf. also Goldenberg (1979) pp. 414–447.

[221] Diamond (2004) p. 122.

[222] Cf. Leviticus 23:3; Diamond (2004) p. 122.

[223] BT: Sab 119a.

[224] BT: Ber 31b.

[225] Cf. also Josephus *Contra Apionem* I, 209 (LCL 186): Jews who pray until evening on the Sabbath.

every day of the year except at Shavuot, Purim and on the eve of Yom Kippur.[226] Thus, there were possibilities of a Sabbath fast in Judaism, but these were rare and unusual.[227] It is more likely that Gentiles considered the seriousness with which the Sabbath was celebrated by Jews a practice as important as fasting.

It is also noteworthy that a fourth century source tells us that at this time in the west, and especially in Rome, there was a so-called "Fast of the Seventh Month".[228] This fast entailed abstention from food and work on Wednesday, Friday and Saturday, during special times of the year. The fast culminated in a solemn vigil from Saturday evening to Sunday morning. The central fasting day was a Saturday. According to Stökl Ben Ezra, this special Saturday fast may have Jewish origins. As we saw before, there were (Roman) Jews who fasted some Sabbaths, and in particular those days connected to Yom Kippur. It may therefore also be true that this specific Christian Saturday fast had Jewish origins. What follows is the question whether other Saturday fasts had a similar influence.

Another possibility, which seems most likely, is that the Saturday fasting practice had no Jewish connotation at all, but that it merely refers to commemorating Christ's entombment. After all, every Friday can be held as Good Friday, followed by fasting on Saturday—cf. the letter of Innocent to Decentius.

One may conclude that the council assumes that fasting took place on Saturday. The question is whether this fasting was an anti-Jewish practice. It seems more likely that the Holy Saturday fasting became a more general weekly fasting practice, possibly originally related to anti-Jewish sentiments. Extending the fast from Saturday to Sunday morning, one presumes, would mean turning the Easter vigil practice into a weekly event. Fasting in the night following Holy Saturday did originally have an anti-Jewish background but this was not the case when performed on a weekly basis.

Whatever the reason for fasting on a Saturday, the council fathers were obviously against extending the fast every Saturday. It makes sense that the council is against this for it should only happen on Holy Saturday until Easter morning. One may assume that the council would

---

[226] BT: Pes 68b.
[227] Diamond (2004), p. 123.
[228] Pope Leo the Great, Sermon 90:1 (PL 54, 447). Cf. Stökl Ben Ezra (2003) pp. 259–282.

wish to avoid turning every weekend into an Easter resemblance. Any Jewish connotation would seem unlikely in this case.

Canon 36

Placuit picturas in ecclesia esse non debere, ne quod colitur et adoratur in parietibus depingatur.

There may be no pictures in the church, lest what is worshipped and adored be depicted on the walls.[229]

The concern of the council fathers is for pictures 'in the church'. One may ask what is meant by 'in the church'—the community, or a building.

The second question to be asked is why the fathers were so concerned about what is 'worshipped and adored' being depicted on walls.

The word *'ecclesia'* can be used to indicate 'the community' or the building where the community meets. In this case, there is no great problem as walls are mentioned in this canon—thus indicating some kind of structure. Furthermore, canon 52 of Elvira speaks against derogatory writings placed in a church (*in ecclesia*)—one may assume there as well the canon is referring to a structure.[230] Whether these were genuine churches or cultic areas, is open to debate.[231]

There are very few churches left in Spain dating to this early period.[232] Actual church buildings did exist, especially in the cities. These are also mentioned in the writings of church fathers, such as Prudentius who described the Santa Eulalia in Mérida.[233] In earlier periods, and especially in the countryside, the meeting places for Christians were, as elsewhere, in houses.[234] As stated, early church buildings are few, and these are often funerary chapels. Some do have paintings on the walls.

---

[229] My translation, Latin text from Hefele/Leclercq (1907) I.1, p. 240.

[230] Blaise (1954) 'ecclesia'.

[231] See below for a discussion on the archeological evidence. According to Souter, the word 'ecclesia' from the fourth century onwards is increasingly associated with the building where Christians meet: Souter (1949). Cf. also the late fourth century councils of Zaragoza (380), canon 2, and Toledo (380/400), canon 5. Even though this council is before 312, I would like to argue in favor of interpreting the word as meaning a building on the evidence of early (house) churches.

[232] Most fourth century structures have been re-used in later structures: Fontaine (1973) p. 43 ff.

[233] Prudentius *Peristeph.* Hymn 3 (Lavarenne (1951) vol. IV).

[234] Cf. Mérida; Puertas Tricas (1975) p. 151.

The best-known chapel is that of Centcelles (Tarragona).[235] It was originally a second century Roman villa with many decorated rooms. Especially interesting are two vast rooms in the center of the building, dating to the third century, with large domed ceilings. One is seriously damaged. The other was eventually turned into a mausoleum, with a crypt beneath. On the ceiling there are many representations. The outer ring contains a hunting scene. The second ring is composed of different biblical scenes including, for example from the New Testament, Lazarus and the Good Shepherd, and from the Old Testament Daniel and Adam and Eve. The inner ring contains representations of the four seasons. It seems likely that a high-ranking person would have been buried here, yet it is uncertain who it was.[236] It is suggested that the artisans may have come from the East or from Rome, as the scenes closely resemble similar examples at Antioch[237] and in the Santa Costanza in Rome.[238]

In Barcelona, underneath the current Gothic cathedral, are the remains of an early Christian basilica with baptistery.[239] The remains of the decoration found show geometric patterns.

A third Christian chapel, or church, with pictures, is found in Troya, near modern day Setúbal in Portugal.[240] On this site there are two large houses dating to the end of the third century. A funerary chapel is decorated with geometric and floral patterns, birds and probably two letters (these are seriously damaged but could represent an A and an Ω).

One may assume then that the Christian community gathered in some type of building—a house church or early church-type of building.

The second question refers to a worry the fathers had about depicting on walls what is worshipped and adored. That what is worshipped and adored, one may assume, refers to the holy and the divine. Why did the council turn against representations of the holy?

---

[235] Palol (1967) p. 236.
[236] Possibly Constant, son of Constantine who died on his way to Spain in 350: Barral i Altet (1996) pp. 61–64; Schlunk (1988) pp. xiv–xv; Arbeiter (1989) pp. 289–331.
[237] Levi (1947) passim.
[238] The funerary chapel of Constantia, daughter of Constantine.
[239] Palol (1967) p. 239.
[240] Palol (1967) pp. 236–9.

According to some church fathers, it is impossible to have an image of the divine. Eusebius in his letter to the emperor Constantine's sister Constantia argues that Christ has two forms (*morphon*), a divine and a servant form. The divine form cannot be represented, it is invisible. The servant form, however, that is to say the human form, was 'mixed up' with the divine form at the Resurrection and the Ascension. Therefore, it is not possible to create an image of Christ.[241] It would be impossible to use earthly means: paint and walls, to capture the brilliance which even the disciples could not view directly at the Transfiguration, according to Eusebius.[242] Eusebius is clear on the matter: no images. Nevertheless, despite rebuking Constantia for requesting an image of Christ, he allows the emperor to adorn the churches being built with pictures.[243] He is equally excited about the statue of Jesus said to have been made for a woman from Caesarea Philippi, cured by Christ, and who consequently had a statue made of the event.[244]

According to Grigg,[245] what the council is against is using material things to represent the divine. It is not a concern for the worship of what is represented, but for representing what is worshipped. God needs no images. Images are man-made and thus subject to decay. Alternatively, the danger also existed of changing the intent of the picture: the *representation* could become the object of worship rather than the divine. In pagan surroundings, this was a genuine threat. Clement of Alexandria realized this and advised that when one needed a ring to be used as a seal, he suggested using symbols recognizable to Christians, such as a dove, fish or a ship, not 'idols' or 'pictures of mistresses'(!).[246]

The council turned against representations in churches—any pictures, for fear of representing what is worshipped and adored. The

---

[241] Constantia had asked Eusebius for an image of Christ: Eusebius *Epist. II ad Constantiam Augustam*; Pitra (1852), cf. also Schönborn (1976) p. 55 ff. Also discussed more recently by Gero (1981) pp. 460–470. For a discussion on the matter of representing the divine, see Besancon (2000) *passim*.

[242] This is an interesting statement by Eusebius, for, as we know, the disciples fell to the ground only when hearing the divine voice, not during the Transfiguration, cf. Matthew 17:6.

[243] *Vita Constant.* Bk. III, 34 f (Cameron (1999)).

[244] *Hist. Eccl.*VII. 18. (SC 41). Cf. also Irenaeus, *Adv. Haer.* I, 25:6 (SC 263 and 264) who scorns Gnostics who claim to have an image of Christ made by Pilate at the time when Jesus was still alive. He as well seems to be against this.

[245] Grigg (1976) *passim*.

[246] *Paed.* III, xi, 59 (SC 158).

divine cannot be represented; the second commandment is against any representations. Mosaic Law was clear on this: no graven images. Even the verbs used (*colitur* and *adoratur*) are the same as the verbs used in the Vulgate translation of Exodus 20:5.

In Scripture the warning is against all graven images. Here it is against representing that which is worshipped and adored (i.e. all that is considered holy). The divine cannot and should not be represented. Why? Several authors have attempted to answer this when discussing this canon.[247]

The concern voiced by Leclercq, as by Nolte, is that when one represents the sacred on walls it can be seen by everyone. The result could be that either the representation could be misinterpreted by those who do not understand the images or that the faithful could be seduced into adoring the pictures: i.e., idolatry or superstition.[248] The viewer might mistake the image for what it depicts.[249] It seems clear to Elliger (1930), following an earlier thought by Funk (1883), that here it concerns a fear of profanation of the holy. This profanation could be caused by either pagans or Jews. After all, according to this author, the whole document from Elvira deals with these issues. The conclusion is that nothing connected to the religious should be represented on walls. The ruling, according to Elliger, is against wall paintings, not against any other art form. After all, according to him, paintings were the earliest Christian art form in Spain. Large, above-ground buildings only attracted people who may have held other convictions.

This thought is further emphasized by Koch (1917) who lists the type of buildings against which this canon speaks. He names cult centers, houses, *memoriae* and *basilicae cimiterialis*. Catacombs are not above ground and thus of no concern. Besides, there are no known catacombs in Spain. As there are no large-scale plastic arts as yet at this period, Koch argues paintings are the object of the council's wrath. Based on an analysis of the verbs used (*colitur* and *adoratur*) he concludes that what are to be avoided are representations of all things

---

[247] Leclercq, H. 'Images' in: *DACL* VII; id. (1907) vol. II, p. 140; Nolte (1877) pp. 482–484; Funk (1883) pp. 270–278; Lenain (1901) pp. 458–460; Koch (1917) pp. 31–41; Elliger (1930) pp. 34–38; Lowrie (1947) p. 29 f; and of more recent date: Grigg (1976) pp. 428–433.

[248] See, for example, the graffito on the wall of a Roman Palatine house mocking the Crucifixion by depicting a crucified ass with text reading 'Alexamenos worships God': Gough (1961) p. 83, fig. 9.

[249] Belting (1994) pp. 144–145.

sacred to Christians: God, Jesus, angels, saints (apostles and martyrs) and Biblical scenes.

The representations could be misconstrued by those who do not understand what is depicted, one may conclude. Also, the divine, as seen in Eusebius and later in Grigg, cannot be depicted, and certainly not with earthly materials.

This canon has also led to the suggestion of possible Jewish influence on the council. The 'Jewish influence' in this case is the second commandment. For example, in his article on the canons of Elvira and the Jews, García Iglesias suggests that this canon cannot be inspired by Jewish thought because the other canons discussing Judaism (c. 16, 49, 50 and 78 as discussed above) are indeed anti-Jewish.[250]

One may assume that the council fathers were indeed thinking of the second commandment when issuing this canon. This is then the 'Jewish' influence: the Old Testament which is a Jewish book.

What is likely is that with the emergence of regular church buildings at this time, representations also seemed likely to adorn the walls. Church leaders wished to halt this—the representations could be images of the holy. Not only can the holy not be represented but the images could also be misunderstood.

That Christian religious structures were built we see at Mérida, Barcelona and at Setúbal. Interestingly, next to each chapel at Mérida and Setúbal is a Mithraeum.

Could this also be one of the concerns of the council fathers: the influence of various religious practices, in too close proximity to each other? Early Christian cult centers were often close to other cultic centers. This is not unusual, especially with the so-called house-churches. These house-churches were often next to other cult centers which more often than not were dedicated to Mithras: cf. here at Setúbal, but also in Rome (the San Clemente is the best known, but also underneath the Santa Prisca church).[251] Christianity was after all brought to Spain through soldiers,[252] who also brought Mithraism.[253] Mithraism was especially strong in the Lusitania and Baetica regions,[254] the area where the council also took place. Mérida has one of the few

---

[250] García Iglesias (1977) pp. 67–69.
[251] MacMullen (1984) pp. 39–40.
[252] Sotomayor (1979) pp. 132–6.
[253] Cumont (1985) pp. 58–59.
[254] García y Bellido (1967) pp. 21–41.

remaining house-churches.[255] The paintings in the house are animals and plants, but these are also full-length figures represented wearing white tunics with purple and gold decoration; one even wears sandals adorned with precious stones. Only the lower part of the bodies is intact.[256] Mérida was also a center for Mithras worship.[257] It is not of course my intention to state that the council fathers turned against possible contamination of Christian religious centers by the Mithras cult alone. I would like to suggest that because of the frequent proximity of house-churches to cult centers of religions attractive to early Christians, such as the Mithras worship, or Judaism for that matter, this would possibly have crossed their minds. After all, similar decorations are often found in the different cult centers of Judaism, Christianity and Mithraism.[258] It would seem likely that the faithful were attracted to many different religious groups. After all, at this time, it would not be so much a question of 'either-or' but rather 'and-and': i.e., a combination of many different religious practices. Mithraism and Christianity shared similar rituals,[259] and the religion closest to Christianity, Judaism, continued to be a strong influence in the lives of many faithful.

The council fathers realized that above-ground structures for Christian worship were being built. In contrast to sepulchral monuments, *ecclesiae* were accessible above-ground meeting places. Representations on the walls of these places could be seen and possibly misconstrued by unbelievers. The fact that some (house) church structures were close to pagan cult centers may well have been a worry.

The most likely reason for this canon is undoubtedly, as stated initially, the concern for representing the divine.[260] The Biblical second commandment makes it clear that God needs no representation and thus *should* not be represented, nor should anything else. An especial concern is when the materials used are subject to decay. The divine is

---

[255] Fontaine claims it is not a house-church, but fails to explain his concern (1973) p. 45

[256] Taracena/Huguet (1947) p. 47.

[257] García y Bellido (1967) p. 23.

[258] Cf. the similar pictures in the Dura Europos synagogue, church and Mithraeum along the western wall of the city: Gutmann (1992) *passim*.

[259] O'Grady (1991) pp. 55–56; Tripolitis (2002) pp. 47–59.

[260] It is especially Bevan who argues that at this time the concern is more about representing the divine than the actual veneration of images. He uses Augustine (*De fide et symbolo* vii, 14) to enhance his argument. Paying homage to images is more of an issue by later times, i.e. the eighth century. Bevan (1940) pp. 114–119, 134, 140–141.

sacred and can never be captured by human hand. Representing the divine is not only impossible, wishing to capture the divine on perishable material was even considered blasphemous.

Whether invoking the second commandment makes this a Jewish-inspired canon seems somewhat forcing the issue. Be that as it may, the likeliest explanation is that the council fathers were influenced by the second commandment.

CANON 61

Si quis post obitum uxoris suae sororem ejus duxerit et ipsa fuerit fidelis, quinquennium a communione placuit abstineri, nisi forte velocius dari pacem necessitas coegerit infirmitatis.

If a man after the death of his wife marries her sister and she is a believer (a Christian), he shall be kept away from communion for five years, unless the pressure of illness demands that peace be given more quickly.

The canon speaks not just of remarriage after the death of a wife. The concern goes further: a man may not marry his wife's sister if this woman is a Christian. The question obviously arises whether marriage would be possible should the woman not be a Christian. The canon also only speaks of the man: would this not be a concern for women?

The punishment is being kept away from communion for 5 years. This punishment occurs frequently.[261] The period may refer to the special period of the catechumenate, the period of preparation before baptism which was five years.[262] The punishment of five years is given for the most diverse reasons, including the above mentioned canon 16 (for the parents of Christian girls marrying Jews or heretics) and canon 78 (a man who commits adultery with a Jewish or pagan woman).

The punishment may be changed should the accused become ill. The wording used is not the usual "communion may be given", but "peace be given". This wording is also found in several other canons,[263] including canon 47 where the phrase "communion of peace" is found. Receiving communion obviously means attaining an inner peace, and peace within the community.

---

[261] Canons 5, 14, 16, 40, 72, 74, 76, and 78.

[262] Canon 11: refers to a female catechumen becoming ill during "the five year period", i.e. of preparation.

[263] Canons 5, 9, 11, 32, 47, 69.

The issue of remarriage is a concern for Christianity and Judaism alike. One may assume that remarriage to an unbelieving woman posed different problems and could be solved through the conversion of the wife. The canon focuses on men remarrying—one may assume that the (re)marriage of women was an issue for the girl's family (see canon 16, above).

What is of concern here is the remarriage of a man to his in-law after the death of his wife. In Judaism, this is known as the levirate marriage. However, the levirate marriage refers to a *woman* who, after the death of her husband, is to marry his brother. The *levir* is the surviving brother of a childless, deceased man. The *levir* is required to marry his sister-in-law, thus entering into a levirate marriage.[264] The ruling is based on Scripture. In Deuteronomy 25: 5–10, it says that if a man dies *without a son* (my italics) the widow should not marry outside the family. The husband's brother therefore must marry her. Their first-born son will continue the family line of the deceased man, "that his name does not disappear". Should the brother not want to marry her, the *halitzah*, removing the shoe ceremony, takes place. The woman must go to the elders, declare that the brother will not marry her, and then take away his sandal and even spit in his face. The sandal after all was a person's cheapest possession. Taking that away ranks him among the poorest of the poor. In this way, he is disgraced.

In Judaism, however, it was the man's *duty* to remarry. In this canon this is not allowed, but if it does happen the man is kept away from the community for five years.

Within early Christianity as well, remarriage after widowhood, especially to close kin, was frowned upon. Various later church laws enforced the ruling of Elvira. The synod held at Rome in 402 (canon 9) prohibits any Christian from marrying his sister-in-law. The Theodosian Code prohibited a man from marrying his former wife's sister, after divorce or the death of his wife, or the former wife of his brother, after divorce.[265] The children of such a union are considered illegitimate. Many church fathers followed this thought and were adamant about forbidding remarriage after the death of one's spouse, especially in the early church where rigorist thoughts influenced church leaders.[266]

---

[264] Neusner (1996) *passim*.
[265] *CTh* 3.12.2 (355).
[266] E.g., Tertullian *De Monogamia* esp. vii, on the levirate marriage (SC 343); Athenagoras *Legatio pro Christianis* 33 (SC 379).

We saw this already in canon 78 on adultery. Ruling was strict: no remarriage.[267] In practice, however, it did seem that widowers sought consolation in a second marriage.[268] Widowers could choose to remain single and follow the church's teachings, however difficult this occasionally may have been.[269] It seems that remarriage, even against the teachings of the church, was an attractive option, especially when there were no children from the previous marriage. In particular, Christians in high positions chose to remarry in order to have offspring, for example, Constantius II who had three wives.[270] His second wife died, and when he married for a third time, to Faustina, she gave him a daughter, Constantia. The emperor Honorius similarly was widowed and remarried, however without offspring, as was his sister Galla Placidia.[271] Christians lower on the social scale as well apparently saw no cause for concern when they remarried after the death of a spouse.[272]

It seems that not all church fathers were equally strict on speaking out against remarriage. Augustine let it depend on the situation, but he was obviously against divorce and remarriage if the marriage had been a regular situation, i.e. no reasons for ending it.[273] There is no mention of widowhood. Ambrose specifically states that if there are children from the first marriage, there is no reason for remarriage.[274]

What seems to be the concern to the council fathers at Elvira is the practice of marrying within the clan after the death of one's spouse. This could have been done in order to keep property within the family. Yet, nothing is said about marrying any other relation of the deceased

---

[267] Crouzel (1971) esp. ch. II–IV.

[268] Incidentally, it is likely that the situation occurred more often to women: after all, they married at a much younger age than men. Thus, the likelihood that they would remain widowed was greater than for men. Cf. Augustine who had to wait two years before his bride-to-be was old enough to be wed: *Conf.* VI:13 (CCSL 27).

[269] Cf. the widower of a woman called Philomethia. She was crippled and thirty years old at the time of her death; her husband was left behind to care for the children. Sidonius Apollinaris *Epistulae* II.viii; text in Latin and French: Loyen (1970).

[270] Jones/Martindale (1971) I, pp. 226, 300–301.

[271] Honorius: Jones/Martindale (1971) I, p. 442; Aelia Galla Placidia whose first marriage was to the Visigothic king Athaulfus: Jones/Martindale (1971) II, p. 888.

[272] Cf. the inscription of a man who mentions his first wife who was a Christian, and the fact that he had married again: Gibson (1978) n. 44. On remarriage following widowhood: Arjava (1996) pp. 168–177; between close kin: p. 30.

[273] Augustine, *De fide et operibus* 35 (CSEL 41); van Geest (2005) pp. 187–209.

[274] I.e., if there are no children was remarriage then possible? Cf. *De viduis* 86 (PL 16, 274).

wife. The Jewish levirate marriage was a duty and linked to procreation. This is not the case here.

The impression one gets is that the council does not just refer to levirate practices where the ruling concerns a duty and procreation. It seems more likely that here again the fathers, influenced by strict asceticism, were against remarriage, and especially between close kin. The specific reference to the sister of the wife may refer to the levirate practice but it is obvious that the council is very much *against* this, due to ascetic influences.

The question asked at the beginning of this section was why the canon specifically mentions a *Christian* woman. Would such a marriage then be possible to a non-Christian? One may assume, based on the above, that the council fathers specifically directed themselves towards their own faithful—they should know better than to remarry, especially to close kin.

4   Conclusion

At Elvira we see the emergence of the conciliar practice as a means of distinguishing between the 'true' Christian faithful and others, and a means of keeping the Christian faithful on the straight path. That the situation as described in this council text was far from ideal, we see in the recurrence of various issues at later councils. The council text at Elvira shows a church spread throughout most of Spain by the early fourth century. The faithful lived in different regions—in towns and the countryside—alongside people of other religious persuasions. They adhered to pagan practices, succumbed to what were considered heretical influences and also found their way to their Jewish neighbors.

We saw in the introduction to this chapter that Jews and Christians arrived in Spain before the fourth century. The fourth century archeological evidence shows that both Jewish and Christian settlements are found at Tarragona, and possibly other places. Interaction between the two groups can be seen in texts of church fathers such as Gregory of Elvira and Prudentius yet the information is vague. Clearer information comes from the letter of Severus of Minorca, yet most noteworthy is the information gleaned from the text of the council of Elvira. Archeology shows the presence of both groups, yet little on the type of interaction that took place. This is found at Elvira in terms of close relations and the borrowing of Jewish practices by Christians.

It is interesting that Judaism as well was so attractive to these Christians considering that Christianity in Spain was probably spread by soldiers and tradesmen. It seems likely that the latter may have been in touch with Jews both at home and in the regions they came to in Spain itself. Many early Christian structures are found in the same areas as early synagogues.

Whoever brought Christianity to Spain, it is clear that relations between the Christian faithful and their Jewish neighbors were close. This we see in the canons at Elvira, less so in the writings of contemporary church fathers. These are theological in nature and contain no visible references to an actual situation concerning Jews or contacts with Judaism by Christians.

One may assume that the choice of these Christian faithful was inspired not just by attraction to the synagogue but more by the proximity and high esteem of the Jews; not much different from the choice for pagan or heretic practices.

Whatever the motives, church leaders were especially concerned about relations with those groups considered too close for comfort: heretics and Jews. This concern is expressed in heavy punishment for relations with these groups. Heretics were considered undesirable partners, but Jews were possibly even less desirable candidates for Christians to associate with.

CHAPTER TWO

THE COUNCIL OF LAODICEA

In the fourth century, on the eastern side of the Mediterranean, a council took place in the Anatolian town of Laodicea. The town of Laodicea lies in southern Phrygia, approximately eleven kilometers south of Hierapolis, in the Maeander Valley—a region known for famous sites such as Aphrodisias. Laodicea lies on the route from west to east leading from Ephesus to Cilicia, and further into Mesopotamia. It was visited by Saint Paul, who mentions the place in his letter to the Colossians (Col. 2:1; 4:15 ff).

The council text contains approximately sixty canons, four of which relate to relations between the Christian faithful and Jews, or relate to supposed judaizing practices.[1]

1 Fourth Century Anatolia: Introduction

Anatolia is known to historians of various periods because of the rich sites it has provided.[2]

Laodicea was one of the most important commercial centers of central Anatolia.[3] The city had been founded by Antiochus II, and was named in honor of his wife, Laodice. The city was mentioned in 220 BC when Achaeus, military leader of Antiochus III, rebelled against his master and proclaimed himself king of that region. In the second century BC it was part of the kingdom of Pergamum during which time it flourished. Later, good relations with the Romans resulted in

---

[1] 'Laodicea' in: *LThK*, 647–648; Trebilco (1991) *passim*.

[2] For example, the Neolithic sites of Çatal Hüyük, Alaca Hüyük and Boğazköy; and for the Iron Age Gordium in Phrygia. Roman expansion from 200 BC onwards meant the defeat of one kingdom after the other. The coastal areas had been colonized by Greek settlements, to these were later added the Roman colonies. Roman rule was mainly located in the western part of the country, and by the mid-first century AD the Roman province of Asia comprised about five hundred cities. Large parts of the east were left untouched, mainly due to the natural barriers formed by mountain ranges.

[3] It was well-known for its textile industry. The glossy black wool of Laodicea was regarded as one of the finest examples and was a source of wealth to the city: Magie (1950) p. 48.

Laodicea becoming a rich and prosperous place which was thoroughly romanized.

During the reign of Augustus, most of Anatolia fell under Roman rule—not through conquest but through annexation upon the death of the ruling princes. Only part of the east and the south Lycian Federation remained relatively independent.[4] Roads were built to enhance transportation, but at Laodicea a stone amphitheater and stadium also appeared for the ever popular gladiator fights. By the late first century, despite much destruction due to an earthquake during the reign of Nero, the city boasted a city gate dedicated to the emperor Domitian, and a marble pavement in front of the Temple of Zeus.[5]

Laodicea lay on the highway at the point where four other roads met: from the north-west, from Sardis; from the south-east, from Pamphylia; from the north-east, from central Anatolia; and from the north. The highway from Ephesus to the east was one of the most important for the history of the region of the Lycos Valley. For example, if anyone of importance traveled from the west to the east, he would necessarily travel along that highway, and would pass through Laodicea, Apamea, Synnada, and Philomelium, probably stopping on the way to visit with local dignitaries and to hold court. The Lycos Valley was, therefore, one of the most important regions as far as transportation was concerned. This road was also important in the spread of Christianity.

Laodicea and Hierapolis became metropolitan sees because of their apostolic origins, but also due to their important location and social and religious significance. Laodicea was the administrative centre and meeting place of the *conventus*, the provincial assembly, of Cibyra. In

---

[4] Magie (1950) p. 466e.

[5] The site of the town of Laodicea occupies a low flat-topped hill. The settlement is contained within the circuit wall, containing three gates. On the north-east side of the slope one finds two theaters. A stadium is located at the south side of the plateau and was dedicated to Vespasian in 79 AD. On the south-east side of the site is a large building—a gymnasium or a bath-house, dedicated to Hadrian and Sabina. A water tower is located nearby, with aqueducts leading into the town from the south. In the centre of the town is the *nymphaeum*, dating to the third century AD. It contains a square water basin with colonnade on two sides connected by semicircular fountains. The basin area was later enclosed, to be approached from one side by steps, undoubtedly reused for Christian purposes. The fountains were walled off and troughs placed in front. In this area, a statue of Isis was found. North of the stadium lies the *odium*, or council chamber. Along the roads leading into the city are found the tombs of the inhabitants: Magie (1950) p. 586.

84 BC Laodicea, Hierapolis, and nearby Colossai had been assigned to the province of Cibyra which became part of the province of Asia in the time of Julius Caesar, and remained thus until the third century AD. It was then renamed Phrygia Pacatiane.

The Lycos Valley continued to be of importance due to its road system during the period when Rome was the capital of the Empire. After the capital was moved to Constantinople (in 330 AD) the Lycos region lost its central location when the roads were re-routed.[6]

1.1   Jewish Evidence in Anatolia[7]

By the first century BC a flourishing colony of Jews existed in Anatolia, enjoying the guarantee of freedom of worship.[8] These Jews were the offspring of approximately 2000 Jewish settlers who, at the end of the third century BC, had been sent by Antiochus III from Babylon to central Anatolia to keep watch at the fortresses and critical points in Lydia and Phrygia. They were given land and were allowed to keep their own laws, with immunity from local levies.[9] In the second century BC a letter was sent by Rome in support of the Jews living in various areas of Asia Minor.[10]

Josephus refers to a large Jewish community at Sardis and at Laodicea.[11] The existence of a Jewish community at Sardis is further corroborated by archeological evidence. The largest ancient synagogue found in the region is that of Sardis, dating to the second to sixth centuries.[12] It seems to have been part of a larger complex of buildings, including not only the synagogue, but a large bath-gymnasium and a colonnade of shops as well. The shops, 27 in total, were occupied by Jews (6 shops) and Christians (10 shops), ten shops show no clear religious affiliation. They were built around the year 400. While pagan

---

[6] Cf. Ramsay (1895) pp. 11–13.
[7] Millar (1986) pp. 20–32; Trebilco (1991) passim; Ameling (1996) pp. 29–56; Trebilco (2006) pp. 75–82; Jewish inscriptions: Ameling (2004) passim.
[8] Trebilco (1991) pp. 5–7; based on 1 Macc. 15: 16–23: Josephus Antiquitates 12: 148–153 (LCL 365).
[9] Josephus Antiquitates 12, 47–153 (LCL 365).
[10] This letter is found in the first book of the Maccabees chapter 15, verses 16 through 23.
[11] Antiquitates 14 (LCL 365).
[12] Mitchell (1993) pp. 32–35. For the synagogue in Sardis, see: Seager (1972) pp. 425–435; id. (1983) pp. 168–190; Mellink (1973) pp. 186–187; Ameling (2004) Inscriptiones Judaicae Orientis, pp. 209–296.

images were destroyed, obviously deemed not acceptable, Jewish and Christian images were left untouched by both faith groups. This would indicate a certain respect, or at least tolerance and peaceful cohabitation of both groups at this time (fourth-seventh centuries).[13]

Interesting to note as well, as far as Christian-Jewish cohabitation in this region is concerned, is the fact that the Sardis synagogue continued to be renovated into the sixth century.[14] This was well after the promulgation of the law by Theodosius II banning the repair and reconstruction of synagogues, in 438 (CJ 1.9.18). A law ignored elsewhere as well it seems, where the reconstruction of synagogues continued, often as here, in close vicinity to Christians: e.g., the Gaza, Beth Alpha and Capernaum synagogues.[15]

Jews and Christians lived at close quarters, apparently peacefully, at Sardis, as can be seen in the shops located so close together. Also interesting to note is that one of the shops owned by a Christian is located right next to the entrance of the synagogue area, closer than that you will not get! There was no segregation in living quarters or trades practices—all was accessible to both groups.[16]

The impressive Jewish evidence from Aphrodisias is, of course, well-known.[17] Chaniotis re-dates the well-known inscriptions of donations to the soup-kitchen for the poor (*patella*) by 68 Jews, 3 proselytes, 54 sympathizers (*theosebeis*, or 'god-fearers'). Reynolds and Tannenbaum (1987) tentatively suggest the second century, Chaniotis suggests fourth to fifth centuries.[18] It shows the existence of Jews at Aphrodisias, but also the attraction the Jewish community had to non-Jews, some who carried obviously Christian names.[19]

However, all was not well in 62 BC when Flaccus, proconsul of the province of Asia, confiscated the gold intended for the Temple at Jerusalem, and turned it over to the public treasury.[20] Sources mention four cities where the money was collected, known as assize centers. The amount collected can now be compared to the other cities and

---

[13] Crawford (1999) pp. 195–196.
[14] Seager/Kraabel (1983) p. 174.
[15] Crawford (1999) pp. 197–198.
[16] Crawford (1999) p. 198.
[17] E.g., Reynolds/Tannenbaum (1987) and references therein; Ameling (2004) *Inscriptiones*, pp. 70–122.
[18] Chaniotis (2002) pp. 209–242; Reynolds/Tannenbaum (1987) *passim*.
[19] Trebilco (1991) pp. 152–155.
[20] Cicero *Pro Flacco* 68–69 (LCL 324).

estimation can be made as to the size of the Jewish population in that city. Laodicea was the assize centre for Cibyratis, the Lycos and Mae-ander valleys. It collected for Hierapolis and Aphrodisias as well. The amount collected is twenty pounds, which in antiquity was indicative for a relatively large community.[21]

Roman sources from Imperial times state that there were Jews living in many different areas, often including Asia Minor.[22]

The various Roman documents show that the Jewish religion was protected, it was a *religio licita*, and that Jews were allowed to keep the Sabbath, follow their own laws and have synagogues.[23] Incidents such as that of the confiscation of gold by Flaccus were merely that— incidents.[24]

Jewish presence in Asia Minor is also attested through Christian texts. Jews are mentioned in Christian texts probably as (negative) examples rather than realistic historical entities.[25] For example:

- the Martyrdom of Polycarp in the second century AD describes the part played by Jews of Smyrna in the martyrdom.[26]
- Jews occasionally opposed Christians living in the region. In Smyrna in 250, for example, pagans and Jews looked on as the Christian Pionius was led away.[27]

For Laodicea itself, only two pieces of literary circumstantial evidence attest to the presence of Jews: the seizure of gold, as stated above, where it seems to have been an assize centre, and in Josephus' *Antiq-uities* where in a letter to the proconsul C. Rubilius the authorities of Laodicea assure him that they will leave the Jews to practice their religion, as ordered from Rome.[28]

---

[21] There is some discussion on when Laodicea was an assize centre: cf. Cicero *Pro Flacco* 68–69 (LCL 324): assize centres at Apamea, Laodicea (: 20 pounds), Adramyt-tium, and Pergamum. Earlier documents do not mention Laodicea: Habicht (1975) pp. 64–91.

[22] E.g., Philo *Leg. Ad Gaius* 214 (LCL 379); Josephus *Antiquitates* 4, 15 (LCL 365); *Bellum* 2, 398, 7.43 (LCL 203).

[23] See e.g. for Sardis and Ephesus: Josephus *Antiquitates* 14.259–264 (LCL 365).

[24] See for instance Josephus *Antiquitates* 16.171.

[25] Lieu (1996) p. 91 on Polycarp and Pionius.

[26] *Martyr.* 12, 13, 17–18 (SC 10).

[27] Martyrdom of Pionius, 3 (transl. Musurillo). Original text (with French transla-tion): Robert (1994).

[28] Josephus *Antiq.* XIV, 10.20 (LCL 365).

Information on Jewish communities closer to Laodicea comes from Apamea, Acmonia, Hierapolis, and Eumeneia.[29]

From *Apamea*, dating to the first century BC, are gravestones with references relating to their Jewish owners.[30] One of the inscriptions, dated to the third century, reads: 'Aurelius Rufus, son and grandson of Julianus, I have made this grave for myself and for my wife Aurelia Tatiana. Let no one else be buried here. If, however, someone buries another (person) here, he knows the Law of the Jews.'[31] Even more interesting are coins with the story of Noah's Ark and the Flood depicted on them, dated to the late second, early third century AD. These are the only known coin types with Biblical scenes.[32] The coins show Noah and his wife inside the Ark, which is box-shaped and on the water. Above the scene are a raven and a dove with an olive branch in its claws. To the left of the Ark, Noah and his wife are shown standing on dry land with arms raised in *'orans'* fashion. The coins can be dated due to the inscription they bear of second century emperors from Severus to Gallus. There is, of course, the question whether these were owned, or made, by Jews, or if the story was copied from Jewish tradition.[33]

At *Acmonia*, an inscription (60–80 AD?) relates the building of a synagogue by a woman called Julia Severa.[34] She came from one of the leading families of the town.[35] She was closely connected to someone called P. Turronius Cladus, who is the *archisynagogos*.[36] The inscription reads: 'This house was erected by Julia Severa; G. Tyrronius Klados, archisynagogos for life, and Lucius, son of Lucius, archisynagogos, and Popilios Zotikos, archon, restored it partly with their own funds and partly with offerings, repared the walls and the roof, reinforced the windows and redid all the decorations. The synagogue as well has hon-

---

[29] Cf. also in Trebilco (1991) pp. 85–103 (Apamea), pp. 58–84 (Acmonia), pp. 99–101 (Eumeneia); Ameling (2004) *Inscriptiones*, Apamea: p. 380, Acmonia: pp. 345–379, Eumeneia: pp. 393–397.

[30] Ameling (2004) *Inscriptiones*, pp. 380–382; Ramsay (1895) no. 399b.

[31] CIJ 774; Ameling (2004) *Inscriptiones*, n. 179; see also Trebilco (1991) p. 100 for translation.

[32] Trebilco (1991) pp. 86–87.

[33] Ramsay (1895) pp. 668–672; Schürer (1986) III, 1, pp. 28–30. The latter sees a Jewish origin. See also discussion in Trebilco (1991) pp. 86–95.

[34] CIJ 766; Ameling (2004) *Inscriptiones*, n. 168; Rajak (1999) 'The Synagogue within the Greco-Roman City', pp. 161–173.

[35] Mitchell (1993) p. 9.

[36] MAMA vol. VI, n. 264.

ored them with a gilded shield on account of their virtuous behavior, goodwill and zeal for the synagogue.'[37]

Two marble capitals may hale from the same building, decorated with a menorah and possibly a partially unrolled scroll.[38]

The synagogue was an obvious, and independent, organization within the Greco-Roman city. Not only Jews, but anyone interested could form some type of financial or religious link or allegiance to the synagogue.[39] In this case it was a Roman lady called Julia Severa, she was possibly a pagan priestess, and was well-known in Acmonia.[40] According to Rajak she may have been what we know from Aphrodisias as a 'god-fearer' (*theosebeis*).[41]

Another inscription, also from Acmonia, may have been part of the same building described above.[42] The inscription is badly damaged and shows six Greek letters and a somewhat longer text in Hebrew, reconstructed as: '[may there be peace upon] Israel and upon Jerusalem and [upon this place to the time] of the end'. The inscription is not dated but Rajak believes it to be later than the Julia Severa inscription.[43]

Several gravestones found at Acmonia are protected by a specific curse formula. Some of these gravestones are considered to be Jewish, not all are clearly so as these curses were also used by pagans and Christians who often copied Jewish formulas out of interest, or respect, for the Jewish traditions.[44] The curses protecting the graves included texts such as: 'the curses which are written in Deuteronomy', or curses called upon the wrongdoers 'children's children'. These texts are found on graves at Acmonia, Eumeneia, Nikomedia, Apameia and Laodicea Katakaumeneand date to the third century CE.[45] Strubbe considers most of the texts published in his work to be Jewish and directed against Jewish violators of the tombs. He doubts whether the

---

[37] CIJ no. 766 for translation.
[38] MAMA VI, no. 347, plate 60.
[39] Rajak (1999) pp. 165–166.
[40] She appeared on the city's coinage: Burnett et al. (1992) n. 3170–3177; Rajak (1999) pp. 163, 167.
[41] Rajak (1999) pp. 168–169.
[42] MAMA VI n. 334, Trebilco (1991) p. 82 ; Ameling (2004) *Inscriptiones*, n. 170.
[43] Rajak (1999) p. 171.
[44] Ameling (2004) *Inscriptiones*, nos. 171–178; Rajak, (1999) p. 173 note 44; Strubbe (1994) 'Curses against violation of the grave in Jewish Epitaphs of Asia Minor', pp. 70–128; Bij de Vaate/van Henten (1996) pp. 16–28.
[45] Strubbe (1994): catalogue, pp. 106–127.

curse addressed pagans (while not mentioning Christians).[46] This conclusion he bases on the fact that the tombs would probably be placed
near the Jewish quarter of the city.

However, several inscriptions also include the payment of a fine and
the threat of a lawsuit. This Strubbe sees as directed against possible
pagan desecrators.[47]

The interaction between Jews and their Gentile surroundings can
be seen in the functions held by the tomb owners, for example that of
Aurelius Phrougianos: who protected his grave 'with the curses that
are written in Deuteronomy'.[48] He was an inspector of sales and military leader.

Near Laodicea lies *Eumeneia*, a city where there is evidence for close
ties between the Christian and Jewish communities: it is often difficult
to even distinguish between Jewish and Christian inscriptions.[49]

he so-called 'Eumeneian formula': 'he [the desecrator] will have
to reckon with God' (ἔσται αὐτῷ πρὸς τὸν θεόν) is found in several
regions, including Acmonia where the epithet 'God most-high' (τὸν
ὕψιστου) is added to the formula. These phrases were used by both
Christians and Jews.[50]

In the town of *Hierapolis*, near Laodicea, several grave stones have
been found; all requesting that should the grave be used by anyone
other than the person who bought the plot, a sum of money should
be paid to the Jewish community.[51] The owner of one of these tombs,
Aelius Glykon, has requested according to local fashion, to have his
tomb decorated with wreaths on the feasts of Passover and Pentecost.[52]

---

[46] Strubbe (1994) pp. 100–105.
[47] For a discussion on the alleged Jewish background of the inscriptions, see: Trebilco (1991) pp. 58–84 and Mitchell (1993) p. 33 who consider these to be Jewish;
Strubbe (1994) pp. 70–105 and Bij de Vaate/van Henten (1996) pp. 16–28 who see
them both Jewish and possibly non-Jewish.
[48] MAMA VI, no. 335a; CIJ 760; Ameling (2004) *Inscriptiones*, n. 173.
[49] CIJ 761; Ameling (2004) *Inscriptiones*, n. 186; Mitchell (1993) p. 35; Trebilco
(1991) pp. 77–78.
[50] Trebilco (1991) pp. 79, 99, 127–144; Mitchell (1993) pp. 40, 58; Bij de Vaate/van
Henten (1996) pp. 24–28.
[51] CIJ 775–780; Ameling (2004) *Inscriptiones*, nos. 187–209.
[52] CIJ 777; Ameling (2004) *Inscriptiones*, n. 196; Trebilco (1991) pp. 178–179; Millar
(1987) pp. 27–28.

1.2 *Evidence for Christians in Anatolia*[53]

The history of Christianity in Anatolia begins where the apostle Paul on one of his first missionary voyages went to Pisidia and Lycaonia: to Antioch in Pisidia, Iconium, and Lystra (Acts 13–14). Probably the earliest Christian text is the Letter to the Galatians, a letter possibly written shortly after his first voyage.[54] Galatia formed the central province of Anatolia in the first century AD.

As far as Laodicea is concerned, we know that there were Christians present from an early period onwards as Paul mentions the city in his letter to the Colossians (2:1; 4:13,15–16). He apparently had some sort of correspondence with the city, as he states: "when this letter is read before you, have it read also in the church of the Laodiceans, and you yourselves (: Tychicus and Onesimus) read the one from Laodicea" (Col. 4:16).[55]

Laodicea is also mentioned in the book of Revelation.[56] It is the seventh city, after Ephesus, Smyrna, Pergamum, Thyatira, Sardis, and Philadelphia to receive a warning. The faithful of Laodicea are accused of being 'lukewarm, neither hot nor cold' (Rev. 3:15). This is due to their wealth, they are 'rich and affluent and have no need of anything' (Rev. 3:17). They are warned to turn around and change their ways. Despite the sorry state its faithful were in, the city remained a bishopric.

Then in the first to second centuries, in various letters Ignatius of Antioch (35–107) mentions Christian settlements in Anatolia, including those at Laodicea and Hierapolis.[57]

Different points of view within Christianity developed throughout Asia Minor. One stream, apocalypticism, we find in the New Testament book of Revelation where the city of Laodicea is mentioned.

Sometimes proponents of a particular stream are only known through the writings of their opponents. Thus, Cerinthus was accused of particular non-orthodox thoughts. Cerinthus ($\pm$ 100?) hailed from

---

[53] See also: Johnson (1958) pp. 1–17; Mitchell (1993) vol. II.

[54] Mitchell (1993) p. 3; Johnson (1975) pp. 77–145.

[55] On the letter from Laodicea mentioned in Colossians, see: O'Brien (1982) p. 258 with bibliography on the subject. Arguing against the validity of the letter is Quispel (1950–1) pp. 43–46.

[56] Revelation 3: 14 ff.

[57] For Laodicea, see: *Ep. ad Heronem* ch. IX (SC 10).

Asia Minor and is known mainly through the work of, amongst others, Polycarp and Irenaeus.[58] Montanism was a typical second century Phrygian movement. Its followers believed in the outpouring of the Holy Spirit upon the church, already to be seen in their prophets and prophetesses. It developed around Hierapolis.[59]

It is not surprising that in the second century already a "council" had been held at Laodicea to discuss differing views within the Christian fold, in this case especially the Easter date. The synod was held between 165 and 175.[60] Bishop Sagaris led this council. He was considered one of the foremost church leaders in Asia Minor at the time.[61] Polycrates of Ephesus speaks highly of him, ranking him among great men such as the apostle John, Polycarp of Smyrna and Melito of Sardis.[62]

Under proconsul Sergius Paulus (164–166), bishop Sagaris of Laodicea died as a martyr (d. 166). He was buried in the town.[63] In the period of the persecutions of Diocletian, several members of the church of Laodicea found an untimely death.[64]

At the council of Nicea (325), bishop Nunechios of Laodicea heads the list of participants from Phrygia.[65] He is then bishop of the still undivided province of Phrygia. This province was divided at the end of the reign of Constantine and Laodicea became the capital of Phrygia Pacatiane.[66]

There is little Christian archaeological evidence for the seven cities mentioned in the book of Revelation. There are shops/residences and remains of church buildings found at Sardis with artifacts indicating

---

[58] Irenaeus stated that Saint John wrote his Gospel against Cerinthus, cf. *Adv. Haer.* 3.11.1 (SC 263–4). For a discussion on Cerinthus, see: Myllykoski, M. 'Cerinthus' in: Marjanen/Luomanen (2005) pp. 213–246.

[59] Eusebius *HE* V.16 (SC 41). For Montanism, see for example the excellent work by Trevett (1996). The work is given a positive review by, e.g., Tabbernee in *JECS* 5 (1997) pp. 595–596.

[60] Eusebius *HE* IV, 26.3 (SC 31). The date is somewhat disputed: cf. Belke/Mersich (1990) p. 323; 'Laodicea' in: *LThK.*

[61] Schultze (1922) p. 442.

[62] Eusebius *HE* V, 24, 2–8 (SC 41).

[63] Eusebius *HE* IV, 26.3 (SC 31); V, 4,5 (SC 41); 'Laodikeia' in: Belke/Mersich (1990) p. 323; Ramsay (1895) pp. 78–79.

[64] Original text: Schultze (1922) p. 442 n. 3; German translation: Lietzmann (1903) p. 13.

[65] Cf. Mansi (1901) col. 695.

[66] Belke/Mersich (1990) p. 323.

a Christian presence (e.g. cross symbols on objects), dating from the second to fourth century.[67]

There is more evidence from *central Phrygia* from the second half of the second century onwards. Approximately 30 kilometers north of Laodicea lies Cadi. From the mid-second century comes a stela with inscription indicating that the owner is a Christian (Χρισ(τ)ιανοί).[68]

The *upper Tembris Valley*, north of Laodicea, offers an early Christian stela with the representation of a man holding in his right hand a dove, in his left hand grapes. On either side of his head is a circle with a cross inscribed, possibly indicating Eucharistic bread. On either side of the figure are grape vines. The Christian connotation of this representation is obvious.[69]

The representation of this type of Eucharistic bread is to be found more abundantly on Montanist inscriptions from *Temenothyrae* (approximately 100 kilometers north of Laodicea).

Dating from the first half of the third century is an inscription mentioning the names of a (Montanist) bishop Diogas and a female presbyter (πρεσβυτερα).[70]

The name of this bishop figures elsewhere as well, this time in an inscription next to a representation of circles with crosses placed on top of tables, possibly representing a portable altar. At this time, it was common for Eucharistic bread to be baked in the shape of an ornamental circle or crown.[71] The bread shown here is round with an inner circle. Between the outer and inner circle is symbolized the rays of the sun, within the inner circle is a cross with semicircular decorations in each corner. The table represented here has stylized legs, yet similar altar tables are shown from the fourth century and later.[72]

Temenothyrae has the largest concentration of Montanist texts, but the movement spread elsewhere in Phrygia as well, including Hierapolis.[73]

---

[67] Hanfmann (1983) p. 166.
[68] Pfuhl/Möbius (1979) Tafelband II, pl. 314 no. 2202.
[69] Pfuhl/Möbius (1979) Tafelband I, pl. 115 no. 783. Date is unclear; cf. Pfuhl/Möbius I, pp. 207–208.
[70] Waelkens (1986) nn. 366–367.
[71] The circular bread with cross representation, or '*panis quadratus*' was already in fashion in the third century: A. Stuiber in: *RAC* col. 617, 'Brot'.
[72] J.P. Kirsch: 'Altar' in: *RAC* col. 338, fig. 20.
[73] Grégoire (1933) pp. 69–76.

By the third century BC Christianity was flourishing in southern Phrygia, the region of Laodicea. Its main centre was possibly Eumeneia where many tombs were found.[74] Most epitaphs contain a formula warning violators of the tomb that they would have to 'reckon with God'.[75]

Eumeneia in the third century even boasted two bishops.[76] The Christians appeared to have been well integrated into the community: some were city councilors, and a certain Helix was even a wrestler![77] Others at Apollonia were from the curial class.[78]

Based on the literary and archeological evidence described above we can see that the development of Christianity in Phrygia went mostly through communities: it had a cellular structure. The development therefore differed depending on the region.[79] It does seem most likely that it spread firstly along the Roman roads, and then along the rivers such as the Maeander to southern Phrygia and along the Tembris to Cadi and Temenothyrae.

Fourth Century Anatolian Church Fathers on Jews and Judaism
The so-called Cappadocian Fathers were Basil of Caesarea (c. 330–379), his younger brother Gregory of Nyssa (c. 330–395) and Gregory of Nazianzus (c. 329–389). The main aim of their writings was combating Arianism. Their writings indicate knowledge of Jews and Judaism yet no clear evidence can be found of any description of Jewish/judaizing contacts and activities.[80] In Basil's works such as the *Hexaemeron*, Judaism is mostly a negative example.[81] Gregory of Nazianzus reflects on this negative attitude.[82]

The only clear reference to actual Jews is in Gregory of Nyssa's laudatory writings on Basil where he describes a great famine which had

---

[74] Mitchell (1993) p. 40.

[75] Cf. e.g., MAMA IV, no. 355 from ± 255: ending with [...ἔστε] αὐτῷ π[ρος] [τον Ξεόν]. No. 357 (ca. 273/4 AD): ἔστε αυτω προς τον ζωντα Ξεόν.

[76] Buckler/Calder/Cox (1926) p. 53 ff., esp. n. 177, 200.

[77] Fox (1986) pp. 295, 302.

[78] MAMA IV, nn. 219–222.

[79] Mitchell (1993) p. 41.

[80] Schreckenberg (1999) p. 293 (Basil), p. 298 (Gregory Nazianzus), p. 300 (Gregory Nyssa).

[81] *Hexaemeron* (SC 26b); *De Spiritu Sancto* 30, 77 (SC 17) ; *Ep.* 263 § 5 (LCL 270). Cf. also: Gain (1985) p. 264.

[82] He suggests that Basil wouldn't be so much 'against the Jews' if they would 'only replace "the Anointed" by "Christ"': *Eulogia de Basilius* 68, 7 (Boulenger (1908)).

taken place in 368 when food needed to be distributed to the hungry. According to Gregory of Nyssa, Basil had sold his possessions in order to feed the people, 'even including Jewish children'.[83]

Gregory of Nyssa, in his catechetical work,[84] instructs catechists on how to deal with specific groups of catechumens, including Jews. The situation is concrete, yet the wording and argumentation are the usual theological rhetoric. Gregory's writings are allegorical—i.e. not referring to a specific situation and describing actual contacts with Jews. Where the object of his attention in the *Oratio Catechetica* is non-(orthodox) Christians, his attitude towards these groups is not particularly positive. Hence his longing to convert them. His more positive view of a Jew is the allegorical Life of Moses.[85] Yet it does not refer to a concrete situation and contacts with Jews in particular.

Gregory of Nazianzus also uses Judaism as a negative example. In his Oration, he uses examples from Judaism to emphasize his point.[86] There is no evidence in his writings of contacts with Jews or judaizing activities. He had spent a few years studying in Palestine so he was familiar with Judaism in general.[87]

Asterius, author of the 'homilies on the psalms', and Diodorus of Tarsus both probably did most of their writing in Antioch, even if they may originally have hailed from Asia Minor. Asterius' homilies were held at Easter time, in late fourth century Antioch.[88] He uses

---

[83] *In laudem fratris Basilii* (Lendle (1990)).

[84] *Oratio Catechetica* 1 (SC 453).

[85] A writing on perfection as the result of man's ascent towards God. Moses, according to Gregory of Nyssa, is the example of someone who came close to perfection. *De Vita Moysi* (esp. at the end; SC 1).

[86] *Oratio* 29, 19; 31, 24 (SC 250).

[87] Norris (1991) esp. the introduction.

[88] Auf der Maur (1967) pp. 5–6: dates it to 325/341; based on the discussion on infant baptisms which took place in the region where the author was, dates the homilies to 385/8: Kinzig (1990) pp. 160–162. As for the place: Auf der Maur suggests Cappadocia, pp. 9–10, due to Sunday celebration of Easter. He claims that Syria kept the Quartodeciman dating. Yet, Kinzig states, Antioch also celebrated Easter on the Sunday, see Chrysostom (Kinzig, pp. 164–226). He suggests rather Antioch or Greek speaking Palestine. Seeing that the homilies for a while were attributed to Chrysostom, Antioch may not be unlikely. However, the homilies also contain several references to angelology (*Hom.* 12, 15, 19 25 and 29). This is well known in Asia Minor as well, as we will see in the reference to angel worship in the council of Laodicea, canon 35. A more recent publication of the psalms can be found in: Kinzig (2002); a commentary by Leonhard, C. can be found in *VC* 59 (2005) pp. 93–102.

well known phraseology to underline his theological argument,[89] interspersed with examples of meetings with Jews.[90] Yet nowhere does he describe actual contacts between Jews and Christians as described at Laodicea.

This is even more the case for Diodorus of Tarsus who came from Antioch and can be placed in the same period and region as the aforementioned fathers. He was bishop of Tarsus in Cilicia from approximately 378 to his death in approximately 393. He was a native of Antioch. In the theological school of that city he came to be the teacher of John Chrysostom and Theodore of Mopsuestia. He is known for his writings against the emperor Julian who, in 362–363, wanted to restore paganism to Antioch. His 'kata Iudaion' is lost to posterity.[91] Diodorus wrote the 'Commentary on Psalms'[92] against the ideas of the Manicheans and Arians, and against Eunomius, Paul of Samosata, Sabellius, Marcellus of Ancyra and Photinus, and against Jewish exegesis.[93]

From slightly more to the north of our area—the Pontus region—and later than our other writings, comes another Asterius, who was bishop of Amaseia in about 400. In his homily on fasting he describes his attitude towards Jews and Judaism. He laughs at the Jews for their clothing, how they fast without knowing why, and how they have not accepted the final redemption of man. He says that they do not understand that what Moses taught was in preparation for the Christ. He then refers to the Jewish fasting, Sukkot, New Year (called: 'Trumpets' by Chrysostom), circumcision, unleavened bread, and bitter herbs. These are all obviously things Asterius has seen and thus knows of.[94] Specific references to Jewish practices and feasts indicate he knew them. His comments indicate that his audience knew the Jewish festivals—pos-

---

[89] Texts published by Richard (1956). According to Gelsi (1978) the commentaries were intended for catechumens (Gelsi, ch. 1). If this is so, the content and use of examples from Judaism are similar to Gregory of Nyssa's *Oratio Catechetica*. Gelsi explains that this is why Asterius is so vehement in his discussion on Judaism: not only out of theological argumentation, but also due to Judaism's 'missionary activities' at this time (Gelsi, pp. 18–20; 48). *Hom.* 8,9; 11,1; 11,14; *Hom.* 5,22; *Hom.* 6,1 ff; 15.1; *Hom.* 6,9; *Hom.* 8.3; *Hom.* 15.6; *Hom.* 11 (Richard 1956).

[90] Cf. a supposed dialogue with Jews: *Hom.* 20. 7–8. Gelsi (1978) p. 10. References to the anger of Jews against those who were to be baptized as Christians: *Hom.* 8.5; Gelsi (1978) p. 65.

[91] Hill (2005a) esp. the introduction.

[92] CCSG 6.

[93] *Comm. in Psalm.* 8 (CCSG 6, pp. 43–50).

[94] *Hom.* 14.8, 14.16 to end (PG 40, 377; 40, 388–390); Meer/Bartelink (1976) pp. 238, 246–247.

sibly even participated in these: "why do you mix that which should be separate?".[95] That is to say, his Christian audience apparently, according to him, was not always aware of the differences between Christian and Jewish celebrations.

In the writings of the above-mentioned church fathers there is little genuine evidence for Jews or judaizing practices. The usual theological statements are made indicating that no concrete knowledge of Jewish practices is needed. Only the description of the famine in Gregory of Nyssa's eulogy on Basil is evidence of Jews in Cappadocia. The Pontic Asterius alone seems to refer to genuine Jews—and even Christians appropriating Jewish festivals. His wording is similar to that of John Chrysostom, on whom more in the next chapter.

It seems clear that by the fourth century there were Jews and Christians in the region of Laodicea. We know little about their relations. Some sources, such as the acts of the martyrs describe a negative relationship, which is not surprising considering the purpose of these texts. The question is to what extent the 'Jews' described in these texts are more likely to be typological examples used in the development of Christian identity.

In the middle of the fourth century a synod was held at Laodicea. The location was undoubtedly chosen because of its easy access, and due to its status as a church center. Several canons of this council may provide different information concerning the relations between Jews and Christians.

2   The Council of Laodicea

The text of the council of Laodicea, as opposed to that of Elvira, does not open with a preamble, or a list of participants, or a date.[96] The text

---

[95] *Hom.* 14,16 (PG 40, 388). My translation.

[96] The text of the council is found in the collection known as the *Hispana* (see discussion on the text of Elvira): Hefele/Leclercq (1907) vol. I.2, p. 989; cf. Gaudemet (1985) p. 75 who mentions that the *Hispana* in this case is based on the fourth century collection known as the "Antioch collection" which contained the text of Laodicea. The Greek and Latin text can be found in: Mansi (1759) vol. II, pp. 563–614 (three versions); and Joannou (1962) vol. 1.2; the Greek text alone is in Hefele/Leclercq (1907) vol. I.2, pp. 746–1028 (who uses Mansi's second version, of Dionysus Exiguus dating to the fifth century). The Latin version of the *Hispana* text can be found in: CCH vol. III from p. 153 onwards. The Latin text of the *Hispana* and the text of Dionysius Exiguus can also be found in: Turner (1899) vol. II (d. 1939) pp. 321–400. The English

consists of approximately 60 canons.[97] The canons have been divided into two groups, depending on the first words used in the statement. Canons one through nineteen open with περι του, while the next canons, 20 through 59, open with ὅτι ου δει. The statements are short, not the long-winded phraseology as found in other eastern council texts, e.g. that of Nicea (325) or Serdica (343).

The council is mentioned by Theodoret of Cyrrhus (c. 393–460) in his Commentary on the Letter to the Colossians.[98] This would give the council, and its document, at least a *terminus ad quem* as far as a date is concerned. It would have taken before c. 430. The *terminus a quo* is a bit more difficult to establish; yet one of the canons mentions how to deal with people who have sought their refuge with other religious groups. Canon 7 mentions the Quartodecimans, Novatianists, and Photinians. It is exactly this last group which gives the council and its text a starting date. Photinus was bishop of Sirmium in approximately 344, and was condemned at the council of Sirmium in 351. The earliest date for the council of Laodicea to have taken place, for some people to have been followers of Photinus, is therefore approximately 345. It appears to some scholars that the council fathers at Constantinople (381) used the text of Laodicea.[99] A likely date for the council to have taken place therefore would be between 345 and 381.

The canons deal with the clergy (c. 3–5, 11–13, 15, 20–26, 41–43, 54–58); liturgy and the sacraments (c. 1, 2, 14, 16–19, 44–53, 59, 85); canon law (c. 14, 40); non-Christians and heretics (c. 6–10, 29–34, 37–39, 54–55); angels and magic (c. 35 and 36); and the canon of Scripture (c. 60).

---

translation of Hefele's text is in Schaff/Wace (1991) vol. XIV. The council text is discussed in: Herbst (1823) pp. 3–46; Boudinhon (1888) pp. 420–427; Amann in: *DTC*, col. 2611–2615; 'Laodikeia' in: *Pauly-Wissowa Realenzyklopädie d. Klass. Altertumswissenschaft* (1925) pp. 712–724; Bardy in: *DDC*, pp. 338–343; Johnson (1950) pp. 1–18; v.d. Horst (1989) esp. pp. 117–118; 'Laodikeia' in: *Der Neue Pauly Enzyklopädie der Antike* (1999) col. 1131–1132.

[97] Sixty canons: 'Laodicea' in: *DTC*, *DDC*, Percival 'Synod of Laodicea' The Seven Ecumenical Councils of the Undivided Church, in: Schaff/Wace (1991) Vol. XIV; Hefele & Leclercq; Herbst (1823) 3–46. Whether fifty-eight or fifty-nine canons: Boudinhon (1888) pp. 420–427. The last entry, canon 60, is questionable. It refers to the canon of the Old and New Testaments, and is of unclear date. Specific references to Jews at the council of Laodicea, see: Trebilco (1991) pp. 101–103; Kraabel (1968) *passim*.

[98] *Ad Colos.* II, 18; III, 17 (Marriott, B.D (1852)).

[99] E. Amann 'Laodicea' in *DTC*: e.g. Laodicea c. 7 and 8 resemble Constantinople c. 7.

The statements, as already observed, are short. They seem to be more of a summary (of a possible earlier text?). Some canons seem to repeat part of the statement made earlier. For example, in canon 22 it says: 'the sub-deacon has no right to wear the stole, or to leave the doors'. Canon 43 seems to continue on a similar theme: 'the sub-deacon may not leave the doors to engage in the prayer, even for a short time'. The canons 10 and 31, on the issue of marriage, show a similar repetition.

The conclusion for some scholars is that the text as we know it now is not the original text.[100]

However, judging by the discussion of the council by Theodoret, it is believed that there was at least *a* council held at Laodicea, between 345 and 381.

Canons 16 and 29

Canon 16

Περὶ τοῦ ἐν σαββάτῳ εὐαγγέλια μεθ' ἑτέρων γραφων ἀναγινώσκεσθαι.

On Sabbath, the Gospels should be read with the other scriptures.

Canon 29

Ὅτι οὐ δεῖ χριστιανοὺς ἰουδαΐζειν καὶ ἐν τῷ σαββάτῳ σχολάζειν, ἀλλὰ ἐργάζεσθαι αὐτοὺς ἐν τῇ αὐτῇ ἡμέρᾳ τὴν δὲ κυριακὴν προτιμῶντας εἴγε δύναιντο σχολάζειν ὡς χριστιανοί. Εἰ δὲ εὐρεθεῖεν Ἰουδαϊσταὶ ἔστωσαν ἀνάθεμα παρὰ Χριστῷ.

Christians should not judaize and refrain from work on the Sabbath, but they should work on that day. As Christians, they should honor the day of the Lord, [and], as much as possible, refrain from work. If they are found out to be judaizers, let them be anathematized from Christ.

Both canons refer to practices on the Sabbath, although each in a different context. Canon 16 will be discussed first. Canon 29 will hopefully provide further information necessary to understand the situation described in canon 16.

The Christian faithful in Laodicea and surroundings had a special relation to the Sabbath. This can be seen in these two canons. Canon 29 seems to turn against making it too special a day—Christians still

---

[100] Bardy, G. 'Laodicée' in: *DDC*; Amann 'Laodicée' in: *DTC*; Boudinhon (1888) pp. 420–427.

needed to work, but (c. 16) apparently there was at some point some type of celebration, or at least a reading of Scripture. Two other canons at Laodicea also discuss the special reverence paid to the Sabbath, even during Lent: canon 49 on Eucharistic celebrations which suggests that 'no bread should be offered during Lent except on the Sabbath and the Lord's day'; and canon 51 which pleads against keeping martyrs' feasts during Lent, these are to be celebrated on the Sabbath and the Lord's day.

Canon 16 provides us with several questions. Firstly, we will assume that the Sabbath mentioned here is to be translated as Saturday. Apparently there was an occasion on the Sabbath when readings took place. These readings were 'other scriptures'. What other scriptures are these? Obviously not the Gospels. What was the occasion when these readings took place? The council fathers ask for the Gospels to be read as well, on the Sabbath. Why especially the Gospels and why on Saturday? Three different answers to these questions have been offered.

The first possibility is that the Christians of Laodicea attended Jewish synagogue services on a Saturday. We know of Jewish presence in the region and the synagogues found at Sardis and Aphrodisias. The Mishnah discusses the readings which took place in synagogue on the Sabbath.[101] Based on canon 29 of Laodicea, which refers to the so-called judaizing tendency to refrain from work on the Sabbath, Trebilco suggests that the Christian faithful of Laodicea may have attended synagogue services.[102] Canon 37 states that the Christian faithful of Laodicea attended Jewish feasts and 'joined their heresies', i.e., attended Jewish practices such as synagogue worship. This is what Trebilco uses as evidence that Christians still attended synagogue services.

The second option is the use by Christians of Jewish origin of Jewish Scripture and practices in their services. This is what several authors discussing both canons suggest. While discussing canon 16, Herbst states that those Christians who came forth from Judaism would naturally still keep to the Jewish custom of reading from the Old Testament on the Sabbath. After their conversion they continued the Saturday liturgy in their 'new' communal gatherings. Saturday was the day dedi-

---

[101] M: Meg esp. 4.
[102] Trebilco (1991) p. 101: '(...) the Council [:Laodicea] attempted to ensure that the members of the Christian communities went to their own service and not the synagogue (...)'.

cated to creation; hence a prayerful meeting seemed logical, with readings from Jewish Scripture, according to Herbst.[103]

A third possibility is that some Christians, not necessarily of Jewish origin, in Laodicea and surroundings may have copied Jewish practices but translated these into their own (Christian) settings. Hefele agrees with Herbst on canon 16 that the canon may be directed towards the practice of Christians keeping Jewish prayer services on Saturday. He also admits the possibility that Christians may have followed the Jewish custom of reading merely excerpts from the Old Testament. Christians of non-Jewish background origin keeping Jewish practices were considered 'judaizers'. However, so Hefele states, 'one no longer encounters many judaizers in the second half of the fourth century'.[104] This thought is also expressed by Kraabel. He states that 'some Christians followed synagogue practice in that they read only the OT (*sic*) at Saturday services, perhaps together with local Jews'.[105]

Before coming to any conclusion, let us first look at canon 29 to see if it provides additional information on the subject of Sabbath worship.

Canon 29 discusses a different aspect of Sabbath observance. It is an issue known to this region—that of observing the Sabbath as a day of rest. Canon 29 shows that this is apparently still an issue in the middle of the fourth century. The council fathers considered keeping the Sabbath as a day of rest a 'judaizing practice'. In their argumentation Sunday is used as the positive example.

Canon 29 appears to contain two separate statements. The first refers to the situation where the faithful apparently refrained from work on the Sabbath. One may ask why they refrained from work on Saturday. Apparently this was considered a judaizing practice. Those who do so are to be punished: they are to be separated from Christ (*anathema para*).

Not many canons at Laodicea contain punishments (c. 9, 34–36). One may assume that the punishment in this canon refers to exclusion from '*communio*': receiving communion and thus forming part of the Christian community.

---

[103] Herbst (1823) pp. 25–26. He unfortunately gives no references to underline this statement.
[104] Hefele/Leclercq (1907) pp. 1008–1009.
[105] Kraabel (1968) p. 137, following Simon (1948) p. 383.

The second part contains an admonition and a suggestion. The faithful should honor the 'day of the Lord'. It is not clear how they should honor that day, but at least refrain from work where possible.

Herbst suggests that canon 29 is directed towards those who keep the Sabbath as a day of prayer. He states that this is the case in the eastern Mediterranean area where Saturday was a day for remembering the creation of the world (cf. Genesis), and religious services as on a Sunday were held. No fasting was allowed on that day.[106] Herbst assumes these people were converted Jews.

Trebilco however states that canon 29 suggests there were Christians who observed the Sabbath, to a certain extent. By enforcing the reading of the Gospel, the faithful would be tempted away from attending synagogue on a Saturday where only Scripture readings would take place, Trebilco argues.[107] As far as he is concerned, the council wished to undo the Jewish character of the Sabbath by enforcing work on that day and encouraging leisure for only the Sunday.[108]

In these two canons, 16 and 29, we see that Christians coming together on a Saturday needed to be reminded to read the Gospels on that day (c. 16). It seems likely that these Christians came together on a Saturday to read from the Old Testament, but not from the New Testament. It also seems likely that these Christians were the ones not willing to work on a Saturday (c. 29).

Whether or not the Christians copied Jewish practices in their services or went to the synagogue, it does seem clear that the Sabbath was held by some in high esteem.[109]

The Sunday was considered by Christians the day of the 'new creation'. They also believed that the Sabbath therefore was the end of the old creation.[110] It was not until the fourth century, however, that legislation protected the Sunday as a day of rest and it thus became a kind of Sabbath.[111]

---

[106] Herbst (1823) p. 26.

[107] Trebilco (1991) p. 101.

[108] Trebilco (1991) pp. 101–102. Cf. also the *Didascalia* 26 (Vööbus (1979) vol. II): one is expected to work on Saturday as the Lord does as well. Real rest will come at the end of time.

[109] See on this topic, Tremel (1962); Rordorf (1962); Kraft (1963); Lecat/Delhaye (1966); Bacchiochi (1977); Carson (1982); Rouwhorst (2001).

[110] Pseudo-Athanasius, approx. 4th c. *De Sabbatis* 4 (PG 28, 137).

[111] Constantine's legislation in the *Codex Justin.* III, 12.3 which encourages rest on Sunday yet allowing those in agriculture to plant and sow. (Scott (1973)).

Despite the increasing reverence for the Sunday as a day of special liturgies, many groups of Christians in late antiquity still kept the
Sabbath. This was of much concern to the church fathers. The longer
version of the letter to the Magnesians by the second century bishop
of Antioch, Ignatius, probably dates to the fourth century.[112] It contains details on how Christians should behave on the Sabbath and the
Lord's day:

> Let us therefore no longer keep the Sabbath after the Jewish manner, and
> rejoice in days of idleness [...] But let everyone of you keep the Sabbath
> after a spiritual manner, rejoicing in meditation on the Law, not in relax-
> ation of the body, admiring the workmanship of God, [...] and after the
> observance of the Sabbath, let every friend of Christ keep the Lord's day
> as a festival, the resurrection day [...]'.[113]

The longer version explains more explicitly how one should behave on
the Sabbath: through meditating the Law, yet not through refraining
from work, however. That is to say, there should be no outward sign
of keeping the Sabbath. That should be kept for the Lord's Day.

It is clear that the author describes two ways of living: the one which
is judaizing, and the other which is following Christ—where the former becomes a Jewish custom of keeping the Sabbath as opposed to
the more 'spiritual' keeping of the Sunday (keeping in mind the specific rituals typical for that day). The contrast is not so much of placing
the Sabbath in opposition to the Sunday, but how to keep the Sabbath
(i.e. spiritually vs. idleness).[114]

Two authors specifically discuss Sabbath observances and Christians
in Asia Minor. As far as Sabbath observance by Christians before the
fourth century is concerned, a link with early (Jewish) Christianity
is evident; yet, why would there be a renewed interest in the fourth
century?

According to Rordorf it is especially in Asia Minor where there is
an increase in Sabbath worship after the first century due to borrowed
Jewish practices and possibly due to superstition.[115] The day of rest on

---

[112] McKay (2001) p. 181, note 31. Cf. comment by Leonhard (2006) pp. 124–9 on
the shorter version. The longer text is much disputed. A redactor published this version in fourth century Antioch. He may have been the same person as the compiler
of the Apostolic Constitutions. See *ODCC*, entry on 'Ignatius, St.'.
[113] Translation in McKay (2001) p. 182.
[114] On Sunday observance, see: *Didascalia* 59, 2–3 (Vööbus (1979) vol. II); Rordorf
(1972) n. 103.
[115] Rordorf (1962) pp. 144–5, using as evidence 'Hippolytus' *Church Order*. Cf. also
Socrates *HE* V, 22 (SC 505) where it is mentioned that 'almost everywhere' a Sabbath

Saturday came to be interpreted in a more spiritual sense. One's devo-
tions to the Lord should take place every day, not be restricted to just
one day. Prayers and praise on Saturday were thus allowed, but then
they should actually take place on every day of the week, and especially
on Sunday. By meditating the Law and celebrating the creation, one
must necessarily also refer to the second creation, i.e., Jesus Christ.
Saturday thus received a more Christological and eschatological interpretation, according to Rordorf.[116]

According to Carson, it is especially in the fourth century again
that more references to Gentile Christians practicing Sabbath observance occur.[117] This would be especially so in those areas where there
were many Jewish communities and Christians easily adopted Jewish
practices. This syncretism was especially obvious in Asia Minor where
Christians came into close contact with Jews. In the second century,
according to this author, this practice was to be expected from Jewish-
Christianity, yet it was again so in the fourth century due to the growth
of Christianity after the last persecutions and the adoption of other
practices.[118]

The question arises why fourth century Christians would again adopt
Jewish practices when they would undoubtedly have been in close contact with their Jewish neighbors since earlier times. What seems likely
is that with the rise of Sunday observance since the time of Constantine, apparently some Christians still kept the Saturday (Sabbath) as
a day of rest, and read from the Old Testament. As far as refraining
from work is concerned, canon 29 clearly states this should only be
so on the Sunday. As far as readings from Scripture are concerned,
canon 16 encourages reading from the New Testament as well. It may
be likely that the two groups were never far apart and that the point
of view of the church leaders concerning Sabbath observance gradually
developed while defining the bounds of their own group as opposed
to the other.

The fourth century was a period of growth for the Christian church
and saw a legal preference for Sunday rest. The council fathers were
thus confronted with an existing situation of faithful (still) following

---

celebration was held. Rordorf, working from a Protestant point of view, sees these
practices as a pagan judaizing influence in Asia Minor. For a discussion on Rordorf's
theories, see Rouwhorst (2001) esp. pp. 226–229, 235–236.

[116] Rordorf (1962) pp. 146–9.
[117] Carson (1982) p. 261.
[118] Carson (1982) p. 261.

Jewish practices while they realized the need to emphasize a more Christian implementation.

What we encounter in these two canons may be that some Christian faithful kept a form of Sabbath observance. Rather than keeping these people away from the fold, the church saw a way to encourage a more Christian implementation of Sabbath practices (canon 16), yet at the same time they attempted to enforce behavior more compatible with a Christian lifestyle (c. 29).

CANONS 37 AND 38

CANON 37

> Ὅτι οὐ δεῖ παρὰ τῶν Ἰουδαίων ἢ αἰρετικῶν τὰ πεμπόμενα ἑορταστικὰ λαμβάνειν μηδὲ συνεορτάζειν αὐτοῖς.

> One should not receive festal gifts sent from Jews or heretics, nor join in celebrating their feasts.

CANON 38

> Ὅτι οὐ δεῖ παρὰ τῶν Ἰουδαίων ἄζυμα λαμβάνειν ἢ κοινωνεῖν ταῖς ἀσεβείαις αὐτῶν.

> One should not receive unleavened bread from Jews nor join their heresies.

Apparently the Christian faithful in Asia Minor not only held the Sabbath in reverence (c. 16 and 29) but also celebrated feasts with the Jews. In canon 37 the reference is to receiving 'festal gifts' and joining in feasts. What feasts which led to the giving of gifts could be referred to here? In canon 38 the occasion seems more specific—the receiving of 'unleavened bread'. Why would Christians need to be kept away from this ritual or any other rituals for that matter (: 'join in their heresies')?

In canon 37, the word 'εορταστικα' is translated as 'festal gifts'. The initial thought could be that this refers to gifts related to the feast of Purim as the book of Esther (9:22) encourages one to 'send portions' (i.e. gifts of food) to friends and to the poor. However, the word for 'portions' (i.e. gifts) in Esther is different from the word used here.[119] Furthermore, any festival, including the Sabbath, is for rejoicing and honoring the day with eating and drinking (i.e., no fasting) and the

---

[119] In the Septuagint: μερίδας for 'portions'.

giving of gifts.[120] It has also been suggested that the Jews of Asia Minor did not celebrate Purim very often. This is based on a story of the visit of the second century rabbi Meir who went to 'Asia' and found that the Jewish faithful had no 'Megillah' (: the scroll containing the book of Esther used during Purim celebrations). The rabbi then wrote out the story by heart so that they would have a text to use.[121] Did the Jews not celebrate Purim because it was known to be politically sensitive? After all, the story is about Jewish resistance to the ruling power. Alternatively, Christian sensitivity to the story which refers to Esther's adversary Haman who was crucified may have prohibited the celebration of the feast.[122] The 'festal gifts' may therefore not necessarily refer to Purim gifts in this canon.

The translation of 'heortastike' is 'festal'. This could also relate to the feast of Passover and its related activities.[123] Several texts use this word in connection with feasts, occasionally Passover: Eusebius,[124] the fifth century Theodoretus,[125] the sixth century Cosmas,[126] and the seventh century *Chronicon Paschale.*[127]

Even though from a different region, the fourth century Syrian Apostolic Constitutions also discuss a similar issue. In chapter VIII, called the Apostolic Canons, in 47.70 it states that:

> if a bishop or other cleric fasts with the Jews or celebrates feasts with them, *or accepts gifts coming from their feasts* (εορτης), *such as unleavened bread* (αζυμα) *or other such items, he is deposed; if it is a layperson, he is excluded.*[128]

---

[120] See: 'Festivals' in: *EJ* vol. 6, pp. 765–771; BT: Pes 118a; M: Besah 1:9 and 5:7.

[121] BT: Meg 18b.

[122] Cf. Seager/Kraabel (1983) p. 183; Kraabel (1992) p. 232; Lieu (1996) p. 75 on Jewish feasts in Asia.

The translation of the story in the Septuagint suggests that Esther's adversary Haman was crucified. Therefore, reference to this aspect during the celebration of Purim by Jews was prohibited in later times: *C Th* 16, 8.18 (cf. Linder (1987) pp. 236–238, n. 36).

[123] Lampe (1961) p. 504 whose translation is 'pertaining to a festival'with the assumption that this festival is Passover; cf. also Müller (1952) p. 508: 'festal', spec. Paschal; Mann (2001) p. 328 n. 2 under 'εορτη': 'feast'.

[124] Eusebius *HE* 7.20; 7.22, 11 (SC 31f; Bardy, G.) who refers to festal letters, not gifts as such.

[125] Theodoretus Cyrrhus (died approx. 458), *Ep.* 72 (SC 98), who refers to 'festal gifts'.

[126] Cosmas Ind. *Top. Christ.* 10 (SC 197) clearly refers to Paschal gifts.

[127] *Chronicon Paschale* 374 (PG 92, 953): celebrating—in an Easter context.

[128] SC 336, (Metzger (1987)).

I would therefore like to argue that canon 37 refers to gifts given at the feast of Passover.

It is obvious that canon 38 refers to this feast as well as it speaks of 'unleavened bread'. The translation of 'αζυμα' is Passover bread.[129]

The conclusion is that the word 'heortastikos' refers to 'festal' and that this was also used in a Paschal context. The Apostolic Constitutions may be from a different region, which we will discuss in the next chapter, yet the parallel is striking. Apparently Christians in that area received gifts such as unleavened bread. In the region of Syria, Christians celebrated Easter 'with the Jews' which was parallel to the 'week of the *Azymi* (unleavened bread)'.[130] (cf. John Chrysostom and Aphraat). In Asia Minor as well there were different ways of celebrating Easter: either on the Jewish date itself, or using the Jewish system and calculating a new date. In the second century there were Quartodecimans. The Jews celebrated Passover, according to the lunar calendar, during the first month of the year, Nisan, on the fourteenth day, the day of the first full moon. By the second century the churches in the eastern Mediterranean (Asia Minor) ended their Lenten fast on the fourteenth day as well, following the Gospel passages on the passion of Christ. They were thus known as 'fourteen-ers', or 'Quartodecimans'.

The dispute over supposed judaizing tendencies of the faithful and the date for Easter, i.e. Quartodecimanism, is not unknown in the second century in the region of Laodicea where the practice even caught the attention of Rome.[131]

There were also other groups in the region that followed similar practices. It should be recalled that many groups existed in Christian Asia Minor, all with different views on keeping Christian traditions: e.g. Montanists and Novatians.[132] Montanists were probably followers of the Quartodeciman Easter date (14th Nisan).[133] Fourth century Novatianism followed the date set by Nicea yet according to Socrates and Sozomen a group of Phrygian Novatians began in the late fourth century to celebrate Easter at the same time as the Quartodecimans, and thus also the Montanists. These two authors thus wished to show

---

[129] Cf. Lampe (1961) p. 40; Athanasius *De Azymiis* (PG 26, 1328 ff).

[130] John Chrysostom *Adv. Jud.* 3.3 (PG 48, 865); Aphrahat *Demonstratio XII de Pascha* 6–8; 12–13 (Cantalamessa (1981)), Syriac Didascalia (Leonhard (2006)); Rouwhorst (2004b) 72–73.

[131] Eusebius *HE* IV, 26; V, 23 (SC 31 f; Bardy, G.). Stewart-Sykes (1998) pp. 155–160.

[132] Cf. Laodicea c. 7 and 8; Maraval (2001) 'L'Asie Mineure', pp. 85–90.

[133] Tabbernee (2007) pp. 366–369.

the diversity of the orthodox and heretic groups in Christian Asia Minor.[134]

It seems likely therefore that these canons are directed against those who celebrated Easter at approximately the same time as the Jewish Passover, not necessarily on the same date, and in this festal period received gifts and unleavened bread from the Jews.[135]

There are two other canons which have been discussed in various sources as referring to judaizing practices, which I would like to discuss below.[136]

CANONS 35 AND 36

CANON 35

> "Ότι οὐ δεῖ χριστιανοὺς ἐγκαταλείπειν τὴν Ἐκκλησίαν τοῦ Θεοῦ, καὶ ἀπιέναι καὶ ἀγγέλους ὀνομάζειν καὶ συνάξεις ποιεῖν ἅπερ ἀπηγόρευται. Εἴ τις οὖν εὑρεθῇ ταύτῃ τῇ κεκρυμμένῃ εἰδωλολατρείᾳ σχολάζων ἔστω ἀνάθεμα ὅτι ἐγκατέλιπε τὸν Κύριον ἡμῶν Ἰησοῦν Χριστὸν τὸν Υἱὸν τοῦ Θεοῦ καὶ εἰδωλολατρίᾳ προσῆλθεν.

> Christians should not abandon the Church of God and turn about and give names to angels and gather to worship [them]. That is forbidden. Should anyone be found involved in this secret idolatry, let him be anathema; for he has abandoned our Lord Jesus Christ, the Son of God, and resorted to idolatry.

CANON 36

> "Ότι οὐ δεῖ ἱερατικοὺς ἢ κληρικοὺς μάγους ἢ ἐπαοιδοὺς εἶναι ἢ μαθηματικοὺς ἢ ἀστρολόγους ἢ ποιεῖν τὰ λεγόμενα φυλαντήρια ἅτινά ἐστι δεσμωτήρια τῶν ψυχῶν αὐτῶν. Τοὺς δὲ φοροῦντας ῥίπτεσται ἐκ τῆς Ἐκκλησίας ἐκελεύσαμεν.

> It is forbidden for priests or clergy to be magicians or enchanters, mathematicians or astrologers, let them cease to make so-called phylacteries [: amulets], which are chains for their souls. Those who wear them should be thrown out of the Church.

---

[134] Socrates *Hist. Eccl.* ch. 4 and 5; Sozomen *Hist. Eccl.* ch. 7; Mitchell (1993) pp. 96–100.

[135] Trebilco (1991) p. 102 who states that as the faithful apparently attended synagogue (cf. the canons on Sabbath observance and readings) they therefore would obviously also attend Jewish feasts. See also for example Christians who were invited to go to the synagogue in Smyrna. The martyrdom of Pionius 13,1 (Robert (1994)).

[136] With many thanks to Professor P.W. van der Horst (Univ. Utrecht) for his useful suggestions.

As these two canons both refer to so-called 'idolatrous' behavior, I would suggest discussing them together. The entry on 'amulets' in the Reallexikon states that these canons refer to amulets with the names of angels on them. They have combined the two canons into one![137]

The canons refer to practices apparently deemed so grave that the punishment is serious—eviction from the church.

The following questions may be asked concerning these canons, and especially canon 35: which practices are referred to; what are the concerns the church leaders had; to what extent do the canons refer to Jewish practices.

Which practices does canon 35 refer to? Is it only the worship of angels or against the worship of certain, unknown angels?

Herbst, writing in the nineteenth century, sees a 'gnostic' origin for the worship of angels. According to him this would therefore be one of the reasons why the fathers were against it.[138] This somewhat dated view is no longer considered very convincing.

Hefele, in discussing this canon, states that the cult of angels flourished in Phrygia and Pisidia because they could be called upon as intermediaries between the High Holy God and mankind. He argues that this canon is not so much against angel worship as such, but more against giving angels other names than those which were known.[139] This argument is also used by Percival who claims that the canon was directed against idolatry which was expressed in giving unknown names to angels.[140] Both authors cite as their source confirming this Charlemagne's *Capitularia Admonitio Generalis*, n. 16 (approx. 789). This text reads as follows: the fathers spoke out "in that council [: Laodicea] also against angels who are imaginary and whose name is not known, [allowing] only those whom we have by authority, which are Michael, Gabriel and Raphael".[141] The source upon which these authors base their argument is rather late for our discussion. The canon seems to be against only the naming of angels. Or is it against the worship of angels in general? There are inscriptions from Phrygia

---

[137] *RAC* I (1950) p. 409.
[138] Herbst (1823) pp. 32–35. 'Gnostic' as seen in the context of the period in which this article was written.
[139] Hefele/Leclercq (1907) I.1, pp. 1017–8.
[140] In Schaff/Wace (1991) pp. 150–151.
[141] My translation, the text is published in: Boretius (1883) p. 55. The source upon which these authors base their argument is rather late for our discussion yet remains of interest for our discussion.

showing the name of for example the archangel Michael,[142] and his worship was widespread in the fourth century with even a major cult center near Colossae.[143] Was this what worried the church fathers in this canon?

The concerns the church fathers apparently had, was that the worship of angels was considered to be idolatrous. This we also see in Theodoretus who, on discussing the council of Laodicea, claims that this canon rules out all angel worship for fear of idolatry.[144] Yet which angels and why we do not know.

We therefore do not know much more than what the canon states: that the worship of angels, possibly all angels, was considered idolatrous behavior.

Canon 35 therefore is on the worship of angels; this is considered idolatrous. Canon 36 concerns certain professions deemed unsuitable for the clergy. Apparently they were also involved in making amulets. This as well was forbidden. The question is whether the practices described in both canons—angel worship and making amulets ('phylacteries')—are *Jewish* practices. Kraabel is very clear on the issue. He sees both practices, angel worship and wearing amulets, as influenced by Judaism.[145] The entry on amulets in the *Reallexikon* even implies that these canons refer to amulets with the names of angels on them. They have combined the two canons into one.[146]

It is difficult to discern whether the cult of angels has Jewish origins. It has been said that pagan interest in Jewish monotheism was especially strong in Asia Minor; a fact also seen in the recurrence of the so-called 'Hypsistos' inscriptions, a title referring to God as the 'Most High'. Inscriptions bearing this title abound in Asia Minor.[147] Votive inscriptions from Asia Minor show that the Most High was considered so far removed from the world of men that intermediaries were called upon. These were called 'theos', 'theos angelos' or 'theos angelikos'. In paganism, 'angelos' was a normal indication for a messenger of a deity: e.g., messengers for Hecate or Hermes. The word 'angelos' was taken from the Greek Old Testament. It appeared more

---

[142] MAMA I, n. 434; IV, n. 307.
[143] 'Engel' in: *RAC* V, esp. p. 251.
[144] *Ad Coloss.* C. II, 18 (Marriott (1852)).
[145] Kraabel (1968) pp. 136–139, discussing the council of Laodicea.
[146] *RAC* I (1950) p. 409.
[147] Nilsson (1961) pt. II, Die Hellenistische und Römische Zeit: 'Der Monotheismus', p. 57.

frequently in Judaism from the moment of more intense contact with its pagan surroundings, for example especially in the period after the exile. The word was borrowed from Greek and adapted to Jewish religious needs.[148]

This is also attested by Shepherd who has published evidence for mostly pagan use of the epithet 'theos hypsistos' often combined with the word 'holy/divine angel' and showing the use of these epithets in paganism and occasionally in Judaism.[149]

In conclusion, it is very difficult to say whether angel worship in Asia Minor was exclusively Jewish in origin and that this was therefore cause for concern at Laodicea. It seems most likely that the origin of calling upon angels for intercession was of pagan *and* Jewish origin. It seems likely that it developed from paganism *and* from Judaism and was then also used in Christianity.

Furthermore, it seems doubtful that the word 'εἰδωλολατρία' found in canon 35 and referring to the practice of angel worship would be used to describe judaizing practices. The word is usually found in reference to pagan practices.[150]

What the council fathers were against seems more likely to be the wrongful worship of angels as it could turn into idolatry, and not so much against supposed Jewish practices.

A similar question may be asked of canon 36. Does the word 'phylactery' refer to Jewish practices?

Herbst, referring to this canon, describes the different types of amulets which existed at the time, including phylacteries, as Jewish.[151] Christians, according to Herbst, wore these as well, but were now banned from doing so through the council of Laodicea.[152] Feldman mentions that phylacteries were seen as magical amulets, and because of Jewish reputation for magic (cf. the council of Elvira, canon 49) they were held in high esteem.[153] He considers the wording as important:

---

[148] Sokolowski, (1960) pp. 228–229.
[149] Shepherd (1980–1) pp. 77–101; esp. pp. 93–94 on the use in Judaism and paganism.
[150] Cf. Lampe (1961) p. 408. Origen *Contra Celsum* VI, 11 (SC 147, pp. 204–7); Petrus I Alexandrinus *Epistula Canonica* 7 (PG 18, 480); Tertullian *De Idol.* (transl. and discussion by Waszink/Winden (1987)); Tertullian *De Pudicitia* 19 (SC 394 and 395).
[151] He refers to the use of the word in Mt. 23:5.
[152] Herbst (1823) pp. 36–39.
[153] Feldman (1993) pp. 380–381.

the '*so-called*' phylacteries (τα λεγόμενα), i.e. a certain type of amulet. These can only refer to Jewish phylacteries, according to Feldman.[154] As his evidence he uses the passage in Matthew 23, v. 5, where the word is used. However, in Matthew 23 the whole passage is on Jewish practices.

In this canon we have only the word 'phylactery'. According to Lampe, the word 'phylactery' can mean any type of amulet, Jewish or not.[155]

We may therefore assume that these amulets and the practices referred to in this canon need not necessarily be Jewish, they could also be pagan.

Neither canon is directed against specific *Jewish* practices but against behavior which was considered undesirable—the worship of angels and possible wrongful religious practices; or professions and ensuing actions which were deemed inappropriate for the clergy.

3   Conclusion

The fourth century Anatolian church fathers discussed above add little to the discussion on Jewish-Christian interaction in the region of Laodicea and only reaffirm the notion that the writings of church fathers are mostly theological in nature with little concrete evidence of actual contacts. This we already saw at Elvira.

However, the text of the council held at Laodicea does suggest that relations between Christian faithful and Jews in the region of Asia Minor were close. Two canons indicate specific relations between Christians and Jews (c. 37 and 38). Other canons describe Jewish practices undertaken by Christian faithful (c. 16 and 29). Two others are often considered to be part of the category of Jewish activities (c. 35 and 36). These last two canons especially show how far the syncretistic activities of the Christian faithful had spread: they included angel worship and activities involving presumed magic. What one sees are far-reaching contacts and the annexation of practices from surrounding groups, including Jews. This is what church leaders in late antiquity wished to end through church council rulings.

---

[154] Feldman (1993) p. 584: n. 49 to ch. 11.
[155] Lampe (1961) p. 1492.

The practices as described at Laodicea concern Sabbath worship by Christians (c. 16 and 29), and Christians participating in Jewish feasts and traditions (c. 37 and 38). These are apparently not issues discussed in Roman imperial legislation.

However, the archeological evidence discussed at the beginning of this chapter does add to our discussion. The evidence from Sardis (synagogue and shops), Aphrodisias (donations inscriptions), and Acmonia, Eumeneia and Hierapolis (grave inscriptions) indicate a close and peaceful interaction between Jews and their surroundings. Especially the grave curses used by both Jews and—often especially—Christians indicate a copying of each other's traditions which is also seen at the council of Laodicea.

CHAPTER THREE

THE APOSTOLIC CANONS

The Apostolic Canons form the penultimate section of Book VIII of the Apostolic Constitutions. They are not a council text as such, however, the composition and phrasing of the rulings indicate that they are a collection of conciliar statements. They appear to have been compiled in the middle to late fourth century, in Syria and most probably in Antioch.[1] They are therefore of importance to our study on conciliar rulings. Furthermore, not without significance is the fact that also from this region and period hails one of the most important church fathers as far as Christian-Jewish relations are concerned—John Chrysostom. It therefore makes sense to look at this collection with reference to this church father.

The Canons form part of the Apostolic Constitutions. The last two chapters of the Constitutions contain prayers which are obviously Jewish, a so-called Christian version of the Jewish *Amidah* prayers ('Eighteen Benedictions').[2] Apparently Christians had appropriated prayers of Jewish origin. As the Apostolic Canons appear in this section of the Constitutions it makes sense to look at them—at least at those rulings which refer to Jewish contacts and 'judaizing' practices by Christians.

1 Fourth Century Antioch: Jewish and Christian Evidence[3]

Geographically and theologically, Antioch's influence spread far. The province of Antioch extended into southern Turkey, and included Tarsus and much of the southern coastal region. Trade routes and major highways leading from the Levant passed through the city and further

---

[1] Turner (1915) pp. 523–538; Gaudemet (1985) passim; Joannou (1962) pp. 1–53. For Antioch as the place of origin, Metzger (1985–7) vol. I, pp. 55–56.

[2] Fiensy (1985) *passim*; Rouwhorst (1997) pp. 72–93; esp. pp. 80–81; v.d. Horst (2000) pp. 228–238. See conclusions to this chapter for further discussion.

[3] For Jews at Antioch, see: Krauss (1902) pp. 27–49; Kraeling (1932) pp. 130–160; Downey (1961) pp. 447–449; Meeks/Wilken (1978) pp. 1–13; Millar (1986) pp. 13–14; Brooten, B. in Kondoleon (2000) pp. 29–37. For the very few Jewish inscriptions found in Antioch: Noy/Bloedhorn (2004) *Inscriptiones Judaicae Orientis*, pp. 116–119.

north and westwards, even via Laodicea in Phrygia. Antioch was the capital of Syria, a military and diplomatic center in the region and later boasted such fine pagan and Christian architecture that many visitors found their way to the city.

The city of Antioch was founded by one of Alexander the Great's generals, Seleucus I Nicator (c. 358–281 BCE).[4] Many Jews who settled at Antioch were retired mercenaries and soldiers of Seleucus' army.[5] The settlement of Jews at Antioch is attested by Josephus[6] and in the Jerusalem Talmud.[7] The gradual growth of the Jewish community and its large-scale organization can be seen in the fact that they had an *archon*, or leader of the community, and even had a court of law.[8] By the fourth century different sources—all literary—attest to Jews who have been at Antioch for at least four generations[9] and speak of at least two synagogues, one at Antioch and one in Daphne, the nearby suburb.[10] There are, unfortunately, very few archeological remains attesting to the presence of Jews at Antioch.[11]

For information on Christians in Antioch, see for example: Downey (1961) ch. 11 ff; Liebeschuetz (1972) ch. 7 and conclusion; Meeks/Wilken (1978) p. 13 ff; Wallace-Hadrill (1982) esp. ch. 1; Harvey, S.A. 'Antioch and Christianity' in Kondoleon (2000) pp. 39–49; Zetterholm (2003) *passim*; Sandwell (2007) pp. 39–40. For Christian archeological remains: Elderlin (1934); Kondoleon (2000) pp. 211–216 (chalices, plaques, medallions), pp. 222–226 (remains of church architecture); for Daphne: Stillwell (1938) pp. 49–94.

[4] Cf. The Chronicle of John Malalas § 200 and § 233, (published and translated by Jeffreys/Jeffreys/Scott (1986)).

[5] Downey (1961) pp. 78–80; Kraeling (1932) p. 131.

[6] *Contra Apionem* 2, 39 (LCL 186); *Antiq.* 12, 119 (LCL 365); *Bellum Jud.* 7, 43 ff (LCL 210).

[7] PT: Sheq. 50a, 52: the suburb of Antioch known as Daphne is mentioned as the place where the Great Sanhedrin met.

[8] Josephus *Bellum Jud.* 7.47 (LCL 210). Names of fourth and fifth century Antiochene rabbis and scholars are mentioned in the BT: Ket 88a and PT: Qid 64d, 71. The visit by three rabbis, Eliezer, Josua and Akiba to Antioch is mentioned in PT: Hor 48a, 45.

[9] Libanius *Orat.* 47, 13 (LCL 452).

[10] In the southern quarter of the city, the 'Kerateion', and at Daphne. John Chrysostom *Adv. Jud.* 1, 6 (PG 48, 852); Meeks/Wilken (1978) p. 8; Daphne: Meeks/Wilken (1978) p. 238.

[11] Meeks/Wilken (1978) ch. II with information on Antioch in inscriptions at Apamea and Beth Shearim; Noy/Bloedhorn (2004) *Inscriptiones Judaicae Orientis*, pp. 116–119, an inscription of uncertain date showing a menorah, and a 3rd–4th c. inscription of Aidesius who was an Antiochene gerousiarch.

As far as Christianity is concerned, we can already see in the New Testament that the city was well known to Christians.[12] It was at Antioch that the conversion of Gentiles was proposed, after which Paul and others embarked on travels elsewhere. It may be that Antioch was the place of conception of the Gospel of Matthew.[13] The second bishop of Antioch, the second century Ignatius, wrote several letters which show the development in Christian thought concerning larger ideological issues and the theological position of church leaders.[14] There were for example discussions in the third century on the thoughts of Paul of Samosata whose views were considered unorthodox.[15] The different strands and points of view within Christianity at Antioch meant that affiliation of Christian faithful with non-(orthodox) Christian groups was a possibility. According to their adversaries, Arians were attracted to Judaism but then so were many more main-stream Christian faithful.[16] We also encounter concerns about Christian faithful associating with other groups in the homilies of the fourth-century preacher John Chrysostom.[17]

Different theological schools thus developed in Antioch. The best known (pagan) school of rhetoric was run by Libanius. His institution knew pupils who were to become great Christian preachers in Anatolia and elsewhere, such as John Chrysostom, Theodore of Mopsuestia, Basil the Great, and Gregory of Nazianzus.[18] Diodorus of Tarsus played a key role in the biblical formation of budding churchmen. His better known students also included John Chrysostom and Theodore of Mopsuestia.[19]

---

[12] Acts 11:26 in Antioch they were first known as 'Christians'; Gal. 2: 11–18 Paul spent much time in the city.

[13] Barton/Muddiman (2001).

[14] *Smyrn.* 8 (on the role of bishops) and *Magn.* 8–10 (on theological issues) (SC 10). See also: Downey (1961) pp. 282–3; Corwin (1960) *passim*; Harvey in Kondoleon (2000) p. 40.

[15] Downey (1961) pp. 310–316; Wallace-Hadrill (1982) esp. pp. 69–70.

[16] Cf. Paul of Samosata and his relations to Jews and Judaism: Philastrius *De Haer.* 64 (CCSL 9).

[17] His *Adv. Jud.* homilies. See also Harvey in Kondoleon (2000) p. 42 ff; Downey (1961) pp. 447–9; Zetterholm (2003) *passim*; Sandwell (2007) pp. 45–46.

[18] Petit (1957) esp. pp. 40–4; Cribiore (2007) *passim*; Sandwell (2007) pp. 47–59.

[19] Hill (2005b) p. 6.

Jews and Christians were part of the city's inhabitants as we saw above. Contacts were close. Local martyrs such as the Jewish Maccabean brothers[20] appear to have been venerated by Christians.[21]

The emperor Julian's brief reign (361–363) undisputedly left its mark on Christian-Jewish relations in Antioch. Just before his arrival in Antioch, Julian had published an edict which made it more difficult for Christians in particular to teach in schools.[22] During his stay in the city he wrote a critique of Christianity, 'Against the Galileans'.[23] He reinstated Apollo in his temple at Daphne and removed the remains of the Christian martyr Babylas back to Antioch.[24] When fire broke out at the temple of Apollo in Daphne, Christians were blamed and their largest church in Antioch was closed down.[25] Julian's attitude towards the Jews only made matters worse. He wooed them in an attempt to create a coalition against the growing influence of Christianity, with promises such as rebuilding the Temple in Jerusalem, amongst others.[26] His untimely death led to rejoicing in Christian Antioch, but his brief reign had only aggravated an already difficult situation in Christian-Jewish relations in the region.[27]

1.1   *Christian-Jewish Relations in Church Father Texts*

The area currently in focus, the region of Antioch, provides us with the best known church father as far as discussions on relations between Christians and Jews in the eastern Mediterranean are concerned: John Chrysostom. This church father—contrary to other patristic sources studied up to now in conjunction with particular council texts—does not only theologize. His arguments are based on concrete examples of

---

[20] 2 Macc. 7.

[21] Rouwhorst (2004) pp. 183–204. It seems likely, Rouwhorst states, that contrary to what was thought before (cf. Liebeschuetz (1972) p. 233; Simon (1936) pp. 413–414), it may have emerged as a *Christian* cult in the later fourth century when they started venerating the (bones of) saints. The building of a sanctuary may also have been a tactical move against judaizers who attended Jewish feasts and may have gone to Daphne where there may have been a Jewish martyrium.

[22] *CTh* 13.3.5. See also Ammianus Marcellinus XXII, 10.7 (LCL 315).

[23] LCL 157.

[24] Ammianus Marcellinus XXII, 12.8 (LCL 315); John Chrysostom *De S. Hieromart. Babyla* (SC 362); Downey (1961) p. 387.

[25] Ammianus Marcellinus XXII, 13.

[26] Ammianus Marcellinus XXIII, 1.2; Meeks/Wilken (1978) p. 28.

[27] Kelly (1995) pp. 9–10; Grissom (1978) pp. 134–140.

interaction between Christians and Jews and thus form a useful addition to the information gleaned from the Apostolic Canons.[28]

John Chrysostom was born in Antioch in approximately 347 CE, and died in Pontus in 407. After an initial period as a hermit, he was ordained a deacon in 381, a priest in 386, and became bishop of Constantinople in 398. He was well known for his many sermons, especially while in Antioch.[29]

In September of 386 he interrupted his series of homilies against the Anomoeans (Arians) to attack the Christians participating in Jewish feasts and Jewish practices. He preached eight sermons known as the '*Adversus Judaeos*' homilies, between the fall of 386 and the fall of 387.[30] Based on their content, some scholars[31] have dated the eight sermons as follows: 1 and 2 in the fall of 386, the third to early 387 and the rest later in 387.[32] The content of the individual sermons can be summarized in the following manner.[33] The first focuses on the 'troubles ahead', i.e. the upcoming Jewish feasts; it is therefore not surprising that the language of this homily is the most virulent: the preacher wished to get off to a 'good start'. The second is more reflective on the

---

[28] On this topic, see also: Meeks/Wilken (1978); Wilken (1983); Kinzig (1991); v.d. Horst (2000); v.d. Horst/Newman (2008) pp. 23–27.

[29] Cf. Quasten (1950) pp. 424–482; Maxwell (2006) pp. 83–84, 140–142.

[30] PG 48, 843ff; Harkins (1999) *Saint John Chrysostom Discourses against Judaizing Christians* (The Fathers of the Church A New Translation); Sandwell (2007) pp. 82–90.

[31] Grissom (1978) pp. 112–118; Maxwell (1966) *passim*.

[32] The first sermon refers to the feast of 'Trumpets, Tabernacles and Fasts' which was about to begin (1.1). These refer to the Jewish fall feasts of New Year, Sukkot, and the Day of Atonement. This homily could therefore be dated to the fall of 386. The second sermon mentions a homily just preached on the same subject and that the fasts were imminent: i.e., September 386. The third homily refers to a different issue, that is to say it speaks of those Christians who calculated the date for Easter in such a manner that they could fast during the Jewish Passover. This calculation obviously did not follow the rules set out by Nicea. This homily could be placed in early 387. This is an internal Christian issue, not related to Christians borrowing from Judaism. That the fifth homily follows the previous one can be deduced from the fact that Chrysostom refers to something he mentioned in the fourth (ref. to Daniel and Passover: 5.1). The fifth sermon is very long; it is therefore not surprising that he complains of hoarseness in the sixth (6.2); which must therefore follow the previous one. In the seventh Chrysostom again speaks of Sukkot and he mentions issues already discussed in sermons four and five (he refers to Jewish celebrations in 7.1). The seventh thus probably follows homilies four through six. In the last, eighth, sermon, Chrysostom expresses his joy that the 'danger', i.e. the Jewish feasts, is past. The homily may be placed either after the first two sermons or after the seventh. We are inclined to place it last seeing that he mentions issues discussed in homilies four and five (8.5).

[33] Cf. Maxwell (1966) pp. lvi–lxvii.

whys and wherefores of Christianity keeping separate from Judaism. The third, as stated in note 31, is on the issue of Easter and the fast preceding it, and the fourth is again the first of several homilies on the approaching Jewish feast days, and recalls some of the rancor of the first sermon. The fifth is a lengthy exegetical exposition on Daniel chapter 9 explaining why Jerusalem fell and would never be rebuilt. Homilies six and seven follow in this vein with an exegetical explanation of Isaiah 53 referring to the death of Christ and the superiority of Christ's sacrifice to Old Testament sacrifice. The eighth homily is again on specific actions and practices undertaken by the Christian faithful.

The discourses, or homilies, were delivered against judaizing Christians.[34] Chrysostom's use of language is virulent, to put it mildly. With the exception of the third one, the homilies were held at the time of year, the fall, when the great Jewish fast and feasts took place. This was apparently the time when most 'judaizing' activities happened. In Antioch, Jews, Christians and pagans lived at close quarters with each other. Appropriating Jewish practices is therefore not surprising. This was seen as unsuitable behavior; after all, wrongful practices meant disruption of the unity of the community and they created division—this was to be avoided.[35] The language used by Chrysostom is focused against deviant Christians, not primarily against the Jews as such.

As far as Chrysostom's homilies are concerned, as stated before, the sermons most likely to contain information relevant to our study are homilies 1, 2, 4, and 8. Homily three is on the Easter date, and five to seven are more theological and exegetical in content.

As was also the case at Laodicea, the faithful at Antioch apparently followed Jewish practices as well as their own religious observance, either in the synagogue or in Jewish homes. However, they may have followed Jewish practices at home as well:

> [*the judaizers*] go to the spectacle of the Trumpets, or rush off to the synagogue, or go up to the shrine of Matrona, or take part in the fast-

---

[34] Grissom (1978) and Wilken (1983, pp. xv–xvii) have called these sermons against judaizing Christians; Smeelik (1985, p. 25) judges the title 'against the Jews' more appropriate. I would like to see a combination of the two: the sermons are addressed towards the Christians of Antioch, but his language is quite obviously virulently anti-Jewish.

[35] Sandwell (2007) pp. 190–198.

ing, or share in the Sabbath, or observe any other Jewish ritual, great
or small[36]

Apparently, the judaizers 'went to the spectacle of the Trumpets', i.e.,
they celebrated the Jewish New Year, and 'took part in the fasting'
which is closely associated with the New Year and the Day of Atonement. Yet, they also 'went to the synagogue' and 'shared in the Sabbath' and observed 'other Jewish ritual[s]'. One may assume that when
the Christians of Antioch were this close to Jewish rituals, the next
step of incorporating part of these practices into their own religious
observances was an easy one to make.

That they were accustomed to incorporating Jewish practices into
their life, is seen elsewhere as well:

> for when they [:the Jews] see that you, who worship the Christ whom
> they crucified, are reverently following their ritual [...][37]

The judaizers followed the rituals of the Jews. The concern is that they
could then possibly negatively influence the other faithful as well. So
Chrysostom advises the others to 'flee and shun their gatherings'. After
all, how can the faithful then not think that the rites performed by the
Jews 'are the best and that our [:Christian] mysteries are worthless'?[38]

These people obviously kept Jewish rituals and sometimes visited
the synagogue.

Chrysostom's greatest concern was for the Christian faithful participating in Jewish festivals, joining their feasts and fasts, especially in the
fall. The Christian faithful attended Jewish services, participated in 'the
festival' and joined Jews in 'observing the fast'.[39] These celebrations
were the great fall feasts of Judaism: the festival of the Trumpets, i.e.
New Year; the feast of Tabernacles, i.e. Sukkot; and the fasts related to
New Year and the Day of Atonement, Yom Kippur.[40]

As far as the third homily is concerned, this is, as stated above
(note 31), a different issue. It concerns fasting and calculating a different date for Easter than was prescribed at the council of Nicea. This

---

[36] *Hom. Adv. Jud.* I, 8. The Matrona was a cave which was a Jewish healing shrine:
Mayer/Allen (2000) pp. 12–13; Feldman (1993) p. 381 (without reference!).
[37] *Hom. Adv. Jud.* I, 5.
[38] *Hom. Adv. Jud.* I, 5.
[39] *Hom. Adv. Jud.* VIII, 5.
[40] *Adv. Jud.* I, 5; Sandwell (2007) pp. 209–210.

was therefore an internal Christian issue, not related to 'judaizing practices'.

The Christian faithful are also warned to stay away from Jewish 'heresies', i.e. their celebrations. Yet, we can see that this was difficult for many. Jewish rituals and practices were attractive: the synagogues were not only places at which to meet for religious ceremonies, but they were also considered of importance in other situations; for example, it was considered the most sacred place for swearing an oath,[41] but also the best place to stay overnight in search of a cure.[42]

Not only their synagogues provided cures; Jews themselves were also seen as those who provided cures where nothing else seemed to help, despite Chrysostom's arguments to the contrary:

> [...] their incantations, their amulets, their charms and spells. This is the only way in which they have a reputation for healing; they do not effect genuine cures[43]

As we have seen elsewhere,[44] the idea of restorative powers ascribed to Jews was of great attraction; apparently at Antioch as well.[45]

To the chagrin of many church leaders these practices and beliefs remained of great interest to the Christian faithful. Council fathers attempted to limit these activities by threatening the culprits with expulsion from the community, keeping the culprits away from the table of the Lord. Chrysostom suggests a similar punishment:

> After you have gone off and shared with those who shed the blood of Christ, how is it that you do not shudder to come back and share in his sacred banquet, to partake of his precious blood? [...] If a catechumen is sick with this disease, let him be kept outside the church doors. If the sick one be a believer and already initiated, let him be driven from the holy table [...][46]

The sermons of John Chrysostom followed the style of rhetoric of the time.[47] This means that the rhetorician's task was not only to bring across a message, but the style was equally, if not more, important.

---

[41] *Adv. Jud.* I, 3.

[42] E.g., at Matrona in Daphne *Adv. Jud.* I, 6.

[43] *Adv. Jud.* VIII, 5; Sandwell (2007) pp. 267–271.

[44] Laodicea c. 35 and 36; Elvira c. 49.

[45] Cf. also Wilken (1983) pp. 83–88 who uses *Adv. Jud.* 8.

[46] *Adv. Jud.* II, 3.

[47] Cf. Kinzig (2001) pp. 652–655; on Chrysostom and his homilies: Siegert (2001) esp. pp. 441–443.

Sermons needed to amuse the public, who would respond by shouting, cheering and applauding. Thus, exaggeration and metaphors form the structure for the message the preacher wished to deliver, as can be seen in the following statement by Chrysostom himself:

> […] but I was not satisfied with prophets nor did I settle for apostles. I mounted to the heavens and gave you as proof the chorus of angels as they sang: "Glory to God in the highest, and on earth peace, good will among men". […] there was great applause, the audience warmed with enthusiasm […].[48]

These skills in oratory can be found throughout Chrysostom's homilies *Adversus Iudaeos*: the judaizers are described as a 'disease' (*Adv. Jud.* 1), for example. He purposely uses this analogy in his first sermon in order to catch his audience's attention. Because he is dealing with what he describes as a 'disease', a 'cure' is needed; this is what John Chrysostom explains in the other homilies, especially the last one:

> This is what physicians do. They tell people in good health what can preserve their health and what can ward off disease. But if people have disregarded their instructions and have fallen sick, physicians do not neglect them […][49]

Other metaphors used to describe the Jews in his homilies are in the same vein.[50] His language appears abusive, thus one would assume the problem of judaizing was great and Chrysostom not a great admirer of Judaism. However, this is not always the case, for in various writings he appears to extol its virtues;[51] however, in general, his view of Judaism is rather negative. The rhetoric seems to delete any subtleties in his opinions. The style fits in with the rhetorical style of the time.[52] That this understanding of style has not always been used properly in the analysis and use of Chrysostom's homilies is unfortunately seen in the misappropriation of parts of the sermons in later anti-Semitic propaganda.[53]

---

[48] *Hom. Adv. Jud.* I, 1.
[49] *Hom. Adv. Jud.* VIII, 3.
[50] Jews described as 'wolves' (IV, 1); 'drunks' (VIII, 1); 'sorcerers' (VIII, 7); synagogues are 'haunts of demons' (I, 3).
[51] Eg., *Hom. 5.1 in Hebr.* 2: 16 (PG 63, 47).
[52] Cf. also Wilken (1983) pp. 95–127. As far as the composition of the audience is concerned: *vide* MacMullen (1989) pp. 503–511; Mayer (1998) pp. 105–139; Sandwell (2007) pp. 11–20.
[53] Wilken (1983) pp. 161–164.

It seems that, in contrast with the church father texts on Jews and Judaism which we have seen in previous chapters, Chrysostom is apparently addressing a genuine situation. We will now turn to the text of the Apostolic Canons to see whether more evidence of Christian-Jewish relations can be found in this document.

2   *The Apostolic Canons*[54]

From an early period onwards, the text of the Apostolic Canons appears as part of the text of the Apostolic Constitutions.[55] Who the author or compiler of the Constitutions was, is widely debated.[56] The Apostolic Constitutions were composed from the third century Didascalia (Apost. Const. bk. 1-6), the first century Didache (bk. 7:1-32), and the Apostolic Tradition (bk. 8). Also found in books seven and eight of the Constitutions are Jewish prayers, or benedictions.[57] These prayers are found in the Apostolic Constitutions book 8, 33 to 38.[58] The prayers are a Greek version of the seven benedictions of the Jewish *Amidah*, 'Eighteen Benedictions', specifically those said in the sabbath morning prayers.[59] The prayers were undoubtedly copied from Jewish synagogue services and incorporated into a Christian setting, indicating a familiarity of Christians with synagogue liturgy.[60]

In book eight, following the reworked Apostolic Tradition and a conclusion (ch. 46), we find the 85 Apostolic Canons (ch. 47). The canons were probably collected by the same person who also compiled the Constitutions.[61] The Canons consist of other canonical collections as well—such as Ancyra (314), Neocaesarea (319), Nicea (325), Antioch

---

[54] Steimer (1992) pp. 87–94.

[55] The text: SC 336; Joannou (1962) vol. I.2. For a discussion see Hefele/Leclercq (1907) vol. I.2: appendix IX p. 1203 ff; Turner (1915) pp. 523–538; Joannou (1962) pp. 1–4; Schreckenberg (1999) pp. 294–295.

[56] 'Apostolic Constitutions' in: *EnEC*; Moreschini/Norelli (2005) pp. 196–7; good survey of literature on the topic: Di Berardino (2006) pp. 656–657; Metzger (1985) vol. III, pp. 9–12.

[57] Fiensy (1985) *passim*; Rouwhorst (1997) pp. 72–93; v.d. Horst (2000) pp. 233–234.

[58] Metzger (1987) Introduction § 6–10.

[59] Fiensy (1985) pp. 165–187; Rouwhorst (1997) p. 81; v.d. Horst/Newman (2008) pp. 3–93.

[60] Fiensy (1985) p. 219; v.d. Horst/Newman (2008) p. 234.

[61] Steimer (1992); Gaudemet (1985) p. 25; Metzger (SC 336). Against the view that it is the same author: Plöchl (1959) p. 110.

(340), and Laodicea (345).[62] Judging by the liturgical practices and daily life described, Syria seems the likely place of origin of the Constitutions and Canons.[63] More precisely, Antioch is suggested as the place of conception.[64] Based on the theological and liturgical content the most likely date, for both Canons and Constitutions, seems to be the late fourth century.[65]

The Greek text was first published as canonical and thus accepted as legally binding in the East, by the sixth century bishop John Scholasticus of Constantinople.[66] The council 'in Trullo' held at Constantinople in 691[67] places the Apostolic Canons at the beginning of its own text and describes it as being authoritative.

In the West the collection was met with more suspicion. This was largely based on several canons dealing with issues concerning heretics.[68] The sixth century Dionysius Exiguus only published in Latin the first fifty canons.[69] Canon 50 was considered too heretical.[70] The early sixth century Codex Veronensis LI contains the Apostolic Canons in Latin, but omits canon 50.[71]

Based on the above, we can conclude that the text was compiled in late fourth-century Antioch as part of the Apostolic Constitutions. More exactly, the Canons are located in the section of the Constitutions where we also find the above-mentioned Jewish-inspired prayers. This could indicate a close relationship between Christians and Jews. It is therefore not surprising that the Apostolic Canons contain references to Christian-Jewish relations (c. 65, 70, 71).

---

[62] Steimer (1992) p. 88; Moreschini/Norelli (2005) p. 196; Di Berardino (2006) p. 658.

[63] Gaudemet (1958) p. 45; for a complete discussion, see Metzger (1985) vol. I, pp. 55–56. Moreschini/Norelli (2005) p. 197.

[64] Moreschini/Norelli (2005) p. 196.

[65] ODCC p. 90; Joannou (1962) p. 1, cf. also note 2; Metzger (1985/87) vol. I, pp. 32, 55–56; Moreschini/Norelli (2005) p. 196; Di Berardino (2006) p. 658.

[66] Mansi (1901) vol. I, pp. 29–48; Beneševič (1937).

[67] Hefele/Lecercq (1907) III.1 pp. 560–578 c. 2 of the council 'in Trullo'.

[68] C. 46 and 47 on re-baptizing heretics; a lengthy discussion on baptism and the Trinitarian formula to be used in c. 50; c. 68 on the re-ordination of heretic clergy and c. 85 on the contents of Scripture excluding the accepted Book of Revelation.

[69] Mansi (1901) vol. I, pp. 49–66.

[70] See above, note 39.

[71] Veronense Cod. Bibl. Capit. LI (49) folio 139–156. Published by Turner (1899) p. 32 ff; Metzger (SC 336): pp. 10–11; Gaudemet (1985) p. 17 esp. note 9; Steimer (1992) pp. 90–91; Mareschini/Norelli (2005) pp. 195–6; Di Berardino (2006) pp. 658–9.

We will now look at the canons which mention this specific inter-action.

Canons with References to Jews and Judaizing Practices

Canon 65[72]

Εἴ τις κληρικὸς ἢ λαϊκὸς εἰσέλθοι εἰς συναγωγὴν Ἰουδαίων ἢ αἱρετικῶν προσεύξασθαι καθαιρείσθω καὶ ἀφοριζέσθω.

If any clergyman or layman shall enter into a synagogue of the Jews or heretics to pray, let the former be deposed and the latter be excom-municated.

Canon 70

Εἴ τις ἐπίσκοπος ἢ ἄλλος κληρικὸς νηστεύει μετὰ Ἰουδαίων ἢ ἑορτάζει μετ' αὐτῶν ἢ δέχεται αὐτῶν τὰ τῆς ἑορτῆς ξένια, οἷον ἄζυμα ἢ τι τοιοῦτον καθαιρείσθω εἰ δὲ λαϊκός ἀφοριζέσθω.

If any bishop, presbyter, or deacon, or any of the list of clergy keeps fast or festival with the Jews, or receives from them any of the gifts of their feasts, as unleavened bread, or any such things, let him be deposed. If he is a layman, let him be excommunicated.

Canon 71

Εἴ τις Χριστιανὸς ἔλαιον ἀπένγκοι εἰς ἱερὸν ἐθνῶν ἢ εἰς συναγωγὴν Ἰουδαίων ἢ λύχνους ἀφοριζέσθω.

If any Christian brings oil into a temple of the heathen or into a syna-gogue of the Jews at their feast, or lights lamps, let him be excommu-nicated.

Another canon which has been suggested as 'judaizing' is canon 7;[73] however, it deals with Christians calculating Easter not according to the council of Nicea but in such a way that their fasting coincided with the Jewish Passover (specifically the 'week of the *Azymi*'). This issue has to do with the discussion on the Easter date rather than with actual *judaizing* tendencies.[74]

The same goes for canon 64 which warns against clergy fasting on the 'day of the Lord' or the sabbath, 'except for the one only' (i.e., Holy

---

[72] The numbering here follows that used by Metzger (SC 320, 329, 336).

[73] Cf. Schreckenberg (1999) p. 294.

[74] These issues are related to Chrysostom's third homily—these are internal Chris-tian discussions and do not refer to Christians appropriating Jewish practices.

Saturday). This is, however, contrary to what some scholars suggest, not a judaizing practice, as we saw at Elvira (c. 26).[75]

The issue stated in canon 65 of praying in a synagogue by Christians has already been insinuated by the canons at Laodicea.[76] There we saw Christians joining in synagogue prayer and feasting with Jews and receiving gifts. This is also found at the later council of Trullo.[77]

Canon 70 is closely related to the same issue of praying and feasting with Jews. The concern voiced here is similar to the issues discussed at Laodicea (c. 37 and 38). Apparently the Christian faithful at Laodicea and at Antioch found their way to the synagogue for prayers, but also to celebrate the (fall) fasts and feasts with the Jews.

This we also see in the homilies of John Chrysostom.

It is interesting to note that Christians apparently received unleavened bread from Jews—which they were not allowed to. We saw this concern also at Laodicea (c. 38).

Canon 71 is somewhat different from what we have seen before. The canon is directed against Christians not only involved in synagogue visits but also in pagan practices. It is, however, the Jewish practices with which we are concerned. The canon is concerned about Christians bringing oil into a synagogue during a feast but also about Christians lighting lamps. Why would these practices be of such concern? What is the specific concern about carrying oil and lighting lamps—or is it specifically the involvement in Jewish feasts? Would they be allowed to bring oil and light lamps at other times?[78]

In Judaism, oil was also used for anointing. It is used on a weekly basis for kindling the sabbath lamp on the Friday evening. Josephus mentions Gentiles who were interested not only in Jewish dietary practices and sabbath observance but also in the 'fasts and the lighting of the lamps'.[79] Oil plays a central role in Jewish feasts, especially that of Hanukkah, when the eight candles of the menorah are lit, one

---

[75] Schreckenberg (1999) p. 294, suggests this canon to be judaizing practice.

[76] Laodicea canon 29 for example, and 38 ('join in their heresies').

[77] Trullo (692) c. 11.

[78] It may be interesting to note that in the eighth century Syriac texrt known as the 'Disputation of Sergius the Stylite against a Jew' (CSCO 339, transl. Hayman), the Jew tells Sergius of Christians who 'associate with us in the synagogue and who bring offerings and alms and oil, and at the same time of the Passover send unleavened bread (and) doubtless other things also' (XXII. 1; 12). The text was supposedly written to warn Christians against judaizing practices: pp. 74–77.

[79] *Contra Apionem* 2.282 (LCL 186).

on every evening of the festival.[80] It could be that the celebration of Hanukkah is meant in this canon.

Whatever feast is referred to here, the canon aims at keeping the Christian faithful away from Jewish synagogues and pagan temples.[81] The issue is similar to that of the other canons (65 and 70) which attempt to distance Christians from synagogue prayer and joining in Jewish feasts and thus appropriating Jewish practices.

3   Conclusion

At Laodicea, which is after all closely connected to this region, we already saw that the Christian faithful kept some sort of Sabbath practice (c. 16 and 29). This is only in passing referred to by Chrysostom.[82] Visits to the synagogue by Christians is referred to at Antioch (Canons 65 and 71) and by Chrysostom (I, 5; I, 8).

More obvious are the references both at Laodicea (c. 37 and 38) and Antioch (c. 70) to Christians celebrating feasts and fasts with Jews. This concern is also voiced by Chrysostom in his homilies.[83]

Chrysostom felt the need to address in strong wording practices which involved adopting Jewish rituals such as synagogue attendance and Sabbath observance, and participating in Jewish feasts and fasts. These practices are also found in the Apostolic Canons. Chrysostom's homilies against the judaizers can thus, to a certain extent, be considered as discussing an actual situation—as described in the council text. This can be said for most of five of the eight sermons. The remainder fit into the category of the homilies which are mostly exegetical arguments with little relevance to actual practices or the situation on the ground.[84] John Chrysostom's homilies *Adversus Iudaeos* are thus a combination of two categories of sermons: exegetical and responding to an actual situation. They are thus the first set of patristic writings which contain references to an actual situation, and not a theological treatise based on a 'Judaism in the mind'—i.e., theological rhetoric. The canons provide the concrete background for John Chrysostom's

---

[80] 'Oil', Neusner (1996).
[81] In classical religion, lamps were lit as votive offerings in sanctuaries and tombs: cf. 'lamps' in Price/Kearns (2003).
[82] *Adv. Jud.* I, 8. Also referred to in the *Constit. Apost.* VIII, 32–34.
[83] *Adv. Jud.* I, 5; I, 8; VIII, 5.
[84] Homilies five to seven.

homilies. In the case of Antioch, therefore, canons and church father texts (John Chrysostom) correspond with each other.

As already noted, the Apostolic Constitutions also include 'Christian sabbath *Amidah* prayers'. It is therefore interesting to note that while the church father uses vitriolic language to persuade his audience to keep away from Jewish practices, the Constitutions include means by which the judaizers would be persuaded to stay within the Christian fold, added on by the Canons and their warnings not to indulge in judaizing sabbath practices. Perhaps a more pastoral way of convincing the faithful than John Chrysostom's homilies, which, according to himself did not have very successful results.[85]

Again, as we saw at Laodicea, there are no references to these type of practices in Roman imperial legislation. The debate on the date for Easter is discussed in Roman law, yet only where it concerns heretic practices (CTh 16.6.6; 16.10.24)—references to the same groups we also saw at Laodicea: Novatians, Protopaschites, and Sabbatians. No reference in Roman law is made to Christians celebrating with Jews or visiting the synagogue, or keeping 'judaizing practices' on sabbath/Saturday.[86]

---

[85] *Hom. in Ep. ad Tit. 3.2* (PG 62, 679); v.d. Horst (2000) pp. 233–236.
[86] Rabello (2000) pt. VIII, esp. 'Conclusions'.

CHAPTER FOUR

GAUL

In this final chapter we will return to the western part of the Mediterranean. Until now, we have seen fourth century council texts referring to interaction between Christians and Jews—mostly through Christians appropriating Jewish traditions. Contemporary church fathers have not offered any additional information in their writings—they mostly refer to a typological picture of Jews and Judaism. The only exception is John Chrysostom in Antioch.

Fifth and sixth century council texts referring to Christians and Jews mostly hail from Gaul. Again, the intention here is to study the relevant documents, place these documents within their historical context and reconsider their relation to the writings of relevant contemporary church leaders.

We will start with a collection known as the *Statuta Ecclesiae Antiqua*, from fifth century southern Gaul. This will be followed by the fifth and sixth century rulings at Vannes (465), Agde (506), Epaon (517), Clermont (535) and the councils of Orléans (533–538), with a brief reference to the fourth council of Orléans (541) and Mâcon (583).

Let us first turn to information concerning Christians and Jews in fifth and sixth century Gaul.

1   *Fifth Century Gaul*

In the fifth century, the area of southern Gaul was divided into 'Narbonensis Prima' (capital Narbonne), and Viennensis (capital Arles). It was the most Romanized region of Gaul, according to the first century Pliny.[1] The geographer Strabo noted that even its produce was Italian: olives, grapes and figs.[2] He continues by saying that in climate, culture and geography, the inhabitants and the area are more like Italy than the rest of Gaul where they "wear tight breeches"![3]

---

[1] *Hist. Nat.* III, 4, 31 (LCL 353).
[2] *Geogr.* IV.1.2. (LCL 196).
[3] *Geogr.* IV.4.3.

The contacts with the Italian peninsula had started in the third century BC. with trade routes set up between Campania and southern Gaul. A military alliance was established between Marseille and Rome after the second Punic War. The region was fully annexed by 120 BC. The new province was named 'Provincia'. The annexed area provided protection for Italy, land routes to Spain, and was opened up to Roman settlement. The local upper classes were closely linked to Rome through commerce, culture and language.[4] By the end of the reign of Augustus, in the first century CE, the region was renamed 'Gallia Narbonensis'.

The year 407 saw a second wave of barbarian invasions. On his way to southern Italy, the Visigothic leader Alaric died. His brother-in-law Ataulf, who had married Theodosius' daughter Gallia Placida, thus securing his dynastic position, succeeded him. Ataulf led his troops into Gaul and in 414 captured Narbonne, Toulouse and Bordeaux. Other groups of Vandals had invaded Spain by 409, and by 429 had entered Africa. Visigothic rule now extended from Spain into southern Gaul. Narbonne had been captured by 462 and Arles by Theodoric at approximately the same time.[5]

By 480, Gaul was divided into three kingdoms: the Burgundian in the west, the Frankish in the east and the Visigothic in the south.[6] The kingdom of the Visigoths stretched from southern Gaul into all of Spain. They had conquered most of this region by the second half of the fifth century. The rich region of Narbonne was of interest to others, so the period was marked by many skirmishes with the Frankish neighbors. The Visigothic rulers were Arians, and converted to Catholic Christianity in the late sixth century. They remained in the region until the Muslim invasions in 711.

1.1　Jewish Evidence[7]

Little is known of the earliest settlement of Jews in southern Gaul. The name does not appear in Scripture either. Some evidence comes

---

[4] Klingshirn (1994) pp. 35–36.
[5] Rivet (1988) pp. 105–8.
[6] Cantor (1993) pp. 104–105.
[7] See for information on Jews in Gaul: Handley, M. 'This Stone shall be a Witness' (Joshua 24.27): Jews, Christians and Inscriptions in Early Medieval Gaul', in: Porter/Pearson (2000) pp. 239–254; Benbassa (1999) pp. 3–7; Perchenet (1988) pp. 19–42; Girard (1986) ch 1.

from Josephus. In the year 6, in the tenth year of his reign, Archelaus, ethnarch of Judea was sent by Augustus into exile to Vienne in Gaul, where he died by the year 16.[8] A similar fate awaited his kinsman Herod Antipas who was tetrarch of Galilee and Perea. In the year 39 he was sent into exile by Caligula and ended up in Lyon, in Gaul. He was accompanied by his wife Herodias and also died in exile.[9] Other early references are much more vague and probably refer to a 'nation far away' rather than specifically Gaul.[10] It is said that the Jews in southern Gaul came either as refugees after the year 70, or through trade. Initially, they enjoyed similar rights to the Roman citizens. In 212 Caracalla had granted citizenship to all residing in various parts of the empire. The ensuing benefits would also help the Jews.[11] It is not until the fifth century that we have more specific written examples of Jews in Gaul.[12]

Jewish archeological evidence does not provide us with any more clues on early settlements in Gaul.[13] What evidence there is, is mostly controversial as the remains are only *alleged* to be Jewish.

There is an oil-lamp from *Bagnols-sur-Cèze*, in the Bouches-du-Rhône region, which allegedly contains the remains of a seven-armed candlestick. It may date to the late fourth-early fifth century.[14]

A presumably fourth-century stamp seal from the region of *Avignon* shows a Jewish candlestick flanked by several letters: an "A", a "V", an "I" and an "N". Blumenkranz interprets these letters as referring to the inhabitants of the city itself, *avinionensis*, or inhabitants of Avignon.[15]

---

[8] Josephus, *Antiquitates* 17, 13, 2 (342–4) (LCL 410).

[9] Josephus *Antiquitates* 18, 7, 2 (252–3) (LCL 433).

[10] Midr Pss XXII, 31: 'It happened that *from Gaul, or Spain, or from such distant country* a man brought his offering' (my italics). A reference to ships sailing between Gaul and Spain: T: t.Yeb 63a.

[11] The Edict of Caracalla: Linder (1987) pp. 103–107; Benbassa (1999) p. 4 ff.

[12] The Sirmondian Constitutions 6 (425) (Pharr (1952)), and church councils and the writings of church fathers—all of which will be discussed later.

[13] For the later period (6th–7th c.), see: Handley (2000) pp. 239–254. The evidence as presented here is hotly contested by Schwartzfuchs (1973) who discards the idea of a representation of a menorah on the lamp from Bagnols (p. 580), the letters and the menorah on the seal from Avignon (pp. 580–3), and the menorahs on the lamp from Orgon which he claims are too vague to discern clearly (pp. 584–5). Goodenough even claims that the seal from Avignon may have magical significance rather than Jewish: Goodenough (1953) Vol. 2, p. 217.

[14] Blumenkranz (1969) pp. 164–5.

[15] Blumenkranz (1969) pp. 166–7.

Noy, however, sees these letters as "I", "A", "N" and "U", and translates this into a name, Januarius.[16]

Another oil-lamp, this one from *Orgon*, in the valley of the Rhône,
arguably shows a representation of two Jewish candlesticks. The lamp
possibly dates to the first century AD.[17]

Much more than this is difficult to find.[18]

1.2 *Christian Evidence*[19]

Early evidence shows that Christianity had reached Gaul by the mid-
second century. There are connections to Christian Asia Minor. This is
verified by the stories of the martyrs of Lyon and Vienne.[20] The second
century bishop of Lyon, Irenaeus, also hails from Asia Minor.[21]

A bishop Marcianus of Arles is mentioned in a letter by Cyprian of
Carthage.[22] Marcianus is accused of 'joining Novatian and distancing
himself from the truth of the Catholic Church' (v.1.1). In the letter,
Cyprian requests the name of Marcianus' replacement in order to be
able to get in touch with him (v.v.2). Two councils are called for in
Arles, indicating that the city must have been an important Christian
center, one in 314 (on Donatism) and another in 355 to discuss the
position of Hilary of Poitiers.[23] Both councils show a situation similar
to Elvira: after the Decian persecutions there were many *lapsi*, so the
church fathers called for meetings to discuss the problem. The council of 314 was attended by the bishops of Arles, Vienne, Marseille,
and Vaison, and priests from Orange and Apt, and a deacon from
Nice. This shows to what extent the church was already established

---

[16] Noy (1993) n. 190. If this name is correct it has obvious pagan connotations: Januarius meaning 'dedicated to Janus', the god at the beginning of the year. CIJ 667.

[17] Blumenkranz (1969) pp. 171–172.

[18] On other, later objects see: Noy (1993) pp. 263–272. Other objects are mentioned
by Blumenkranz yet without references: Blumenkranz (1972) pp. 13–14. See also:
Duval et. al. (1995–1998) *Les Premiers Monuments Chrétiens de la France*, 3 vols.

[19] For a good introduction on Arles and southern Gaul in the later Roman Empire,
cf. Klingshirn (1994) pp. 33–71; and esp. Fevrier (1978) pp. 127–158; Loseby (1996)
pp. 45–70. For Christians in other parts of Gaul as well, see: Pietri (1997) pp. 393–411;
and a special edition of the *Mélanges de Science Religieuse* (oct.–déc. 1993) with several
articles.

[20] Cf. the martyrs of Vienne under emperor Marcus Aurelius. Cf. Eusebius who
mentions reports sent by the Christians of Lyon and Vienne to their co-religionists in
'Asia and Phrygia' (*HE* V, 1–2; SC 41).

[21] Griffe (1964) pp. 20–27.

[22] *Ep.* LXVIII (CCSL IIIc).

[23] Hefele/Leclercq (1907) vol. I.1 p. 275 f.; vol. I.2 p. 869 f.

by this time.[24] In 407 Arles became the capital of the diocese and seat of the prefecture of Gaul.[25] Arles received ecclesiastical primacy in 417 when pope Zosimus established the bishop of the city as primate over the southern provinces of Viennensis, and Narbonensis I and II.[26] The resulting opposition from Patroclus of Narbonne and Proculus of Marseille was not solved easily. The primacy of Arles was contested by Vienne as well through claims of antiquity in their Christian presence.[27]

The original capital of the southern province of Gaul, Narbonensis, was Narbonne. Prudentius mentions a third-century bishop of Narbonne named Paul.[28] No bishop of Narbonne, however, is mentioned for the council held at Arles in 314. The first bishop mentioned in pontifical letters dating to between 417 and 422 is a Hilarius. He was apparently succeeded by Rusticus who is known through inscriptions and texts dating to 427–458.[29]

As far as Marseille is concerned, there is the well-known legend of Mary Magdalen who was joined by Mary and Lazarus on their flight from Palestine after the death of Jesus. According to this legend they landed near Marseille. Needless to say, it is but a legend.

The first bishop known for Marseille is mentioned at the council of Arles in 314, Oresius.

For Béziers and Nîmes, there is mostly circumstantial evidence as far as literary sources are concerned. The bishops from these places are mentioned in late fourth and fifth century council texts.[30]

Fourth to sixth century sarcophagi in Gaul were made in different places. Rome was an important production center, and remained in use until the early fifth century. Roman-made sarcophagi are found throughout Gaul and were decorated with biblical scenes, figures and scenes from nature. Regional workshops existed as well. There was a small center at Marseille and a larger one in south-west France, near the Pyrenees, called *Lugdunum Convenarum* (Valcabrère). These sarcophagi as well knew different types of decoration—both stylistic and

---

[24] Rivet (1988) ch. 7.
[25] Fevrier (1978) p. 153.
[26] Griffe (1964); Vanneufville (1996) p. 62.
[27] Fevrier (1978) pp. 153–4.
[28] Prudentius *Peristephanon* IV, 34–35 (Lavarenne (1951).
[29] Fevrier/Barral (1989) pp. 15–23.
[30] Fevrier/Barral (1989) pp. 33–38; 53–60.

figurative.[31] Most sarcophagi from the Provence were made in Rome, occasionally in Marseille, one in Arles and possibly in Ravenna. In Arles and Marseille the sarcophagi can be found *in situ* (Arles at Alyscamps and Trinquetaille, in Marseille at St. Victor). All are Roman-made, except one in Arles which may have been made in Ravenna, and are all decorated with stylistic and figurative (biblical) scenes.[32]

The city of Arles provides us with much Christian archeological and literary evidence. It seems likely that within the western section of the medieval abbey, now the area of Saint-Jean du Moustier, the early cathedral and monastery, as described by bishop Caesarius in his Rule for monks and nuns,[33] can be found. The fourth century city not only boasted a large cathedral, but still contained the vestiges of the Roman city: an amphitheater, baths, a circus, and a basilica.[34] The suburb of Trinquetaille is the site of the martyrdom of Saint Genesius which is now covered by the church of St. Genest. He was buried in the southeastern part of the city where the cemetery was (now St Genes aux Alyscamps). This is also the burial place of Honoratus and Hilarius. In this area more fourth century sarcophagi have been found.[35] Documents also mention a basilica dedicated to Saint Stephen; this is now probably under the ninth century Saint Trophime. The same holds for other early buildings which are also undoubtedly to be found under later church structures.[36] Arles was ideally situated for economic development such as trade via the Mediterranean and northwards through the Rhône valley. It is therefore not surprising that it received civic and ecclesiastical primacy by the fifth century.

In Marseille, cathedral foundations from the fourth to fifth century have been found, together with a fourth century baptistery with mosaics.[37] The basilica of Stephen, mentioned by Gregory of Tours, was replaced in the Middle Ages by a chapel and cannot be recovered. The same goes for different abbeys and monasteries mentioned in various

---

[31] Immerzeel (1996) esp. ch. 6 and 7 (pp. 95–151) and conclusion (pp. 160–166); Christern-Briesenick (2003) *passim*.

[32] Immerzeel (1996) pp. 120–131; Christern-Briesenick (2003) no. 32–142 (Arles), no. 283–315 (Marseille).

[33] Caesarius *Regula* (for monks), rule 3 (SC 398); *Statuta sanctarum virginum*: rule 9, 45, 51 (SC 345).

[34] Fevrier (1978) pp. 127–158. See also: Heijmans (2004) pp. 83–243.

[35] Fevrier (1978) pp. 127–158.

[36] Fevrier, 'Arles' in: Biarne (1986) pp. 73–84.

[37] Guyon, J. 'Marseille' in: Biarne et al. (1986) pp. 121–133.

texts.[38] The only remaining fifth century oratory is now to be found in the crypt of the Saint Victor.[39]

In Narbonne, inscriptions and part of the lintel of a monumental gate dating to around 445 have been found. The ruins of the church burnt in 441 have probably been built over again. Outside the city walls a decorated room with polychrome mosaics dating to the fourth century, together with fourth to sixth century sarcophagi, was discovered within another structure. Also found in the area is a fourth century basilica which was built over a Roman house.[40]

As far as Avignon is concerned, the only Christian textual evidence comes from fifth century council texts, but within the ruins of the fourth century abbey church of Rufus fifth and sixth century sarcophagi were discovered.[41] On the sarcophagi found, possibly dating to the fourth century, are representations of Christ giving the keys to Peter.[42]

At Apt one of the sarcophagi shows Christ bearing a cross-shaped staff, flanked by two figures wearing the pallium.[43]

Several sarcophagi from Aix contain elaborate representations: Christ giving the law to Peter who holds the cross-shaped staff and apostles on either side, biblical scenes of Abraham sacrificing, the raising from the dead of Lazarus, an *orante* figure, the curing of the blind and the woman suffering from hemorrhages, and Moses and the bush, or scenes from the arrest of Jesus, including a scene of Judas' embrace at Gethsemane.[44]

Despite a lack of concrete evidence for early settlements of Jews and Christians in Gaul, from the fourth and fifth centuries at least literary sources show that here as well there were contacts between the two communities.

---

[38] Guyon, *ibidem*.
[39] Mâle (1950) p. 155.
[40] Fevrier (1989) pp. 15–23; sarcophagi found: Christern-Briesenick (2003) no. 359–393.
[41] Biarne (1986) pp. 113–119; Christern-Briesenick (2003) no. 153–168.
[42] Christern-Briesenick (2003) no. 154.
[43] Le Blant (1886) n. 201.
[44] Christern-Briesenick (2003) no. 19–27; esp. no. 22.

1.3   Christian Authors on Jews and Judaism

That there were contacts between Christians and Jews is affirmed through the writings of several church leaders. Various Christian authors from this region and period wrote about Jews and Judaism.[45] These fathers can be grouped into the categories mentioned in the Introduction:

- theological treatises: Evagrius (*Altercatio Simonis*); Eucherius (exegetical works); Sedulius (a poem); and Prosper of Aquitaine (*Chronikon*).
- 'historical' texts: Sidonius Apollinaris (letters); Gregory of Tours (a History); Venantius Fortunatus (Poem *Carm*. V, 5; *Vita S. Germani* 63).
- the homilies of Caesarius of Arles.

1.3.1   Theological Treatises

The first three Gallic church fathers to be studied within the framework of this period and region are Evagrius, Eucherius of Lyon, and Prosper of Aquitaine. These three church fathers refer to Jews and Judaism in their writings which can be described as theological and exegetical texts.

Evagrius was a monk in southern Gaul, who is mainly known through the writings of Gennadius.[46] In approximately 430/440, Evagrius wrote the treatise *Altercatio legis inter Simonem Iudaeum et Theophilum Christianum*.[47] The Jew Simon and the Christian Theophilus are in conversation and Simon poses questions on the usual topics such as the virgin birth, circumcision, and the crucifixion of Jesus. Theophilus responds by using Old Testament quotes to show that Jesus was foretold by the prophets to be the Messiah. In the end, the Jew Simon converts to Christianity.[48]

---

[45] See also Geisel (1998) pp. 231–360.

[46] *De vir. ill.* 50 (Bernoulli (1968)).

[47] CCSL 64.

[48] Cf. Schreckenberg (1999) pp. 367–8; Quasten (1950) vol. IV, pp. 509–510; Blumenkranz (1963) pp. 27–31 who sees this as a text directed against judaizing Christians, hence topics such as circumcision, Sabbath observance and dietary restrictions.

The dialogue seems reminiscent of the conversation between the Jew Priscus, Gregory of Tours and king Chilperic.[49]

Eucherius, bishop of Lyon between 432 (or 434) and 441, entered the monastery of Lérins with his wife and sons, and died in approximately 450. He is mostly known through the writings of Gennadius.[50] Eucherius wrote two exegetical texts: the *Instructiones ad Salonium*[51] and the *Formularum Spiritalis Intelligentiae*.[52]

The two works date to the period of his episcopacy and are dedicated to his sons. The texts again consist of a series of questions and answers, again attempting to prove the usual issues: that the natural law was given to Old Testament leaders before Sinai, an allegorical explanation of dietary laws, the crucifixion, and the world since the coming of Jesus.[53]

Prosper of Aquitaine was a theologian who lived from approximately 390–463. He also can be found in Gennadius.[54] He wrote a chronological work called the *Chronicum*.[55] Prosper Tiro of Aquitaine, as is his full name, lived in Marseille and corresponded with Augustine. He went to Rome in 431 where he wrote the Chronicle shortly before his death. The Chronicle is a history of the world from its origins to 455. For the initial parts Prosper uses the works of Eusebius and Jerome; from about 412 it becomes his own work.[56]

What he writes is that many Jews had been killed in Jerusalem in the year 71 because they had killed the Savior. As a result of their bad behavior their land had to be deserted, and thus came an end to their prophets, sacrifice and liturgies. For this part of the Chronicle, Prosper relies heavily on Jerome, thus these are not his own thoughts.[57]

---

[49] *Hist. Franc.* VI, 5; Krusch/Levison (1951).
[50] *De vir. ill.* 63 (Bernoulli (1968)).
[51] CSEL 31.
[52] CSEL 31.
[53] Cf. Schreckenberg (1999) pp. 375–376; Quasten (1950) pp. 504–507; Blumenkranz (1963) pp. 22–23 who suggests the author knew no Jews as there is no evidence in the text (p. 23); 'Eucherius (von Lyon)' in: Döpp/Geerlings (1998) pp. 234–235.
[54] *De vir. ill.* 85 (Bernoulli (1968)).
[55] Mommsen (1892).
[56] Cf. Schreckenberg, op. cit., pp. 381–382; Quasten (1950) pp. 551–558; Blumenkranz (1963) pp. 37–38; Muhlberger (1990) ch. 3.
[57] Markus (1986) pp. 31–45.

These theological treatises are similar to those seen in the previous chapters and contain, as expected, very little concrete evidence on Jews, Judaism and the relations between Christians and Jews.

1.3.2 'Historical' Texts

Cajus Sollius Modestus Apollinaris Sidonius was born in Lyon in 431. His grandfather was praetorian prefect of Gaul; he was the first in his family to convert to Christianity. Sidonius married the daughter of the Visigothic king Avitus. In 469 or 470 Sidonius became bishop of Clermont. The city of Clermont suffered many attacks by the Gauls, and Sidonius was exiled and imprisoned at least once during his office as bishop. Reinstated, he wrote many poems and letters.[58]

It is in his letters that he mentions Jews. Sidonius writes about a Jew called Gozolas who is a client of Magnus Felix of Narbonne, a school friend of Sidonius. Sidonius has charged Gozolas with delivering his letter to Felix. In the letter, he says that he could like Gozolas 'if only he weren't a Jew', and: '[...] a man I should like if I could only overcome my contempt of his sect.'[59] The reason why this Gozolas was traveling from one place to the other could be trading activities; he could thus transfer the missives as well.[60]

Gozolas is again mentioned in another letter,[61] also to M. Felix, where Sidonius writes the cryptic message: 'your Gozolas (God grant he may become our man) acts once more as the carrier of my letter'.[62]

In a further letter, this one to Eleutherius, bishop of Tournai, he commends a Jew to the bishop.[63] Sidonius is obviously not in favor of the Jewish religion: 'not because I approve a sect pernicious to those involved in its toils'. Yet, he does not want to discard them completely: 'for while there is any possibility of converting them, there is always a hope of their redemption'. Sidonius ends his letter requesting a proper defense for the man, for 'much as you may attack his heresy, you can fairly defend him as a man'.

In a fourth letter, this one to Nunechius, bishop of Nantes, Sidonius speaks with joy of a certain Promotus, 'by birth a Jew', but 'he has pre-

---

[58] LCL 296, 420. Geisel (1998) pp. 234–236.
[59] *Ep.* III, 4.1.
[60] Cf. Blumenkranz (1963) pp. 43–44.
[61] *Ep.* IV, 5.1.
[62] Several authors assume he refers to a hoped-for conversion of the Jew: Blumenkranz (1963) p. 43; Régné (1908) pp. 2, n. 2.
[63] *Ep.* VI, 11.

ferred to be numbered with those chosen by faith rather than blood; [...] by grace of the Spirit which makes alive he has rejected the letter that kills. [...] for he ceased to belong to the handmaid Hagar when he exchanged the servitude of conformity according to law for the freedom which comes of grace.'[64] His joy at the conversion of Promotus is expressed in the poetic language he uses.

Gregory of Tours was born in c. 538 in Averna (modern Clermont, where Sidonius had been bishop). His family was of Roman origin. Gregory became bishop of Tours (Turones) in 573 and remained thus until his death on November 15th 594. He was much involved in the politics of his time, often endangering his life. Gregory had had a cursory education with little knowledge of the classics or grammar. Despite this, he was a prolific writer. His work can be divided into two categories—hagiographies and 'histories'.

His hagiographical works include miracle stories involving Jews. His 'miracles of St. Martin' served to establish his position as bishop of the city of which Martin was the patron saint. Gregory further consolidated his authority in Tours by writing other saints' lives in the 'Glory of the martyrs', 'Glory of the confessors', and the 'Life of the Fathers'.[65]

Miracle stories served a useful catechetical purpose: to show the power of orthodox faith over 'non-believers' (here, Jews) and 'mistaken believers' (heretics).[66]

In the 'Miracles of Saint Martin' (III.50), Gregory describes how Lupus, a priest of the town of Bordeaux, was ill and wished to visit the tomb of St. Martin. On his way to the cathedral he encountered a Jew who told him that a dead person would never be able to help him. Ignoring the Jew, Lupus continued into the cathedral and eventually was cured. The Jew, of course, was afflicted for a year by the same fever Lupus had had, but his 'iniquitous character never converted'.[67] Illness was seen as the result of sinful behavior, a cure usually resulted not only in the healing of the body but also of the soul.[68]

---

[64] *Ep.* VIII, 13.
[65] Arndt/Krusch (1985).
[66] Monroe, W.S. '*Via Iustitiae*: The Biblical Sources of Justice in Gregory of Tours' in: Mitchell/Wood (2002) pp. 99–112, esp. pp. 103–107.
[67] Bordier (1860).
[68] Van Dam (1993) esp. p. 86 ff; p. 114.

In the 'Glory of the Martyrs' (ch. 9) Gregory describes how a Jewish boy befriended Christian boys and went to Mass with them. His father found out that he had received communion and in anger threw him in the furnace. The boy survived the ordeal unscathed due to the protection of the Virgin Mary whom he had seen in a vision. The boy and his mother became Christians, his father was killed.

Chapter 21 describes how a Jew, annoyed by the presence of an image of Christ on a church, removed it, but the image started bleeding. The trail of blood led the search party to his house, the image was retrieved and the Jew killed. In chapter 99 a Jew is cured and converts after visiting the shrine of a local saint. Christians angered at his cure destroy part of the church but those with illnesses are cured nonetheless, probably much to their surprise.[69]

The 'Glory of the Confessors' chapter 95 describes how through the intercession of the relics of an ascetic a boat manned by Jews was stopped in order that the Christian passenger on the boat could go on land to visit the monastery of Lérins.[70]

The least specific reference to Jews in Gregory's writings of the Fathers is in his description of the funeral of Gallus of Clermont where 'even the Jews followed the procession in tears'.[71]

In Gregory's 'Glory of the Martyrs' (ch. 79), he describes a dinner party where the Catholic hostess invited a Catholic priest but her heretic husband invited an Arian priest. Gregory describes the Arian as a glutton—a major sin according to the author. The Arian dies as a result of his eating habits, obviously much to Gregory's joy. Yet, the purpose of the story is rather to show the incompatibility of orthodox Christians and others at joint meals; an issue also discussed where Jews and Christians are concerned, at the councils of Vannes (465, c. 12), Agde (506, c. 40), and Epaon (517, c. 15).[72]

Gregory of Tours also wrote a monumental work called the 'History of the Franks'.[73] The work contains various references to the Jewish inhabitants of the Merovingian kingdoms. Some references are only passing remarks. These references can be grouped into:

---

[69] Arndt/ Krusch (1985): *Liber in Gloria Martyrum.*
[70] Arndt/Krusch (1985): *Liber in Gloria Confessorum.*
[71] Arndt/Krusch (1985): *Vitae Patrum.*
[72] See also Effros, (2002) p. 18.
[73] Krusch/Levison (1951).

- Jews and trade and money:
  - Bishop Cautinus of Clermont was known to 'respect nothing'. For example: he was on familiar terms with Jews as he 'bought goods from them' (IV.12).
  - A priest Ephrasius wanted to succeed Cautinus after the latter's death. Hoping to influence the king in his decision on the new bishop, Euphrasius sent him gifts 'which he had obtained from the Jews' (IV.35).
  - Armentarius, another Jew, and two Christians went to collect their payment on some bonds. Initially they were received kindly, but in the end were killed. No-one was punished for the murder (VII.23).

- There are longer references to Jews which involve a more religious discussion:
  - Leonastus of Bourges had recovered his failing eyesight after visiting the church of Saint Martin. However, having asked a Jew for medical advice to further improve his eyesight, he lost his eyesight again, according to Gregory because he had 'sinned' by consulting a Jew. After all, 'what fellowship does righteousness have with unrighteousness' (V.6).[74]
  - A lengthy account registers the discussion between king Chilperic, Gregory and a Jew called Priscus whom they attempt to convert to Christianity. Priscus was the king's trade agent. At the beginning of the conversation the king and Priscus discuss the purpose of the coming of the Son of God. When the king falls silent Gregory takes over. He tries to convince Priscus by stating that Jesus had to be born for the redemption of mankind. Using quotes from the Old Testament he explains how mankind's sins meant God had to send His Son. Despite Gregory's attempts, Priscus would not be convinced to convert to Christianity. (VI.5)
  - Despite a peaceful parting of the ways after the aforementioned example, Chilperic, no doubt frustrated by the failed attempt to convert Priscus, ordered a group of Jews, including Priscus, to be baptized. That this forced conversion had little effect can be seen in the fact that some Jews still 'clung to [their] beliefs' and

---

[74] Cf. the council of Trullo (Constantinople 691) c. 11 against receiving medical advice from Jews.

continued observing the Sabbath while appearing to honor the Lord's day. Priscus did not consent to the forced conversion and was imprisoned—if he did not convert, he would be forced. Through bribes he got out of prison, ostensibly for his son's marriage, and promised to convert after the wedding. He didn't, as a matter of fact, but continued in his faith. A converted Jew eventually killed him as he went to the synagogue on a Sabbath. (VI.17)

- A description of the forced conversion of Jews is the incident involving bishop Avitus of Clermont. At Easter, a Jew wishing to convert to Christianity was accosted by a fellow Jew who poured rancid oil on him. The bishop managed to keep the people from attacking the Jews, but they destroyed the synagogue ten days later. Afterwards, the bishop gave the Jews an ultimatum: convert to Christianity or leave Clermont. A large group ('more than 500') converted at Pentecost; those who didn't left for Marseille. (V.11)

  In a letter from Pope Gregory I to the bishops Vergilius of Arles and Theodore of Marseille he writes that 'many Jews have been brought to baptism through force rather than by teaching'. However, he emphasizes that the conversion process should be accompanied by enforcement from Holy Scripture. For, anyone brought to baptism by compulsion and not by preaching may 'return to his former superstition'. Thus, emphasis is placed on preaching rather than pressure.[75]

- King Guntram visiting Orléans is acclaimed by many, including Jews 'in their own tongue'. The king reacts angrily for he assumes they want him to rebuild their synagogue 'destroyed some time ago by the Christians'. He refuses to do so because the 'Jewish people [are] evil, treacherous and full of deceit'. (VIII.1)

These references appear to relate to specific situations and they seem to refer to genuine Jews, not fictitious examples. What we see is interaction between mostly clergy and Jews, involving trade issues. Jews were involved in trade; undoubtedly, as we saw earlier, one of the reasons for their presence in Gaul. The information above points to close contacts between Christians (clergy) and Jews. That Jews were also known

---

[75] Gregory I, *Reg.* 1:45 (591 CE) (CCSL CXL, p. 59).

for their medical advice we see elsewhere as well; but it apparently also occurred in Gaul, as Gregory describes in the encounter of Leonastus and the Jew in Bourges. Gregory is not happy about Leonastus' choice of medical advisor.

The more negative example of Christian-Jewish relations is found in several of Gregory's stories. These involve conversions, or at least the attempt thereat and the resulting problems. Apparently, conversions by Jews to Christianity, or vice versa, posed severe problems.[76]

Gregory's account of the conversions of Jews serves a purpose similar to the miracle stories.[77] This does not mean that the events did not take place, rather that the numbers involved and especially the significance of the people and the event itself had a purpose.[78] The task of a bishop was to convert the unbelieving—pagan, Arian and Jew alike.[79] That conversions are not always completely successful we see in the forced conversion by Chilperic where the converted continued their Jewish practice of observing the Sabbath while also keeping the Lord's Day. According to Brennan this is not surprising: according to him, Gregory was deeply involved in the factional quarrel for the bishopric and as such highly in favor of bishop Avitus.[80] All Avitus' contenders are thus shown in a negative light. This means that the events may have been as Gregory perceived them but the (positive) emphasis on Avitus' role is thus explained.

The success for Avitus is re-emphasized in the poem written by Venantius Fortunatus at the request of Gregory.[81] The story is the same in both sources, but Venantius' account of the conversion of the Jews of Clermont is more graphic, Avitus more patient, and the Jews more bellicose. The only 'positive' reference to Jews in the writings of Venantius is found in his account of a Jew in Bourges who had converted to Christianity.[82]

---

[76] Geisel (1998) on Jews at Clermont: pp. 261–297; on Priscus: pp. 305–309; on the image of Christ ('Glory of the Martyrs'): pp. 315–321.

[77] See also: Rose (2002) p. 308; Goffart (1985) pp. 473–497; Brennan (1985) pp. 321–337; Rouche (1979) pp. 105–124.

[78] Rose (2002) p. 308 note 5.

[79] *Hist. Franc.* II, 31 (pagan); IX, 15 (Arians): Krusch/Levison (1951).

[80] Brennan (1985) pp. 321–337.

[81] *Carm.* V, 5 (Venance Fortunat *Poèmes* T. II, L. V–VIII; Reydellet (1998)).

[82] *Vita Germ.* 63 (Krusch (1981)). This story is the only evidence for Jews in Bourges: Prevot/Barral I Altet (1989) p. 20. Cf. also on Venantius and Jews: George (1992) pp. 127–129.

It appears that there is no period of preparation for the 'converts'. Noteworthy as well is the use of Christian feasts to mark the timing of the events: the initial incident takes place at Easter, the resulting attack at Ascension, and the conversion at Pentecost. The question arises whether this was normal practice in Gaul. Was there a period of preparation for converts from Judaism, and did these resulting initiation ceremonies normally take place during the Easter period? We will return to this point when discussing the *Statuta Ecclesiae Antiqua* (c. 16) and the council of Agde (c. 34).

The statements in Gregory's 'Histories' and Venantius' poem emphasize a growing tendency to single out non-believers, especially Jews, in an attempt to create the image of a Christian kingdom and good Christian bishops. The references in these works to Jews and incidents involving Jews may, once again, refer to genuine situations—yet ecclesiastical politics and theological argumentation certainly colored the description of the events.[83] However, the texts do show that contacts between Christians and Jews existed—not only on a friendly level but certainly also in a more hostile situation.

1.3.3 Homilies: Caesarius of Arles

Caesarius of Arles was born in 470 in Chalon-sur-Saône, became a monk at Lérins and finally deacon, priest and even bishop at Arles (502–542). He had been born in the Burgundian kingdom yet became bishop of Visigothic Arles; his loyalties would often be questioned. Caesarius is mostly known for his sermons.[84]

Caesarius presided over the council held at Agde in 506, the rulings of which contain two canons on Jews.[85] His name was associated with the text of the '*Statuta Ecclesiae Antiqua*', though this seems incorrect.[86] This was due to the fact that the ideas expressed in the document so closely resemble Caesarius' own thoughts on church and Christian society.[87] It is said that his influence is also seen in the results of the council held at Orléans in 538, even if he did not attend it.[88]

---

[83] See also Goffart (1985) pp. 473–498.
[84] See also Klingshirn (1994) *passim*.
[85] C. 40 on joint meals and c. 34 on a lengthy catechumenate for Jews.
[86] Cf. a.o. Malnory (1894).
[87] Klingshirn (1994) p. 82.
[88] Klingshirn (1994) p. 258.

In the 'Life of Caesarius'[89] there are several references to Jews. The 'Life' is obviously an embellishment of the life and works of the bishop, written by close associates of his.[90] To what extent the 'Life' therefore is based on Caesarius and his views or rather the view of his biographers is a matter of conjecture.

In the first part of the 'Life', the siege of Arles is described. Arles was part of the Visigothic kingdom which extended from Spain into southern France. In 507 it was besieged by Franks and Burgundians. Apparently the Jews were responsible for defending part of the city walls. However, they wanted to help the enemy in a 'Trojan-horse' situation. It failed, however, despite the 'treacherous and cruel intent' of the Jews.[91] One assumes that, real or not, the Jews in this incident proved a useful scapegoat.[92] They are here represented as a typology even if their presence in the city is a historical reality. They may have provided a useful diversion to keep the bishop free from suspicion. Yet, the final part of the episode is more interesting. Caesarius, according to this 'Life', was in favor of paying ransom for those captured rather than have them become slaves and thereby run the risk of conversion to Arianism or Judaism.[93] The more general, and thus less reliable, reference to Jews in the *Vita* is at the very end where 'everyone' wept at the bishop's passing: 'good and evil, just and unjust, Christians and Jews'.[94] This does not necessarily refer to specific examples but typifies 'all of society'.

The sermons of Caesarius contain various different types of references to Jews and Judaism, and topics relevant to our study.

There are sermons where Caesarius uses exegesis to explain Old and New Testament passages. In these homilies, the usual comparison is made between Jews and Christians and synagogue and church—i.e., the old and the new covenant. What he does is to show the differences between Judaism and Christianity in order to convince his audience

---

[89] *Vita*: PL 67. See also Mikat (1996); Courreau (1970) pp. 92–112.

[90] Cyprianus, a close associate and bishop of Toulon for part I, and the second part by two diocesan clerics who had attended him: Messianus and Stephanus: Klingshirn (1994b) p. 1.

[91] *Vita* I, 29–31 (PL 67, 1011–1012 n. 21–22). See for a discussion on the issue of loyalties, Mikat (1996) pp. 11–23.

[92] Klingshirn (1994) pp. 108–110.

[93] *Vita* I, 32 (PL 67, 1012, n. 23), Mikat (1996) pp. 24–25.

[94] *Vita* II, 49 (PL 67, 1042: n. 35).

of the superiority of Christianity.[95] In *sermo* 104 Caesarius states that Christianity had been promised since the creation of the world and had been foretold by the prophets. The complete homily is dedicated to describing the difference between the church and the synagogue, with obvious emphasis on the superiority and legitimacy of the church. Even where he mentions the possibility of explaining this superiority to Jews (and pagans), conversion is not his purpose. Rather, he wishes to emphasize good behavior and pride in their faith to his audience (*sermo* 104, 6).[96] Despite admonishing his flock against too close contacts Caesarius does suggest the possibility of conversing with each other as a medium towards spreading the Christian message. In the sermon Caesarius encourages his flock to 'explain clearly, not only to Jews, but also to pagans, the mystery of the Christian religion, at all times and in all places'. And: 'those who can show Jews, pagans and wicked Christians the proper way of living will receive eternal recompenses'.[97]

Yet, the Jews served a useful purpose as well. While trying to convince his audience of the church's superiority as opposed to the synagogue's inferiority, he was very well aware of the shortcomings of his flock. In order to emphasize that good behavior only enhances this vision of the church's superiority, he used Jewish practices as positive examples of how to act. For example, the Jews' abstention from work on a Saturday (*sermo* 13, 3) and his high regard for Jewish almsgiving (*sermo* 1, 8). Thus, Judaism also provided a useful support for his arguments.

This is again seen in *sermo* 183. Caesarius is once again looking for opportunities to correct the behavior of his flock and warns them that if they steal from a Jew it gives a wrong impression and prevents possible conversion of the Jew.[98]

In *sermo* 163, Caesarius discusses the parable of the prodigal son.[99] Much of this homily seems to have been borrowed from Augustine.[100] The eldest son represents the Jews who have always been loyal to God and to the writings of the Old Testament. The younger son represents

---

[95] *Sermo* 96, 104, 107 (CCSL CIII).
[96] SC 447.
[97] *Sermo* 104, 6 (SC 447); Mikat (1996) p. 27.
[98] *Sermo* 183, 6 (CCSL CIV) p. 748.
[99] Lc. 15: 11 ff.
[100] *Quaest. Evangeliorum* II, 33 (CCSL XLIVB, p. 73). For discussion see: Klaassen (1996) pp. 95–108; Blumenkranz (1948) pp. 102–105. Mikat (1996) pp. 27–28.

the pagans. Caesarius hopes for the redemption of both at the end of time.

The relatively mild language where Jews are concerned in this homily is indicative of the manner in which Caesarius viewed them, as opposed to heretics and pagans.[101] Jews are described as 'unfortunate'.[102] He deplores their obtuseness in not recognizing the signs in Scripture, and their blindness.[103] Even where he describes the misfortune of the Jews—their dispersion after the destruction of Jerusalem—he hastens to add an admonition to his listeners against pride and for humility. He warns that similar things can happen to those who do not pursue a proper lifestyle.[104]

Despite the traditional references to Jews and Judaism found in all contemporary church father writings, Caesarius seems more positive about this group than when he refers to heretics and especially pagans. The positive examples of the Jews, as stated earlier, could be based on experiences with the Jews living in and around Arles. He admonishes his flock to improve their church attendance and observe Sunday rest as Jews do, and extols Jewish almsgiving. The Jews can serve the Christians as the slaves carrying books for their masters: after all, the Jews brought the books of the Old Testament for all peoples when they were scattered to every land. Thus they can be of use when trying to convince pagans of the relevance of Scripture.[105]

A last sermon to discuss in this context is without number and placed at the end of the volume containing Caesarius' homilies, as published by the *Corpus Christianorum* series.[106] It is not clear whether it is by Caesarius. The obviously negative description of Judaism is contrary to all we have seen until now, only adding to the doubt that it may be by Caesarius. Nevertheless, the content of the very short homily is on joint meals of Christians and Jews. In it, the homilist states that Jewish food and drink is 'accursed' and 'so are the Jews for they crucified the Lord'. Therefore, they lost their land, cult, prophets, law, priests, and temple.

---

[101] Cf. Correau (1970) pp. 92–112; esp. pp. 101–106. For heretics and pagans, cf. *Sermones* 99, 123 (SC 447) where the 'cunning' of the heretics is described as resembling the third plague of Egypt.

[102] *Sermones* 83; 102, 3 etc. (SC 447).

[103] *Sermo* 102 (SC 447).

[104] *Sermo* 127, 2–3 (CCSL CIII).

[105] *Sermo* 86, 3 (SC 447).

[106] *De esca uel potu iudeorum prohibendis* (CCSL CIV, p. 967).

It seems likely that Caesarius' relatively 'mild' view of the Jews is based on a theological argument rather than describing personal experiences. He seems to have been inspired by Augustine's view on Jews and Judaism which was based on the notion that the Jews had a role to play in the redemption of mankind, and that their presence testified to the truth of Christianity.[107] Jews are useful examples in the Christian discussion on the development of their own identity. They provide examples of how not to be, and are seen as objects for possible redemption through conversion; however, redemption only when they agree, not via forced conversion. In this we can also look at the rulings of the council of Agde which was presided over by Caesarius himself. At the council, canon 34 asks for a lengthy catechumenate for Jews wishing to convert. This council and the canon mentioned will be discussed in section 3, below. Hence, forced conversion such as described, e.g., by Gregory of Tours at Clermont in 576, was not desired.

The Jews may appear to play a special role in the theology of Caesarius: they are exemplary and thus serve a purpose and must therefore be 'protected'.[108] This does not, however, mean that the Jews are therefore a fictive entity in the writings of Caesarius. The council of Agde and the descriptions in the homilies prove otherwise.

1.4   Conclusion

In general we may say that the last-mentioned church father writings, and especially the historical texts, add some relevant information to the meager picture provided by the archeological and earlier literary sources on relations between Christians and Jews in late antique Gaul.

Whether Jews served as a typological example or useful (negative) example, Caesarius of Arles shows that even in that case church fathers need not necessarily only have a negative view of Jews and Judaism.

Thus we see that apart from the theological treatises by the first-mentioned church fathers, the homilies of Caesarius and especially the 'historical' writings of Gregory of Tours convey specific information on Christian-Jewish relations.

---

[107] Fredriksen (1996) 29–54.
[108] Geisel (1998) pp. 236–247; Mikat (1996) pp. 34–38; Drews (2006) pp. 194–196 on Augustine's view of Jews as exemplary figures in Christian theology and the effects this had on later authors; Daly (1970) pp. 1–29, esp. pp. 9–17.

Let us now turn to the council texts from fifth and sixth century Gaul to see what specific information they provide. We will then return to the relevant church father texts to reconsider the content thereof.

2   *The Text of the* Statuta Ecclesiae Antiqua

The text of the *Statuta Ecclesiae Antiqua* has come to us through various manuscripts. The version mostly used in early publications is the collection we have already met in Elvira and Laodicea, the *Hispana*. The *Hispana* collection suggests that this collection of canons belonged to a 'fourth council of Carthage', which was supposedly held in 398.[109] It was not until 1757 that the Ballerini brothers corrected this view. They argued that it was not made up of a council held in Carthage but is rather a collection of council rulings from southern Gaul, dating to the second half of the fifth century.[110] Maassen placed the collection in Arles, and dated it to the end of the fifth century.[111] Munier then gave the compiler a name: Gennadius of Marseille.[112]

The canonical collection can be found in approximately 30 different manuscripts. These can be divided into three main groups: a collection of manuscripts containing the councils of Gaul; the 'Italian' collection, called the '*Statuta Antiqua Orientis*'; and the Spanish collection known as the '*Hispana*'.[113]

Munier, in his critical edition, uses the earlier manuscripts from Gaul.[114] The *Hispana* collection uses Roman numerals for the canons—

---

[109] PL 84, 199–208 (*Hispana* text). For a discussion on the *Hispana*, see part 3 of the first chapter on the council of Elvira.

[110] Ballerini (1887) (PL 56, 103 ff : discussion on Carthage 398; 879–889: text). The text of the *Statuta* can be found in: Hefele/Leclercq (1907) II, 1: using the text of the *Hispana*, published under the chapter title 'conciles de Carthage', but the authors indicate this is wrong. They believe it is a collection of African/Eastern councils. Text of the first ten canons in Latin, remainder in French. On the editions of the *Hispana* and the *Statuta* see: Martínez Diez (1966) *CCH* vol. I, pp. 103–146; 206–255; 286–288. Munier (1960): critical edition based on earlier manuscripts from Gaul (see discussion below). Text in Latin, no translation, lengthy discussion on manuscripts. Munier (1963) (CCSL CXLVIII) pp. 162–188, dates the text to 475 and from Gaul. Limmer (2004) vol. I: pp. 141–149: discussion on the canons, canons in German only. For further discussion on the text: Morin (1913) pp. 334–342; Coquin (1961) pp. 193–224; Gaudemet (1985) pp. 84–86; Munier (1987) pp. 170–180; Linder (1997) pp. 564–572.

[111] Maassen (1956) pp. 386–394.

[112] Munier (1960) pp. 55–73.

[113] Munier (1960) pp. 55–71.

[114] Munier (1960) pp. 74–100.

this is also used in the edition by Hefele whose publication uses the *Hispana*. We will follow the numbering used by Munier in his critical edition based on the Gallic documents.[115]

The date of the *Statuta* text has a possible *terminus a quo*: the text uses the rulings of the councils of Orange (441) and Vaison (442); this is especially obvious in the disciplinary canons.[116] The dating *ante quem* is seen for example in *Statuta* canons 25–27 which have been used by the council of Agde (506).[117] It may be that the *Statuta* collection of canons was gathered during the reign of the Visigothic king Euric (476–485) as it was a period of relative calm.[118]

As stated above, the compiler may have been Gennadius of Marseille.[119] This is based mainly on the profession of faith by the candidate for ordination as found in the prologue of the text of the *Statuta*. This follows the outline of the first chapters of the *liber ecclesiasticorum dogmaticum* which was redacted by Gennadius. The style of the *Statuta* is similar to Gennadius' *De viris illustribus*.[120]

The collection is composed of 102 canons. These can be divided into various sections: regarding church and liturgical functions;[121] on penance and disciplinary actions;[122] on heretics[123] and on the consecration of virgins, on widows and marriage.[124]

The *Statuta Ecclesiae Antiqua* give a good impression of Christian life as it had developed in (southern) Gaul by the late fifth century. Especially the liturgy and the role of the clergy is described in detail in the collection of canons. Yet, there are—here as well—references to Jews (c. 16) and Christians appropriating Jewish practices (c. 83).

We will now turn to the discussion of these canons.

---

[115] For a further history of the text of the *Statuta*, see e.g. Coquin (1961) p. 193 ff. The article contains a helpful list of the numbering systems used for the canons of the *Statuta*.

[116] Munier (1960) p. 146; Gaudemet (1985) p. 86.

[117] Munier (1960) pp. 157, 209, 223.

[118] Munier (1960) p. 235; Gaudemet (1985) p. 86; Klingshirn (1994) pp. 69–70.

[119] Malnory (1894) p. 50 ff: prefers to see Caesarius of Arles as the author; Morin (1913) pp. 334–342 who argues against Caesarius being the compiler but offers no alternative name.

[120] Munier (1960) pp. 107–124, ch. III.

[121] C. 1–22; 25–29; 31; 34–35; 40; 42–48; 50–51; 53–62; 65; 70–82; 84–85; 87–98.

[122] C. 18–24; 30; 32–33; 36–39; 41; 49; 52; 63–69; 83; 86; 102.

[123] C. 80–82.

[124] C. 99–102.

Canon 16[125]

Ut episcopus nullum prohibeat ingredi ecclesiam et audire verbum dei, sive gentilem, sive haereticum, sive iudaeum usque ad missam catechumenorum.

A bishop shall not prohibit anyone from entering a church and listening to God's word, whether he is a pagan, heretic or Jew, until the dismissal of the catechumens.[126]

The canon refers to the issue of non-believers entering a church. Apparently there were bishops who did not allow non-believers to enter a church!

The purpose of allowing these groups into a church in this canon is closely connected to Christian liturgical celebrations, especially the Mass. The first part of the Mass consists of readings from Scripture and the homily, after which those who had not yet been received into the church would be dismissed.[127] The first part of the Mass was open to non-believers, and especially the catechumens.[128] The emphasis of this part of the celebration was the instruction, or conversion, of those not (yet) part of the Christian fold.[129] The traditional period of adult preparation for baptism was Lent. Instruction has always been the goal of the homily, during all liturgical periods. Non-believers and catechumens would be dismissed after the first part of the Mass, the latter for their own instruction elsewhere.[130] One may assume that those offici-

---

[125] Number in Hefele/Leclercq (1907) II.1: n. 84 (the *Hispana* document).

[126] The last part of the canon which refers to the 'missa catechumenorum' is translated as 'until the mass of the catechumens' by Hefele/Leclercq, vol. II.1, p. 119, and Linder (1997) p. 565. However, this does not make sense. The point is that non-believers were allowed into church during the first past of the mass, the 'missa catechumenorum'. They were then dismissed. The word 'missa' means 'dismissal': Blaise (1954) p. 535; see also the council of Valence (524), c. 1 where it is translated as such 'dismissal of the catechumens' (Hefele II.2, p. 1067 n. 4), and Klingshirn (1994) p. 178. Hence my translation as it is.

[127] Cf. the council of Valence, c. 1, which refers to the first part of the Mass in conjunction with possible conversions.

[128] *Trad. Apost.* 17,18,19 (SC 11b); the council of Orange (441) c. 18: the Gospel should be read to the catechumens (Hefele II.1); the council of Lyon I (518–523) the catechumens remain until after the prayer of the faithful, which is said after the Gospel; Beck (1950) pp. 142–3.

[129] One would assume that this was the part of the celebration which someone like Augustine would have attended as well, as he was a catechumen for a large part of his life, cf. Finn (1997) 215.

[130] The council of Valencia (513) refers to the dismissal of the catechumens after the Gospel and sermon: Akeley (1967) p. 49.

ating would hope for converts who, after hearing several convincing homilies and appropriate readings, may wish to enter the Christian fold.[131] One may also assume that the expression 'pagan, heretic or Jew' here, as elsewhere, means 'everyone who is not an orthodox Catholic'.

The presence of non-believers was undoubtedly encouraged in order to enhance the possibility of conversion.[132] This counted for pagans and heretics but also for Jews. We have seen in the historical writings of some Christian authors that Jews specifically were singled out for conversion—for example, Sidonius on Gozolas and Promotus, Gregory of Tours on Priscus and the Jews of Clermont, and Venantius on the conversions in Bourges.[133]

The canon is directed towards Christians (bishops) and their relationship with non-Christians, including Jews. It is not specifically aimed at Jews, but they are part of a general group of 'non-believers'.

Not many conclusions can be based solely on this canon. The only observation one can make is that apparently everyone was admitted to the first part of the Mass—hoping thus that pagans and heretics but also Jews would convert. That the conversion of Jews was an issue can be seen in the 'historical writings' of church authors.

CANON 83[134]

Auguriis vel incantationibus servientem a conventu ecclesiae separandum; similiter et iudaicis superstitionibus vel feriis inhaerentem.

Those who trust auguries and incantations will be placed outside of the community of the church; just as those who depend on Jewish superstitions or feasts.

---

[131] The council of Valence (524) c. 1: 'the Gospel should be read before the offertory and before the departure of the catechumens, after the reading of the Epistles, in order that not only the faithful but also catechumens, the penitents and everyone else may hear the word of the Lord and the bishop's sermon. For it is known that many have come to the faith on hearing the sermon.' (Hefele II, 2). The seventh century Antiphonary of León speaks of readings and the homily being especially directed towards the making of candidates for Christian initiation; i.e., the conversion of the listeners. They would be dismissed after the offertory with a special blessing (Akeley (1967) p. 148). See also canon 31 of the *Statuta* which states that 'anyone leaving the church during the sermon is to be excommunicated'!

[132] Cf. the council of Agde (506) where c. 34 states that the catechumenate of Jews was to last 8 months. See discussion on Agde in the following section 'Later Gallic Councils'.

[133] See above in the section on Christian authors on Jews and Judaism.

[134] Number in Hefele/Leclercq (1907) II. 1: n. 89 (*Hispana* document).

The canon consists of two sections. One deals with auguries and incantations and the punishment for those adhering to these practices. The other part concerns those who are attracted to Jewish 'superstitions and feasts'. Jewish 'superstitions and feasts' would usually be taken to mean the Jewish faith and its rituals.[135]

The letter of Gregory I (c. 591 CE) to the bishops of Arles and Marseille refers to Jewish converts to Christianity. He writes that baptism should only take place after preaching and the use of Scripture lest they return to their 'former superstition'.[136]

The Jewish religion is also referred to as a 'superstition' in the fourth council of Orléans (541 CE). Canon 31 states that 'should a Jew allow a newly converted to convert to Judaism or lead him to the *Jewish superstition* once he has become a Christian (etc.)'.

In this canon the reference is to Jewish religious practices and feasts. The reference to Jewish feasts is slightly complicated as it is not exactly clear which feasts could be referred to. The issue of celebrating Jewish feasts was also seen at Laodicea (c. 37, 38), yet there it clearly referred to the Passover season. Here, we do not know.

It is interesting to note that even at this period and in this region as well the Christian faithful were apparently (still?) attracted to Jewish religious practices.

The canons of the *Statuta Ecclesiae Antiqua* offer some insight into Christian-Jewish relations in early (southern) Gaul. The Christian community was concerned with the conversion of non-believers, and focused as well on converting Jews. As for admonitions towards the Christian faithful—c. 83 shows that Christians (still) celebrated with Jews, also in this western Mediterranean region.

Further insight is given in other council texts from Gaul. These we will look at next.

3   *Later Gallic Councils (c. 465–541)*

In the period following the *Statuta Ecclesiae Antiqua*, until the late sixth century, seven councils deal with relations between Christians and Jews. Most canons of the councils discussing Jews and judaizing

---

[135] Harmening (1979) pp. 39–40.
[136] *Ep.* 1, 45 (CCSL vol. CXL).

behavior concern the issue of joint meals and marriages between
Christians and Jews, yet several new topics are addressed as well.

3.1   *Vannes*[137]

The council of Vannes was held around 465. It was initiated by the
bishop of Vannes, Paternus. Of the sixteen canons issued, one discusses relations with Jews.

CANON 12

> *Omnes deinceps clerici Iudaeorum convivia euitent nec eos ad conui-
> uium quisquam excipiat; quia cum apud Christianos cibis communibus
> non utantur, indignum est atque sacrilegum eorum cibos a Christianis
> sumi; cum ea, quae Apostolo permittente nos sumimus, ab illis iudicentur
> immunda ac sic inferiores incipiant esse clerici quam Iudaei, si nos quae
> ab illis apponuntur utamur, illi a nobis oblata contemnant.*

> All clergy must avoid eating with Jews, nor should anyone entertain them
> to a meal. For they do not consume food in common with Christians, so
> it should be shameful and sacrilegious for Christians to eat their food;
> for what is allowed by the Apostle and what we consume they consider
> impure, and thus clergy would be more unworthy than the Jews when
> we consume what they serve, while they despise what we offer.

Joint meals between Christians and Jews were already discussed at the
council of Elvira (c. 50). The difference with this canon is that instead
of the '*cibum sumpserit*' (food that is partaken) at Elvira, in this case
'*conuiuia*' (meals, banquets in classical sense) are mentioned.

Also added is the argument that Christians are able to eat other foods
than Jews do, hence the incompatibility of joint meals. Clergy would
become unworthy when partaking of meals with Jews. The warning is
given that Christians may eat all that 'the Apostle has allowed'—probably referring to the discussion on impure foods by Paul in 1 Corinthians 10: 23 ff.

Jews of course may not eat with gentiles because of purity issues, but
Christians are less restricted.[138] The argument here is that eating with
Jews makes one inferior.

Also interesting is that here only the clergy are mentioned. What
would be the situation for lay people?

---

[137] Text: CCSL CXLVIII, p. 150 ff; text and some discussion: Linder (1997) pp.
465–466; Limmer (2004) p. 133 ff; Blumenkranz (1977): on the specific canon.

[138] Except of course for the references in early texts such as the *Didache*.

3.2   Agde[139]

The council of Agde was held in 506. It was called together under the
authorization of Alaric II, king of the Visigoths. Caesarius of Arles
presided at the council. Two canons were issued discussing relations
with Jews, of the 47 canons issued.

CANON 34

> *Iudaei quorum perfidia frequenter ad uomitum redit, si ad legem catholi-*
> *cam uenire uoluerint, octo mensibus inter catechumenos ecclesiae limen*
> *introeant, et si pura fide uenire noscuntur tunc demum baptismatis gra-*
> *tiam mereantur. Quod si casu aliquo periculum infirmitatis intra prae-*
> *scriptum tempus incurrerint, et desperati fuerint, baptizantur.*

> If Jews, who in their perfidy frequently return to their vomit, should
> want to join the Catholic law, they shall enter the church up to the
> threshold among the catechumens for eight months, and if they should
> be recognized to be joining out of pure faith, only then shall they deserve
> the grace of baptism. But if they should incur an accidental health risk
> during the prescribed period and should be in a desperate condition,
> they shall be baptized.

Added to what we saw in the *Statuta Ecclesiae Antiqua* (c. 16), Agde
gives a specific length of preparation for catechumens from Judaism.
Also here at Agde it is specifically mentioned that non-baptized people
would not be allowed into the church building prior to their acceptance into the fold and thus remained 'on the threshold' ('*ecclesiae
limen*') during the period of preparation. This period as mentioned
here is not the duration of Lent, as was usual, but eight months. This
may be because of the proximity of the Jewish faith to Christianity and
the possibility of relapse to their former faith. This possible relapse we
encountered in the writings of Gregory of Tours (on Priscus and Chilperic) and in the letter of Gregory I (*Reg.* 1: 45). In the latter the same
word for former faith: '*uomitum*' is used. The unpleasant simile referring to a return to one's former mistakes (as a dog would to its vomit)
is taken from Proverbs 26: 11 and the second letter of Peter 2: 22.

The issue here at hand, similar to that of the *Statuta Ecclesiae Antiqua*, c. 16, is typical for church law as it concerns the catechumenate.
This is not a topic discussed in civil legislation.

---

[139] CCSL CXLVIII, pp. 189–228; some discussion: Linder (1997) pp. 466–467; Limmer (2004) p. 152 ff.

CANON 40

Omnes deinceps clerici sive laici Iudaeorum convivia euitent nec eos ad conuiuium quisquam excipiat; quia cum apud Christianos cibis communibus non utantur, indignum est atque sacrilegum eorum cibos a Christianis sumi; cum ea, quae Apostolo permittente nos sumimus, ab illis iudicentur immunda ac sic inferiores incipiant esse Catholici quam Iudaei, si nos quae ab illis apponuntur utamur, illi vero a nobis oblata contemnant.

All clergy and lay people must avoid eating with Jews, nor should anyone entertain them to a meal. For they do not consume food in common with Christians, so it should be shameful and sacrilegious for Christians to eat their food; for what we consume is allowed by the Apostle, they consider impure, and thus Catholics would be unworthy when we consume what they serve, while they despise what we offer.

The issue of joint meals is discussed above at Vannes, yet here again it is repeated. Both at Vannes and at Agde the warning is given that Christians may eat all that 'the Apostle has allowed', as opposed to Jews. It is also interesting to note that at Vannes the canon is directed towards the clergy, at Agde towards the clergy and lay people (just as at Elvira and Epaon) and at Orléans III (c. 14, see below) against 'all Christians'.

3.3   Epaon[140]

The council of Epaon was convened by Sigismund, king of the Burgundians, in 517. Amongst the 24 bishops attending the council was Avitus of Vienne. Of the 40 canons issued, one is dedicated to Christian-Jewish relations.

CANON 15

Si superioris loci clericus heretici cuiuscumque clerici conuiuio interfuerit, anni spatio pacem ecclesaie non habebit. Qoud iuniores clerici si praesumserint, vapolabunt. A iudaeorum uero conuiuiis etiam laicus constitutio nostra prohibuit, nec cum ullo clerico nostro panem comedat, quisquis Iudaeorum conuiuio fuerit inquinatus.

If a cleric of a superior position should take part in a meal with any heretical clergy, he shall not have the peace of the Church for the duration of one year. And if junior clergy should dare to do it, they shall be flogged. As for meals with Jews, our law prohibited even laymen to take

---

[140] CCSL CXLVIIIA, pp. 20–37; SC 353 pp. 93–125; Linder (1997) p. 468; Limmer (2004) pp. 174–183.

part in them, and anyone defiled by a meal with Jews should not eat bread with any of our clergy.

The canon declares that clergy of a 'superior position' should not eat with heretical clergy. What happens to lay people? As far as meals with Jews are concerned, nobody is apparently allowed to partake of meals with them; otherwise they may not eat with clergy. Would they be allowed to eat with others? And still remain in communion with the church?

3.4   Orléans II[141]

The second council of Orléans was held in the year 533, and was convened by the three sons of Clovis. Of the 26 canons one is dedicated to Jews.

CANON 19

> *Placuit, ut nullus Christianus Iudaeam neque Iudaeus Christianam in matrimonio ducat uxorem, quia inter huiusmodi personas illicitas nuptias esse censuimus. Qui si commoniti a consortio hoc se separare distullerint, a communiones sunt gratia sine dubio submovendi.*

> It has been resolved that no Christian should take a Jewess in matrimony to be his wife, nor a Jew a Christian woman, for we have decreed that marriages between such people are illegal. Those who postpone severance from this association though warned shall be removed from the communion's grace.

The topic of mixed marriages was also addressed at the council of Elvira (c. 16), yet it is the first reference in Gaul. In this canon a warning is given first, but apparently there were those who chose to ignore this. The result is exclusion from communion.

The issue of mixed marriages in Roman imperial law we already discussed in canon 16 of the council of Elvira, referring to CTh 3.7.2, 9.7.5. and CJ 1.9.6. It is repeated in the Breviary of Alaraic dating to 506 (3.7.2 and 9.4.4), where the wording is the same as in the Theodosian Code.[142]

---

[141]   CCSL CXLVIIIA, pp. 98–103; SC 353 pp. 194–207; text and some discussion: Linder (1997) pp. 468–9; Limmer (2004) pp. 208–212.

[142]   See also: Sivan, H.S. 'Why not marry a Jew? Jewish-Christian Marital Frontiers in Late Antiquity' in: Mathison (2001) pp. 208–219.

3.5   Clermont[143]

The council of Clermont was held under the presidency of Honoratus, bishop of Bourges, on November 8th 535. It was attended by fifteen bishops from different parts of the region, and issued sixteen canons, two of which discuss Jews. The council rulings repeated and expanded dealings with the clergy already stated earlier at Orléans II (533).s

CANON 6

> *Si quis Iudaecae pravitati iugali societate coniungentur et seu Christiano Iudaea siue Iudaeo Christiana mulier consortio carnali misceatur, quique horum tantum nefas admisisse dinoscetur a Christeanorum coetu atque conuiuio et a communione ecclesiae cuius sociatur hostibus segregetur.*

> If anyone should join the Jewish depravity in a conjugal union and if a Jewess should have intercourse with a Christian or a Christian woman with a Jew, anyone known to have admitted to such a great wickedness should be segregated from Christian society and meals as well as from the communion of the Church, whose enemies he had joined.

The topic of mixed marriages was also addressed at the second council of Orleáns (see above). A slight variation is found here, in the text of the council of Clermont. In this canon the point seems to go beyond conjugal union and also applies to Christian men and women having sexual relations with Jewish women and men. The punishment at Clermont also offers some new thoughts: the culprit is not only excluded from receiving communion but is also excluded from Christian company ('*coetu*') and meals ('*conuiuio*'). At Clermont the point is made as well that the Christian man or woman admits his/her fault—admits to having joined in a (prohibited) inter-religious union.

CANON 9

> *Ne iudaei christianis populis iudices praeponantur.*

> Jews should not be appointed as judges over Christian people.

A '*iudex*' was a person with judicial authority. The plural '*iudices*' usually refers to members of a jury.[144] The '*iudex*' can be anyone acting in a judicial capacity, and this may include any higher official. Almost

---

[143] CCSL CXLVIIIA, pp. 104–112; SC 353) pp. 208–225; Linder (1997) pp. 469–470; Limmer (2004) pp. 212–216.

[144] Blaise (1954) 'iudex'.

all high officials had judicial and administrative functions and were judges in cases that came within their jurisdiction. Hence, the word refers to anyone in this function, not necessarily a professional judge but someone on 'jury duty', so to speak.[145]

Jews were citizens of the Roman Empire and could thus hold a position in the *ius honorum*: the right to hold public office. Public office could include being a member of the judiciary. The organization of law courts in (late) antiquity was tied to the administration of the different regions. This meant that most higher-placed officials held both judicial and administrative functions. In the fourth century a *defensor civitatis* was introduced in order to ease the workload of the provincial courts. The *defensor* acted as judge in minor civil and criminal cases.[146] That Jews could also serve as *defensor* can be seen in the Letter of Severus of Minorca where he speaks of a Theodorus, head of the local synagogue, who served in this capacity.[147] By 438 imperial law stated that 'no Jew [...] shall enter upon any honors or dignities; to none of them shall the administration of a civil duty be available, nor shall they perform even the duties of a defender'.[148]

Mikat rightly comments that until this time any ruling on Jews in public office was restricted to secular law.[149] In discussing this canon, Geisel claims that this is the beginning of the exclusion of Jews from the public sphere.[150] The church became more and more involved in secular law, which resulted in an increasingly difficult position for Jews—e.g. as civil lawyers, just as Geisel states.

In civil law one sees a similar development taking place at the same time. In March 418, under Theodosius II entrance to the state service was closed to those 'living in the Jewish superstition' (Cod. Theod. 16.8.24). Linder defines this 'state service' as referring to the various branches of public service offices in the military and the civil service.[151] At this point, however, Jews were still allowed to 'practice as advocates (lawyers)'. This changed by 425 under Valentinian III. In the Sirmondian Constitutions (no. 6) it literally states that 'we also deny to the

---

[145] Bowersock (1999) 'law courts'; 'iudex' in: *LMitt* Bd. V, pp. 793–4.
[146] This all refers to secular cases; there were also ecclesiastical law courts—the *episcopalia audientia*. Cf: Bowersock (1999) p. 540.
[147] Severus of Minorca *Ep.* 3 (Bradbury (1996)).
[148] *Nov. Th.* 3.2. Cf. also *CJ* 1.9.18 (439), Linder (1987) p. 332.
[149] Mikat (1995) pp. 32–36.
[150] Geisel (1998) pp. 114–133.
[151] Linder (1987) pp. 280–283.

Jews, and to the pagans, the right to practice law and serve in the state service; we do not wish people of the Christian law to serve them, lest they substitute, because of this mastery, the venerable religion by a sect.' That is to say, Jews could 'misuse' their power over Christians. This was part of the general policy of expelling Jews (and pagans and heretics) from positions of authority.[152] Still later, Jews and heretics were no longer allowed to act as witnesses in trials involving orthodox Christians (Theodosius II, Nov. 3; 438 and CJ 1.5.21, July 531).

In 409, Honorius had already declared the Jewish religion ("perversity") as 'alien to the Roman Empire' and stated that 'anything that differs from the faith of the Christians is contrary to the Christian law (= religion)' (CTh 16.8.19). He thus established that Jews, heretics and pagans were considered deviant groups. Their rights were consequently reduced and eventually their position in society deteriorated.[153]

3.6   Orléans III[154]

The third council of Orleáns was held on May 7th in the year 538. It was attended by bishops of the Merovingian kingdom of Childebert, and included bishop Gallus of Clermont, who we have already encountered in the discussion of the council of Clermont. The metropolitan bishop of Lyons presided, bearing the colorful name of Loup. The council issued 36 canons, several dealing with Jews.

CANON 14

> De mancipiis Christianis, quae in Iudaeorum seruitio ditenentur, si eis, quod Christiana religio uetat, a dominis inponitur aut si eos, quos de ecclesia excusatos tollent, pro culpa quae remissa est, adfligere aut caedere fortasse praesumpserint et ad ecclesiam iterato confugerint, nullatenus a sacerdote reddantur, nisi praecium offeratur hac detur, quod mancipia ipsa valere pronunciaverit iusta taxacio. Christeanis quoque omnibus interdicimus, ne Iudaeorum coniugiis misceantur. Quod si fecerint, usque ad sequestrationem, quisque ille est, cummunionem pellatur. Idem Christeanis conuiuia interdicimus Iudaeorum; in quibus si forte probantur, annuali excummunicatione pro huiuismodi contumacia subiacebunt.

---

[152] Linder (1987) pp. 305–308.
[153] Linder (1987) p. 65 f.
[154] CCSL CXLVIIIA, pp. 113–130; SC 353, pp. 227–263; Linder (1997) pp. 470–471; Limmer (2004) pp. 216–224.

Concerning Christian slaves who are kept in the service of Jews, should something which the Christian religion forbids be imposed upon them by their masters, or if they [the masters] dare punish or beat them [the slaves], whom they had taken from the church after they had been pardoned, because of the sin which had been pardoned, and if they again seek refuge in a church, the priest should never return them [to their masters], however a price should be offered and given which a correct estimate would establish the slaves are worth. We also prohibit all Christians from intermingling in marriage with Jews. If they should do it, whoever he will be, he shall be driven out of communion until he effects separation. We also forbid Christians to take part in meals with Jews; if anyone should be found guilty of this, they shall undergo excommunication for a year as punishment for such insolence.

As for the reference to joint meals and mixed marriages, see above in the discussion on the council of Agde.

This canon refers as well to Christian slaves owned by Jews. These slaves had been pardoned by the church for a sin they had committed. Nobody should be allowed to punish them again. That is why the slaves sought refuge in the church. The canon states that no priest should therefore return them to their owners but rather pay the owners compensation. These Christian slaves made use of the (Christian) right of sanctuary which their Jewish owners ignored. In canon 14 the wording is: '*quos de ecclesia excusatos tollent*'. Blaise translates '*excusatos (tollent)*' as 'pardoned'—referring to slaves who had sought refuge in a church.[155] They would then be allowed to return to their master without further punishment. The Jewish owners of the Christian slaves would not be very pleased with this arrangement, hence the financial compensation.[156]

CANON 31

Quia persuasum est populis die dominico agi cum caballis aut bobus uehiculis itinera non debere neque ullam rem ad uictum praeparari uel ad nitorem domus uel hominis pertinentem ullatenus execeri, quae res ad

---

[155] Blaise (1954) 'excusatus'.

[156] The Theodosian Code explains what to do when slaves are freed. Should a slave be freed, he will then need to recompense his redeemer by working for him for five years (*CTh* 5.7.2.). Later on these slaves, if they are Christians, would be turned over to the church (*CTh* 16.8.22—here specifically referring to Jewish owners of Christian slaves). There is no mention in this canon of what to do once the slaves are freed. Pakter (1988) pp. 88–91; and (1985) pp. 3–4.

iudaicam magis quam ad christianam obseruantiam pertinere probatur,
id stauimus, ut die domenico, quod ante fieri licuit, liceat. De opera tamen
rurali, id est arata uel uinea uel sectione, messione, excussione, exarto
uel saepe, censuimus abstinendum, quo facilius ad ecclesiam uenientes
orationis gratiae uacent. Quod si inuentus fuerit quis in operibus supra
scriptis, quae interdicta sunt, exercere, qualiter emundari debeat, non in
laici districtione, sed in sacerdotis castigatione consistat.

The people have been persuaded on a Sunday not to travel with horses,
cattle or vehicles, nor prepare any foods, nor perform any cleaning tasks
in the house or on persons, since this comes closer to Jewish observance
than Christian. We have therefore ruled that it is allowed on a Sunday to
do all that was allowed before. However, as far as working in the fields
is concerned, that is to say, ploughing, viticulture, scything, harvesting,
threshing, clearance and fencing in, we have decided that one should
abstain from these in order to facilitate going to church and attend to the
benefit of prayers. If one should be found performing any of the prohibited works, let the punishment be by a priest not by a lay person.

The point in hand is that the people apparently were used to approaching activities on a Sunday in a manner, according to the council,
resembling Jewish practice. Whether the people did so consciously or
not is unclear. They abstained from certain activities but out of which
conviction is unclear. What is clear is that the council fathers deem
this to be judaizing behavior.

Geisel assumes that the people were judaizing and connects this to
Sabbath observance by the Christian faithful—practice which we have
seen at Laodicea and which he also mentions.[157] This Sabbath observance, Geisel states, still happened even at a much later date—at the
council of Frioul. There it says that 'peasants' (*rustici*) still celebrated
Sabbath 'as the Jews do'.[158]

Bachrach goes even further by suggesting that here at Orléans it is
said that the Christian faithful celebrated the Jewish Sabbath.[159] One
wonders on what reading of this canon he bases this assumption.

Were the faithful of the council of Orléans involved in judaizing
practices? Whether consciously or not, it is interesting to note that the
list of agricultural activities which the council fathers would not allow
on a Sunday is similar to that found in the Mishnah, in the tractate on

---

[157] Geisel (1998) pp. 147–8.
[158] Council of Frioul (*Forum Iuliani*, Aquileia, 796) (PL 99, 301): which admonishes
the faithful to celebrate Sunday starting on Saturday evening, and not already on Saturday 'as the Jews, which is what peasants do'.
[159] Bachrach (1977) p. 51.

the Sabbath.[160] Scripture mentions only 'no ploughing or harvesting'.[161] The Mishnah adds a more specific list. The council fathers seemed to have followed this list—possibly in anticipation of what the faithful would or would not do?

In Justinian's Code one finds a discussion on the type of work that can be done on a Sunday and what cannot, where it says that landowners should be allowed to work in the fields on a Sunday as it may be the best moment to do so, while all others should revere this day.[162]

One wonders why the Christian faithful of this region believed this was the correct behavior for a Sunday. Despite a lack of serious archeological evidence for the presence of Jews in Gaul, literary material does show they were present, in close vicinity to other inhabitants of the region.[163] The Mishnah seems to provide a list of prohibitions very similar to that mentioned in this canon. It seems that there were Christians in the region who kept the Sunday as if it were a Jewish Sabbath. They may have been influenced by the Old Testament (Exodus 34). Yet, the list in the Mishnah is more in agreement with what is mentioned in this canon than what is listed in Exodus. What we see here in Gaul is a curious intermingling of Judaism and Christianity. It is also noteworthy that Caesarius of Arles used the Jewish observance of the Sabbath as a very positive example for his audience.[164]

Whether or not the behaviour of the Christian faithful in the Merovingian kingdom was Jewish inspired or not, the council fathers apparently thought it was so and considered it wiser to call a halt to it.

CANON 33

Quia Deo propitio sub catholicorum regum dominatione consistimus, iudaei a die cenae Domini usque in secunda sabbati in pasca, hoc est ipso quatriduo, procedere inter christianos neque catholicis populis se ullo loco uel quacumque occasione miscere praesumant.

As we live, by the grace of God, under catholic kings, Jews may not, from the day of the supper of the Lord until Easter Monday, that is those

---

[160] M: Shab 7:2—prohibited on the Sabbath are ploughing, reaping, binding, harvesting, grinding, building; in 12:2—pruning and gathering are added.

[161] Exod. 34: 21.

[162] *CJ* III.12.2, from 321 CE. Cf. discussion on Sabbath behavior on a Sunday: Rordorf (1962) pp. 165–171; and specifically on this canon: Huber (1958) pp. 107–109.

[163] Gregory of Tours *Hist. Franc.* VIII, 1 (Krusch/Levison (1951)).

[164] *Sermo* 13, 3 (see above in the discussion on Caesarius, section 1.3.3).

four days, be present among Christians, nor mingle for whatever reason among the catholic population.

This ruling is directed towards the Jews rather than against the Christian faithful. The Jewish population is not allowed to be amongst Christians from Holy Thursday to Easter Monday.[165] The issue of Jews during the Triduum is only mentioned in one other council text.[166]

Suntrup wonders why the Jews were not allowed out during the Triduum: for their protection, or as punishment?[167] After all, Good Friday and the commemoration of the death of Jesus are a likely cause for anti-Jewish feelings.[168] This thought is also voiced by Mikat.[169] The anti-Jewish feelings could go both ways—perhaps the ruling was intended to protect the Jews. We have seen the results at Clermont in 576.[170] The aspect of protection is also the reason for Lotter to assume that the canon should be interpreted in favour of the Jews. He then cites several examples of synagogue burnings, expulsions and 'persecutions' in Gaul in the sixth and seventh centuries.[171]

Seeing that the opening statement of the ruling voices a sense of relief at having a Catholic ruler, one may wonder whether the statement should rather be interpreted as *against* the Jews rather than for their protection. At least, that is what Geisel would have us believe.[172] We may assume the ruling was intended to protect the Jews. After all, the Easter Triduum, and especially Good Friday, would be cause enough for anti-Jewish rioting.

---

[165] Blaise (1954) 'sabbatum', spec. 'secunda sabbati' which is a 'feria secunda', i.e. the Monday (of Easter).

[166] Mâcon (583) c. 14.

[167] Suntrup (2001) p. 172.

[168] Cf. e.g., Yuval (2006) ch. 2.

[169] Mikat (1995) pp. 37–42.

[170] Gregory of Tours *Hist. Franc.* V, 11 (Krusch/Levison (1951)).

[171] Lotter (1997) pp. 849–880, esp. pp. 874–5.

[172] Geisel (1998) pp. 142–151. Suntrup sees this as the beginning of the policy that the 'faith of the king is the faith of the people', i.e. anyone believing differently is thus excluded: Suntrup (2001) pp. 172–3. It is interesting to note that in the Mishnah (but also Talmud and Tosephta) at the beginning of the tractate Abodah Zarah it says that Jews are forbidden to do business with gentiles for three days before the gentiles' festivals, and in M: AZ 1: 2 also for three days after. Although the Mishnah refers to purity issues, it is interesting to note that the text refers to interaction between Jews and non-Jews at the time of non-Jewish festivals.

3.7   Orleáns IV[173]

The fourth council held in Orléans took place on May 14th 541. A representative from Arles attended representing the well-known bishop Caesarius as he was too old by that time to hazard the voyage. The representatives hailed from many parts of France, even including Normandy, and from the north, east and south. Again, Gallus came from Clermont. This council issued 38 canons, again containing several on Jews.

CANON 30

> *Licet prioribus canonibus iam fuerit definitum, ut, de mancipiis christianis quae apud iudaeos sunt, si ad ecclesiam confugerint et redemi se postulauerint, etiam ad quoscumque christianos refugerint et seruire iudaeis noluerint, taxato et oblato a fidelibus iusto pretio ab eorum dominio liberentur, ideo statuimus, ut tam iusta constitutio ab omnibus catholicis conseruetur.*

> Although it has already been established in previous canons in regard to Christian slaves held by Jews, that if they should flee to a church and demand to be redeemed or even flee to any Christians and refuse to serve Jews, their just price should be estimated and paid by the faithful and they should be liberated from their ownership; we decree, therefore, that such a just law should be observed by all Catholics.

In this canon, contrary to canon 14 at Orléans III, it is not specified why the Christian slaves should flee to a church. We may assume that the comment "and demand to be redeemed" refers to the same issue as at the third council of Orleáns—that they had committed a crime and had been pardoned. What is added in this canon, contrary to canon 14 at Orléans III, is that slaves may also "flee to any Christians", not just the church. The text goes further than Orléans III, c. 14, by referring to all Christian slaves owned by Jews.

CANON 31

> *Id etiam decernimus obseruandum, ut, si qui cumque iudaeus proselitum, qui aduena dicitur, iudaeum facere praesumpserit aut christianum factum ad iudaicum superstitionem adducere uel si iudaeo christianam ancillam*

[173] CCSL CXLVIIIA, pp. 131–146; SC 353, pp. 264–295; Linder (1997) pp. 471–473; Limmer (2004) pp. 225–233.

suam crediderit sociandam uel si de parentibus christianis natum iudaeum sub promissione fecerit libertatis, mancipiorum amissione multetur.

Ille uero, qui de christianis natus iudaeus factus est, si sub condicione fuerit manumissus, ut in ritu iudaico permanens habeat libertatem, talis condicio non ualebit, quia iniustum est, ut ei libertas maneat, qui de christianis parentibus ueniens iudaicis uult cultibus inhaerere.

We also state that if a Jew dares convert to Judaism a proselyte, which is called a newly arrived one, or leads him to the Jewish superstition once he has become a Christian; or if he believes that his Christian slave woman should be joined to a Jew as his wife; or if a Jew converts to Judaism a slave born of Christian parents while promising him freedom, that he be punished by losing all his slaves. As for a man who, born of Christian parents, becomes Jewish, under the condition that he be freed, if he continues following the Jewish rite, this is not valid, for it is not allowed for someone born of Christian parents to be connected to the Jewish cult.

In this canon, the issue approaches the concern underlying all further canons on Jews owning slaves—namely the possibility of conversion.[174] This is something which underlies all concerns the church had on Christian slaves.

Why would Jews not be allowed to own Christian slaves? The answer lies in our second canon: the possibility of conversion to Judaism. This is what most authors discussing this canon see as the reason behind this legislation.[175] The concern for Christians involved in judaizing practices as seen in many council texts is related to the issue in hand here: appropriating Jewish practices—also an issue when it concerns Christian slaves in a Jewish household.[176]

Secular law addresses the problem of Jews owning non-Jewish slaves from an early period onwards. In the third century, Jews are forbidden to circumcise slaves (Paulus' *Sententiae* 5.22.3–4); this is repeated in the fourth century.[177] The laws are in general against Jews keeping non-Jewish slaves for fear of circumcision of the slaves (i.e. conver-

---

[174] On Jews and slaves: Mâcon (583) c. 16, 17; Reims (624) c. 11; Clichy (626) c. 13.

[175] Most recently: Pakter (1988) pp. 88–91; Geisel (1998) pp. 133–140; Mikat (1995) ch. V.

[176] See also *CTh* 3.1.5: in order to avoid that the Christian slave be 'contaminated with Jewish religious rites'.

[177] *Constitutio Sirmondiana* (335) 4; *CTh* 16.9.1 (336), 16.9.2 (339), 3.1.5 (384), 16.9.3 (415), 16.9.4 (417); *CJ* 1.10.1 (529), 1.10.2 (527–534). The last is against all non-orthodox Christians, including Jews, holding Christian slaves; this is further developed in 534, *CJ* 1.3.54.

sion). Only *CTh* 16.9.3 (from 415) allows Jews to keep Christian slaves as long as they may remain Christian.

The general prohibition on Jews keeping Christian slaves for fear of possible conversion is also found in Alaric's *Breviarium* (3.1.5 and 16.4, from 506).

According to Linder, Jews were required to convert their non-Jewish slaves because of halachic law.[178] Various jobs in and around a Jewish household can only be performed by Jews. Gradually the idea of Jews serving as masters over Christians (slaves) was considered intolerable (CTh 16.9.5: 'mastery of impious buyers [of Christian slaves]'). The strongest motivation was however the fear of conversion to Judaism by the non-Jewish slaves.

The topic of the possible conversion of Christian slaves owned by Jews is the clearest example of the close cooperation between state and church legislation. This was of course because of the religious nature of the issue (: possible conversion) but also because the Church was initially entrusted with the care for the Christian slaves after their release. The Church also served as a sanctuary when Christian slaves fled from their non-Christian masters. Initially, the Christian slave was only to be freed, later the owner was paid in compensation. Occasionally, the slave after release was placed in the ownership of the Church but by the sixth century, slaves were to be emancipated and no longer transferred to other ownership. In secular legislation, the punishment for converting non-Jewish slaves to Judaism was the death penalty.

4   Conclusion

At the end of the discussion of the canons of various Gallic councils, we may return to what was said earlier in the section on church father texts. What we can conclude now is that even if the focus may differ slightly, the canons of the Gallic councils and the relevant church fathers corroborate each other.

Several church father writings refer to possible or genuine conversions—specifically of Jews to Christianity.[179] Sidonius' letters describe

---

[178] Linder (1987) pp. 82–85.
[179] Sidonius in his Letters; Gregory of Tours on Priscus (HF VI.5) and the Jews at Clermont (HF V.11, and Venantius); and Caesarius of Arles in his homily (*Sermo* 183).

two examples of Jews he hopes will convert, and one other who has converted. Gregory of Tours' description of the conversion attempts of the Jew Priscus follows this thought. Venantius Fortunatus in his 'Life' of Germanus of Paris briefly mentions a Jew who had converted, to be followed by many others. These examples refer to possible voluntary conversions of individual Jews.

A less positive conversion story—that is to say a forced conversion—can be found in Gregory of Tours and Venantius Fortunatus who describe the incident at Clermont in 576.

These literary historical sources show that there were conversions and attempts towards the conversion of Jews. These sources agree with what we see in the *Statuta Ecclesiae Antiqua*, c. 16, and at Agde, c. 34. The literary sources and the council texts consolidate and complement each other.

Christians were also concerned about the possibility of Christian slaves converting to Judaism. The issue of Christian slaves and their possible conversion to Judaism is addressed by Caesarius.[180] After the siege of Arles in 507, many inhabitants of the town were captured. Rather than have them remain in the hands of Jews, and others, and thus possibly falling prey to conversion tactics, Caesarius pays a ransom to have them released.

The canons show that Caesarius' comments are not unique but part of a larger problem.

The problem of intermingling of faiths is also the underlying concern in the canons on joint meals and intermarriage. These issues are a recurring concern for the council fathers of all regions and in all times. It is therefore surprising not to find any references to these meals and marriages in the writings of the church fathers.[181]

Another interesting point is the Sabbath observance. In the third council of Orléans, canon 31 is issued against those people who keep the Sunday as if it were a Jewish Sabbath. It seems as if there is an interesting intermingling of Jewish practice and Christian faith—something the council fathers wish to avoid. However, Caesarius actually praises the Jewish Sabbath while the canon is more ambiguous.[182]

---

[180] Caesarius *Vita* I, 32.
[181] Except in '*de esca uel potu iudeorum prohibendis*', said to be by Caesarius.
[182] *Sermo* 13, 3.

What we do not find in the council texts but in several church father writings are other examples of contact between Christians and Jews. Christians sought out their Jewish neighbors for various needs; this we see in the writings of Gregory and Caesarius. Consulting non-(orthodox) Christians in times of need is mentioned by Gregory in the case of Leonastus of Bourges who sought medical advice from a Jew.[183] However, in various homilies, Caesarius warns against those who seek solace in consulting seers or magicians, or those who hang phylacteries, amulets and magic letters upon themselves for protection.[184]

Texts of several church fathers from fifth and sixth century Gaul give specific examples closely related to the issues mentioned in council texts. Again, as at Antioch with John Chrysostom, we see that the Jews mentioned are not theological examples, a 'Judaism in the mind', but specific people and incidents. The canons also mention issues not found in church father texts (e.g. Jewish judges), yet both church father texts and council rulings indicate that contacts between the two groups—Christians and Jews—in fifth and sixth century Gaul remained closer than the ecclesiastical authorities liked.

We have seen that several issues discussed in council texts also appear in secular legislation: e.g. interfaith marriages and relations, Jews as judges and keeping non-Jewish/Christian slaves. Yet, some issues are apparently too much within the realm of Church policy and are therefore not found in secular legislation: i.e., on meals, the catechumenate, Christians celebrating Jewish feasts, observing the Sunday, and Jews on the streets during the Triduum.

The relative paucity of archeological remains is obviously more than made up for in the literary source material.

---

[183] *Hist.Franc.* V.6.
[184] *Sermones* 50, 51, 52, 54, (SC 243); 184 (CCSL CIV).

SOME FINAL THOUGHTS

This seems a possible point at which to end the discussion on council texts on Christian judaizing and Christian relations with Judaism. Councils do still address the issue of Christian-Jewish relations yet the issues seem to repeat themselves. Only occasionally a new topic is addressed.

Comparing imperial, secular, law on Jews and Judaism to canon law, one sees a gradual shifting in focus. Imperial legislation contained laws which protected, but eventually also limited, the functioning of Jews in the public sphere. Until the early fifth century, the terms *'religio'* and *'superstitio'* could both be applied to Judaism. The former, *'religio'*, an objective definition of a religion, had no negative connotations. The latter, *'superstitio'*, in essence applied to all religions different from and considered hostile to Roman religion. Judaism was a *'religio licita'*, yet depending on the spirit of the law, the terminology *'superstitio'* could also be used to describe it. This applied to practices performed in name of a religion which were considered unlawful under Roman law. After the early fifth century, *'religio'*, however, was reserved for the Christian religion while Judaism would be referred to as a *'superstitio'*, but in this case the definition was based on Christian philosophy rather than secular law.[1]

Where initially as a *'religio licita'* Judaism was often protected under secular law, gradually, as it would be increasingly defined in negative terminology, non-orthodox Christian groups, including Jews saw legislation turn against them. This we also see in canon law when 'Jews, pagans and heretics' are addressed.[2]

As seen above, Roman legal texts also focused on specific religious groups such as the Jews. Laws on Jews date from the middle of the second century to mid sixth century. The texts from the second to third centuries are remains of pagan legislature.

As far as Roman imperial law was concerned, two types of laws concerning the Jews existed: laws dealing with all non-Romans (the *Ius gentium*), including Jews. Secondly, laws dealing specifically with Jews

---

[1] Linder (1987) pp. 55–58.
[2] Linder (1987) pp. 62–63.

when in contact with their non-Jewish surroundings. These included rights and privileges but also duties and restrictions. Specific internal question were not dealt with by Roman law as these were included in their own *halachah*, or Jewish law. The Roman authorities considered these Jewish religious issues as non-Roman affairs.

That Roman law did not interfere with internal issues of specific religions is seen in our discussion on Jewish rites and feasts, with these the Roman authorities were not concerned. We therefore also see later that there are no Roman laws on Jews and Christians celebrating feasts together.

Specific topics discussed in Roman legal texts concerning Jews can be divided into three categories: relations between Jews and the government; relations between Jews and non-Jews; and relations between Jews and other Jews. It is the second group with which we are mostly concerned.

The issues discussed in each category are:

– for Jews and the government: recognition of the Jewish religion, and the political situation of Jews—in municipal and imperial administration, and Jews before the law. The latter was initially a fair situation, but much changed after the early fifth century when Jews were excluded from the legal profession and often judged differently from Christians. By the sixth century, Jews were judged similarly to pagans and heretics.
– in the relations between Jews and non-Jews, the topics refer to possible conversions—either from or to Judaism, keeping non-Jewish slaves and interreligious marriages, but also interreligious conflict.
– as far as relations among Jews were concerned, laws were few and mostly concerned with Jewish religious practices.

When studied by century, the topics discussed in Roman legal texts on Jews increase gradually. In the second to third centuries, topics were concerned with Jewish religious rites (including circumcision) and the civil status of Jews in cities. In the fourth century, the topics also turn to allowing Jews in the curia, protecting converts from Judaism, the protection of Jewish religious offices, protecting non-Jewish slaves, against Christians participating in pagan, Jewish and Manichean rites and by 388 also against interreligious marriage, and against Jewish marriage rites, yet also protecting synagogues against Christian attacks. The topics repeat themselves in the fifth century and after, but then also include laws against heretics, 'god-fearers' and pagans, the 'prohibition to mock Christians on Purim', the protection of the Christian cult against Donatists, heretics, Jews and pagans, and again the protection of synagogues but also slaves and converts, on curial and legal duties of Jews. These laws were in effect for the whole population of the (Eastern and/or Western) Empire. They were issued on topics which extend far beyond the topics raised in church father texts.

The significance of council texts as compared to the other sources studied (archeological, patristic, and Roman imperial legal sources) is that these concern the Christian faithful specifically, in their contacts with Jews. Roman imperial legislation is, as far as this study is concerned, directed against Jews, and occasionally also when in contact with Christians. As Judaism was still a *religio licita*, Roman imperial law would occasionally still protect the Jews, canon law will not as it is directed towards the Christian faithful in an attempt to keep them away from contacts with Jews. Examples of this we have seen in the previous chapters.

Then there is another difference. Roman imperial laws are directed towards the empire as a whole (East and/or West). It is a question how these were received in the various regions. Council texts are much more local, regional, and show us the practicalities of daily life in areas as diverse as Spain and Asia Minor.

Specific topics found in canon law will also not be found in secular law, such as feasts celebrated by Christians and Jews together and Christian liturgical issues.

FURTHER DEVELOPMENTS

After the Gallic councils discussed in the last chapter, chronologically the next council is that of Macon (583). The issues are similar to what we have seen before: no Jews to be placed as judges over Christians (c. 13), Jews not to be allowed on the streets between Holy Thursday and Easter Sunday (the Triduum, c. 14), against meals partaken by Jews and Christians together (c. 15) and against Christians held as slaves by Jews (c. 16 and 17). New is the ruling against Jews entering women's convents for private conversation (c. 2).

At the council of Narbonne (589) we see for the first time a ruling against Jews singing psalms as they carry the deceased to the grave (c. 9). Not new is the issue of the Sunday rest which at Narbonne is discussed in canon 4. At this council the issue of Christian involved in Jewish 'magical practices' also appears (c. 14).

The Sunday rest is also discussed in relation to Christians keeping the Sabbath. This is prohibited, as after all Christians should keep the day of the Lord as holy: Benevento (900) c. 9—also on Jewish magic, judges, communal meals, slaves; Christians keeping the Sabbath: Oviedo (1050) c. 6; on Sunday: rest Szaboles (Hungary 1092) c. 26.

The topic of Jews in public office is discussed at the councils of Paris (614) c. 17; Toledo IV (633) c. 65; Pavia (Italy, 856) c. 54; Siponto (900); Rome (1078) c. 22.

While Christian slaves held by Jews we see again at (626) c. 13; Reims (627) c. 11; Châlon (647) c. 9; Toledo IV (633) c. 66; Toledo X (656) c. 7; Meaux-Paris (845)—also on meals, judges, Triduum, marriage, and feasts and gifts (quoting Laodicea and Gallic councils); Rouen (1074) c. 14.

The issue of intermarriage is discussed again at: Toledo III (589) c. 14; Toledo IV (633) c. 63; Rome (743) c. 10—also on slaves; Szaboles (Hungary, 1092) c. 10.

Communal meals of Christians and Jews proves to be a recurrent theme and is again seen in the rulings of the councils of Metz (893) c. 7 and Oviedo (1078) c. 6.

Christians receiving gifts from Jews is an issue at the fourth council of Toledo (633) c. 58.

The Toledo councils are mostly directed towards the conversion of Jews: Toledo IV (633) c. 57, 59, 60, 61, 62, 64; Toledo VI (638) c. 3 and Declaration; Toledo VIII (653) c. 10, 12; Toledo IX (655) c. 17; Toledo XII (681) c. 9—also on other issues; Toledo XVI (693); Toledo XVII (694)—the Toledo councils limited the rights of Jews, in favor of forced conversions, limited Jews practicing their faith. The topic of converting Jews is also discussed at Erfurt (932).

The reason for ending the current discussion in this book, at this point in time is the fact that from here the canons, on the whole, tend to be directed more towards Jews, and less against the Christian faithful involved in Jewish practices. This may have a logical explanation.

When Chlotar I, the last surviving son of the Merovingian king Clovis, died in 561, the Frankish kingdom was divided amongst his four sons. Rather than a peaceful solution, this division led to civil war. Guntram received Burgundy but his power was weakened by unrest. This civil instability probably meant that the king sought the support of the church, wishing to re-establish his royal power, and he therefore called the many councils which took place at this time. The council of Mâcon had been called by Guntram in 583. During this time, there were many claims on his throne. Guntram's bishop, Theodore, rallied support for the king and sought a scapegoat for the troubles. The bishop found this in the Jews, for they had supposedly welcomed Guntram's opponent with much enthusiasm. The royal power, or rather weakness, had an influence on further civil and religious policy concerning the Jews. This may be the reason for the fact that the canons on Jews in the following Gallic councils are directed mainly against them and, in general, less against the Christian faithful—thus reaffirming the argument to end here our discussion on Christian-Jewish relations in council texts. The negative feelings towards the Jews were now initiated on a royal level, from a legal point of view and apparently added to the Church's theological concern for keeping the faithful away from their Jewish neighbors.

As far as council rulings on relations with Jews are concerned, the other part of the western Mediterranean studied earlier is Spain. The rulers of Spain and southern Gaul (Narbonensis) from the mid-fifth century were Visigoths. Until 589, the Visigothic kings were Arians. Their policy towards the Jews was no different from other rulers. After their conversion to orthodox Christianity, the policies of the Visigothic kings were directed against non-Christians, and in particular the Jews. The council texts, especially from the numerous councils held at

Toledo reflect this policy. On the whole, here as well the canons are directed more against the Jews, less against Christian faithful. From Reccared to Gundemar (approximately the sixth to mid-seventh century) the policies on the Jews were relatively lenient, yet by Sisebut, in 612, this had changed drastically. The Visigothic state and church now worked together towards the (forced) conversion of the Jews. Hence the change in attitude in the rulings on Jews and Judaism.

CONCLUSIONS

What we have seen in the previous chapters, based mainly on the canons of council texts and archeological information where available, is that contacts between the Christian faithful and their Jewish neighbors were often close. On the level of the ordinary faithful, practices considered as 'judaizing' continued even when church leaders wished for these to end. During this period of the development of the church's own identity and theology, clear rules needed to be set in order to keep the faithful on the right path. These rules seem to have been inspired less by anti-Jewish feelings than by concerns for establishing clear boundaries between the two, so closely connected, faith groups.[1] Specific examples given by the canons of the council texts depict a situation in the fourth to sixth centuries in the western and eastern Mediterranean, which indicates that the Christian faithful borrowed from Judaism and found their way easily to their Jewish neighbors. Archeological evidence corroborates the textual evidence. It was not only a matter of borrowing from Judaism, but the conclusion seems more likely that the borders between the two groups of faithful—Christians and Jews—was not as clear as in later times. Occasionally Roman imperial law followed along similar lines as canon law, often topics were different.

This study is based on the rulings issued at church councils. However, it is interesting to note that in the Judaism of late antiquity attention was also given to Jewish faithful interacting with other groups—gentiles. The Mishnah is concerned with who is and who is not part of 'Israel'—those who accept the authority of Torah and Jewish Law. Gentiles do not accept these and are defined as idolaters. The tractate on how to relate to these gentiles is the Abodah Zarah.[2] The tractate Abodah Zarah is found in the Mishnah, in the Tosefta and in the Talmuds. In the first part, Jews are reminded that it is 'forbidden to do business with' gentiles before the gentiles' festivals.[3] Other

---

[1] For an interpretation of the council texts as 'anti-Jewish', see authors mostly writing in the 1950's and 1960's: e.g., Simon (1948) and Parkes (1979).

[2] Neusner (2004) ch. 3.

[3] m AZ 1:1.

examples of intermingling with gentiles are mentioned which are forbidden to Jews. Could these gentiles eventually refer to contacts with Christians? The statements indicate that contacts existed, at times were close, and that here as well the religious leaders were concerned. This is an interesting source which could possibly offer information from another—the Jewish—side on what we have seen from the Christian perspective.

The discussions as stated in the introductory chapter focused on two main issues. The first concerns the question whether Judaism was in decline after the first century (Harnack). Whether or not Judaism was an active missionary religion (Feldman), it seems from the evidence presented in the previous chapters that it was certainly not a faith in decline. The council texts show that Christians found their way to their Jewish neighbors, often borrowing from their tradition, much to the chagrin of—e.g.—John Chrysostom who attacks his faithful at the moment when they are most likely to find their way (again) to the synagogue. The evidence goes beyond a merely literary situation (Taylor, Fredriksen). The social reality indicates close interaction resulting in an expected reaction from church leaders.

The second issue concerns the parting of the ways. At what point a parting of the ways seems imminent is still not clear. According to church leaders, and in church father texts, the partition had already happened. Yet, the situation 'on the ground' appears much more complex. Rather than assume an early and clear partition, the evidence from the council texts, with additional information from archeology and the homilies of John Chrysostom, proves otherwise.

The steady Christianization of the Roman Empire from the fourth century onwards meant that the church gradually gained a certain position within society. This situation led to a growing need for clearer identity.

Within this context we must place the council texts—as attempts at establishing boundaries within which the Christian faithful were assumed to stay. Yet, we see that contacts between Christianity and Judaism on the level of the ordinary faithful remained close, and for a much longer period than the church leaders would have liked.

BIBLIOGRAPHY

Primary Sources

Legal Texts (Including Church Councils)

Codex Theodosianus (CTh)	Mommsen, Th. and Krueger, P. (Eds.) (Weidmann Berlin 2006) Text in Latin.
Novellae	Mommsen, Th. And Meyer, P.M. (Eds.) *Codex Theodosianus* Vol. II (Weidmann Berlin 2006). Text in Latin.
Codex Justinianus (CJ)	Mommsen, Th. and Krueger, P. (Eds.) *The Digest of Justinian* 4 vols. (University Pennsylvania Press 1985). Text in Latin and English.
Councils:	Ballerini, P. & H. (1887) *Ad opera sancti Leonis Magni Rom. Pontif. appendix De Antiquis Collectionibus et collectoribus canonum* Pt. II *De Antiquoribus collectionibus Latinis* (PL 56).
Elvira	Hefele/Leclercq (1907) I.1, pp. 221–264. Martinez Diez *CCH* vol. IV, pp. 233–268.
Laodicea	Greek text: Hefele/Leclercq (1907) vol. I. 2, pp. 746–1028; Latin version: CCH vol. III, p. 153ff.
Apostolic Canons	Metzger (1987) vol. III (SC 336); Joannou, P.-P. (1962) *Discipline Générale Antique (IVᵉ–IXᵉ s.) vol. I. 2 Les Canons des Synodes Particuliers* (Fonti Fasc. IX Pontificia Comissione per la Redazione del Codice di Diritto Canonico Orientale Grottaferrata/Rome).
Gaul	Munier, Ch. (1960) *Les Statuta Ecclesiae Antiqua* (Presses Universitaires Paris). Munier, C. (1963) *Concilia Galliae A 314–A 506* (CCSL CXLVIII, Brepols Turnhout). De Clercq, C. (1963) *Concilia Galliae A 511–A 695* (CCSL CXLVIIIA, Brepols Turnhout).

Classical Sources

Ammianus Marcellinus	*Rerum Gestarum* (LCL 300, 331, 315; Rolfe, J.C., 1956–1958).
Cicero	*Pro Flacco* 68–69 (LCL 324; Lord, L., 1937).
Julian	*Contra Gal.* (LCL 157; Wright, W.C., 1923).
Libanius	*Orationes* 47, 13 (LCL 452; Norman, A.F., 1969–1977).
Plato	*Symposion* (LCL 166; Lamb, W.R.M., 1975).
Pliny	*Hist. Nat.* III, 4, 31. (LCL 352; Rackham, H., 1942).
Plutarch	*Quaestiones Convivales* (in: *Moralia* vol. VIII, LCL 424; Clement, P.A., 1969).
Strabo	*Geografikon* IV (LCL 196; Jones, H.L., 1927).
Suetonius	*Augustus*: (in: *Suetonius*, LCL; Rolfe, J.C., 1920).

Jewish Sources

Mishnah (M)	There are various reprints. Indicated here are the editions used in this study.

	Original text: Beer, G. and Holtzmann, O. et al. (Ed.) *Die Mischna* (Töpelman Giessen, 1912–); transl.: Danby, H. *The Mishnah Translated from the Hebrew with introduction and brief explanatory notes* (Oxford University Press, 1933).
Babylonian Talmud (BT)	Epstein, I. *Hebrew English translation of the Babylonian Talmud* (Soncino Press London, 1980). In Hebrew and English.
Jerusalem Talmud (PT)	There is no complete critical edition and no proper translation to accompany this. Again, indicated here are the editions used in this study for the tractates *berakhot, horayot, qiddushin*. Original text: Guggenheimer, H.W. (Ed.) *The Jerusalem Talmud Edition, Translation and Commentary* (Studia Judaica, W. de Gruyter Berlin, 2000–7); for the tractates used in this study, transl.: Hengel, M. *Übersetzung des Talmud Yerushalmi* (Mohr Siebeck Tübingen, 1990).
Tosefta (T)	Original text: Zuckermandel, M.S. and Liebermann, S. *Tosephta* (Wahrmann Books Jerusalem, 1970); transl.: Lieberman, S. *The Tosefta* (Jewish Theological Seminary of America New York, 1955).
Midrash Rabbah (Midr)	Original text: Margaliyot, M. *Midrash Wayyikra Rabbah* (Critical Edition Jerusalem 1953–1960); transl.: Israelstam, J. and Slotki, J.J. *Midrash Rabbah Leviticus* (Soncino Press London, 1971).
Targum Jonathan	Original text: Sperber, A. (Ed.) *The Bible in Aramaic* vol. I II *The Latter Prophets According to Targum Jonathan* (Brill Leiden, 1962); transl.: Cathcart, K.J. and Gordon, R.P. *The Targum of the Minor Prophets* (The Aramaic Bible Vol. 14, Edinburgh, 1989).

Josephus	– *Antiquitates* (LCL 242, 281, 326, 365, 410, 433, 456; Thackeray, H./Marcus, R./Feldman, L., 1930–1981). – *Bellum Iudaicum* (LCL 203, 210; Thackeray, H., 1927–1928). – *Contra Apionem* (LCL 186; Thackeray, H., 1926).
Philo	*Legatio ad Gaium* 214 (LCL 379; Colson, F.H., 1962).

Christian Sources

Adon	Dubois, J. & Renaud, G. (1984) *Le Martyrologe d'Adon Texte et Commentaire* (Éditions du Centre Nationale de la Recherche Scientifique, Paris).
Ambrose	– *De viduis* 86 (CPL 146; PL 16, 247). – *Epistola* 19 (CPL 82; PL 19, 1024–1036).
Aphrahat	*Demonstratio XII de Pascha* 6–8; 12–13: Cantalamessa, R. (1981) *Ostern in der Alten Kirche* (Traditio Christiana IV, Peter Lang Berlin/Frankfurt am Main).
Asterius of Amaseia	*Homiliae* (CPG 3260; PG 40, 377; 40, 388–390).
Asterios Sophistes	CPG 2815; Richard, M. (1956) *Asterii Sophistae Commentariorum in Psalmos* (Symbolae Osloenses Fasc. Supplet. XVI, Oslo).
Athanasius	– *Apologia ad Constantinum* 4 (CPG 2129; SC 56b, Szymusiak, J., 1987). – *De Azymiis* (CPG 2237; PG 26, 1328 ff).

Athenagoras — *Pro Christianis* 33 (CPG 1070; SC 379, Pouderon, B., 1992).

Augustine — *Confessionum* VI: 13 (CPL 251; CCSL XXVII; L.M.J. Verheijen, 1981).
— *De fide et operibus* 35 (CPL 294; CSEL 41, Zycka, J., 1900).
— *Epistola* 36, 16 (CPL 261; CCSL XXXI, 140–141; Daur, K.D., 2004).

Basil of Caesarea — *Hexaemeron* (CPG 2835; SC 26b, Giet, S., 1950);
— *De Spiritu Sancto* 30, 77 (CPG 2839; SC 17, Pruche, B., 1947);
— *Ep.* 263 § 5 (CPG 2900; LCL 270, Deferrari, R.J., 1961).

Caesarius of Arles — *Sermones* (CPL 1008; CCSL 103,104; Morin, G., 1953SC 447, Courreau, J., 2000);
— *Regula* (CPL 1012; SC 398, Courreau, J., 1994);
— *Statuta sanctarum virginum* (CPL 1009; SC 345, de Vogüé, A., 1988);
— *Vita S. Caesarii Episcopi* (CPL 1018; PL 67, 1001).

Chronicon Paschale 374 (CPG 7960; PG 92, 953).
John Chrysostom — *Homiliae Adversus Judaeos* (CPG 4327; PG 48, 843);
— *Homilia* 5.1 *in Hebr.* 2: 16 (CPG 4440; PG 63, 47);
— *De S. Hieromartyre Babyla* (CPG 4347; SC 362; Grillet, B., 1990).
Clement of Alexandria *Paedagogos* III, xi, 59 (CPG 1376; SC 158; Marrou, H.-I., 1960).
Clement *Epistola ad Corinth.* (CPG 1001; SC167; Jaubert, A., 1971).
Constitutiones Apostolorum (CPG 1730; SC 320, 329, 33; Metzger, M., 1985–7).
Cosmas Ind. *Topographia Christiana* 10 (CPG 7468; SC 197; Wolska, W., 1973).
Cyprian of Carthage *Epistolae* (CPG 1760; CCSL IIIc; Diercks, G.F., 1994).

Didache (CPG 1735; SC 248; Rordorf, W., 1998).
Didascalia (CPG 1738); Vööbus, A. (1979) *The Didascalia Apostolorum in Syriac* II (Corpus Scriptorum Christianorum Orientalium Vol. 407, Scriptores Syri 179, Louvain).
Diodorus of Tarsus *Commentarii in Psalmos* (CPG 3818; CCSG 6; Olivier, J.-M., 1980).

Disputation of Sergius the Stylite against a Jew (CSCO 339, Scriptores Syri 153, Hayman, A.P., 1973)

Eucherius of Lyon — *Salonium* (CPL 489; CSEL 31, Wotke, C., 1894);
— *Formularum Spiritalis Intelligentiae* (CPL 488; CSEL 31, Wotke, C., 1894).
Eusebius — *Epistola II ad Constantiam Augustam* (CPG 3503); Pitra, J.-B. (1852) *Spicilegium Solesmense, complectens Sanctorum Patrum scriptorumque ecclesiasticorum* (Didot Paris);

180 BIBLIOGRAPHY

- *Historia Ecclesiastikes* (CPG 3495; SC 31, 41, 55, 73; Bardy, G., 1952–1960);
- *Vita Constantini*: (CPG 3496); Cameron, A. and Hall, S.G. (1999) *Eusebius Life of Constantine* (Clarendon Ancient History Series Oxford).

Evagrius   *Altercatio legis inter Simonem Iudaeum et Theophilum Christianum* (CPL 482; CCSL 64, Demeulenaere, R., 1985).

Gennadius   *De viris illustribus* (CPL 957); Bernoulli, C.A. (1968) *Hieronymus und Gennadius De Viris Inlustribus* (Minerva Frankfurt).

Gregory of Elvira   *Tractatus Origenis* (CPL 546; CCSL LXIX; Bulhart, V., 1967).

Gregory Nazianzus
- *Eulogia de Basilius* 68, 7: (CPG 3010); Boulenger, F. (1908) *Discours Funèbres* (Librairie Alphonse Picard & Fils Paris);
- *Oratio* 29, 19; 31, 24 (CPG 3010; SC 250; Jourjon, M., 1978).

Gregory of Nyssa
- *In laudem fratris Basilii* (CPG 3185); Lendle, O. (1990) *Gregorii Nysseni Sermones* Pt. II (Gregorii Nysseni Opera X, 1, Leiden);
- *Oratio Catechetica* 1 (CPG 3150; SC 453; Winling, R., 2000);
- *De Vita Moysi* (CPG 3159; SC 1; Daniélou, J., 1942).

Gregory of Tours
- *Historiae*: (CPL 1023); Krusch, B. and Levison, W. (Eds.) (1951) *Scriptores RerumMerovingicarum* Tomus I Pars I *Gregorii Episcopi Turonensis LibriHistoriarum X* (Monumenta Germaniae Historica, Hahn Hannover);
- *S. Martin.*: (CPL 1024); Bordier, H.L. (1860) *Les Livres des Miracles et autres opuscules de Georges Florent évêque de Tours* vol. II (Libr. de la Société de l'Histoire de France, Paris);
- *Vitae Patrum*: Arndt, W. and Krusch, B. (Eds.) (1985) *Scriptores Rerum Merovingicarum* Tomus I *Gregorii Episcopi Turonensis Opera* (Monumenta Germaniae Historica, Hahn Hannover): *Vitae Patrum*; James, E. (1985) *Gregory of Tours Life of the Fathers* (Translated Texts for Historians Latin Series I Liverpool University Press);
- *Liber in Gloria Martyrum*: Arndt, W. and Krusch, B. (Eds.) (1985) *Scriptores Rerum Merovingicarum* Tomus I *Gregorii Episcopi Turonensis Opera* (Monumenta Germaniae Historica, Hahn Hannover): *Liber in Gloria Martyrum*; Van Dam, R. (1988) *Gregory of Tours Glory of the Martyrs* (Translated Texts for Historians Latin Series III Liverpool University Press);
- *Liber in Gloria Confessorum*: Arndt, W. and Krusch, B. (Eds.) (1985) *Scriptores Rerum Merovingicarum* Tomus I *Gregorii Episcopi Turonensis Opera* (Monumenta Germaniae Historica, Hahn Hannover): *Liber in Gloria Confessorum*; Van Dam, R. (1985) *Glory of the Confessors* (Translated Texts for Historians Latin Series IV Liverpool University Press).

Gregory I   *Epistola* 1, 45 (CPL 1714; CCSL CXL; Norberg, D.L., 1982).

Hermas   *Pastor, Similitudines* (CPG 1052; SC 53; Joly, R., 1958).

Ignatius of Antioch   *Epistolae* (CPG 1025; SC 10; Camelot, P.Th., 1958).

Innocent I   *Epistola* XXV, 4 (CPL 1641; PL 20, 555).

Irenaeus   *Adversus Haereses* (CPG 1306; SC 263 and 264; Rousseau, A., 1979).

Isidore of Seville   *De Ecclesiasticis Officiis* (CPL 1207; CCSL CXIII; Lawson, C.M., 1989).

Jerome — *Ep.* LXXI.6, *Ad Lucin. Baetic* (CPL 620; CSEL 61, 1; Hilberg, L., 1996);
— *De Viris Illustribus* (CPL 616); Richardson, E.C. (1896) *Hieronymus Liber de viris inlustribus* (Texte und Untersuchungen XIV, 1 a; Hinrich Leipzig);
— *In Isaiam* (CPL 584; CCSL LXXIII A; Adriaen, M., 1963).

Justin Martyr — *Apologia* (CPG 1073; SC 507; Munier, Ch., 2006).

Martyr. Pionius — Musurillo, H. (1972) *The Acts of the Christian Martyrs* (Clarendon Press Oxford).

Origen — *Contra Celsum* (CPG 1476; SC 132, 136, 147, 150, 227; Borret, H., 1967–1976).

Philastrius — *Liber de Haeresibus* 64 (CPL 121; CCSL 9; Bulhart, V., 1957).

Prosper of Aquitaine — *Chronicum* (CPL 2257); Mommsen, Th. (1892) *Chronica minora* I (Teubner Berlin).

Prudentius — *Apotheosis* (CPL 1439; LCL 387 and 398; Thomson, H.J., 1949);
— *Liber Peristephanon*: (CPL 1443; Lavarenne, M. (1951) *Prudence*, Association G. Budé, Éd. Les Belles Lettres, Paris).

Pseudo-Athanasius — *De Sabbatis* 4 (CPG 2244; PG 28, 137).

Severus of Minorca — Bradbury, S. (1996) *Severus of Minorca Letter on the Conversion of the Jews* (Clarendon Press, Oxford).

Sidonius Apollinaris — *Epistolae* (CPL 987; Loyen, A. (1970) *Sidoine Apollinaire* T.II *Lettres*, Association G. Budé, Éd. Les Belles Lettres, Paris); (LCL 296, 420; Anderson, W.B., 1936–1965).

Socrates — *Historia Ecclesiastica* V, 22 (CPG 6028; SC 505; Maraval, P., 2006).

Sozomen — *Historia Ecclesiastica* (CPG 6030; SC 306, 418, 495; Bidez, J., 1983–2005).

Tertullian — *Ad Uxorem* (CPL 12; SC 273; Munier, Ch., 1980).
— *Adversus Judaeos* VII, 4 (CPL 33; CCSL II, 1354–1355; Gerlo, A., 1954);
— *De Monogamia* (CPL 28; SC 343; Mattei, P., 1988);
— *De Oratione* 19, 1 (CPL 7; CSEL 20, Reifferscheid, A., 1890);
— *De Pudicitia* 19 (CPL 30; SC 394 and 395; Munier, Ch., 1993).

Theodoret of Cyrrhus — *Ad Colos.* II, 18 (CPG 6209); C. Marriott, B.D. (1852) *Bibliotheca Patrum Ecclesiae Catholicae* II (John Henry Parker Oxford);
— *Epistolae* 72 (CPG 6240; SC 98; Azéma, Y., 1964).

Traditio Apostolica — (CPG 1737; SC 11b; Botte, B., 1984).

Venantius Fortunatus — *Fortunat Poèmes* T. II, L. V–VIII (CPL 1033; Reydellet, M. (1998) Association G. Budé, Éd. Les Belles Lettres, Paris).
— *Vita S. Germani* 63 (CPL 1039); Krusch, B. (1981) *Venantius Fortunatus* (Monumenta Germaniae Historica Auctores Antiquissimi, IV.2, Munich).

Victorinus of Pettau — *De fabrica mundi* 5 (CPL 79; SC 423; Dulaly, M., 1997).

182   BIBLIOGRAPHY

Secondary Sources

Akeley, T.C. (1967) *Christian Initiation in Spain 300–1100* (Darton, Longman and Todd London).
Albl, M.C. (1999) *"And Scripture Cannot be Broken" The Form and Function of the Early Christian Testimonia Collections* (Suppl. To Novum Testamentum Vol. XCVI, Brill Leiden).
Ameling, W. (1996) 'Die jüdischen Gemeinden im antiken Kleinasien' in: Jütte, R. and Kustermann, A.P. *Jüdischen Gemeinden und Organisationsformen vor der Antike bis zur Gegenwart* (Böhlau Verlag Wien) pp. 29–65.
Ameling, W. (2004) *Inscriptiones Judaicae Orientis Bd. II Kleinasien* (Texts and Studies in Ancient Judaism 99, Mohr Siebeck).
Ando, C. and Rüpke, J. (Ed.) (2006) *Religion and Law in Classical and Christian Rome* (Potsdamer Altertumswissenschaftliche Beiträge Bd. 15, Franz Steiner Verlag Stuttgart).
Arbeiter, A. and Korol, D. (1989) 'Der Mosaikschmuck des Grabbaues von Centcelles und der Machtwechsel von Constans zu Magnentius' in: *Madrider Mitteilungen 30*, pp. 289–331.
Arjava, A. (1996) *Women and Law in Late Antiquity* (Clarendon Press Oxford).
Attridge, H.W. and Hata, G. (1992) *Eusebius, Christianity and Judaism* (Brill Leiden).
Aubert, J.-J. and Sirks, B. (Ed.) (2005) *Speculum Iuris Roman Law as a Reflection of Social and Economic Life in Antiquity* (University of Michigan Press).
Auf der Maur H. (1967) *Die Osterhomilien des Asterios Sophistes* (Trier Theologische Studien Band 19, Paulinus Verlag Trier).
Bacchiocchi, S. (1977) *From Sabbath to Sunday* (Pontifical Gregorian University Rome).
Bachrach, B.S. (1977) *Early Medieval Jewish Policy in Western Europe* (University of Minnesota Press).
Bareille, G. 'Elvire (concile d') in: *DTC* col. 2386.
Baron, S. (2007) "Population" in: *EJ*.
Barral i Altet, X. (1996) *L'Art Espagnol* (Bordas Barcelona).
Barton, J. and Muddiman, J. (2001) *The Oxford Bible Commentary* (Oxford University Press).
Basso, M. (1986) *Guide to the Vatican Necropolis* (Vatican City).
Bauer, J.B. (1952) 'Die Früchtesegnung in Hippolyts Kirchenordnung' in: *Zeitschrift für Katholische Theologie 74*, pp. 71–75.
Bean, G.E. (1971) *Turkey beyond the Maeander* (Ernest Benn Ltd. London).
Belke, K. and Mersich, N. (1990) 'Laodikeia (1)' in: *Phrygien und Pisidien* (Tabula Imperii Byzantini, Band 7 Verl. Österr. Akad. Wissensch. Vienna).
Beck, H. (1950) *The Pastoral Care of Souls in South-East France during the Sixth Century* (Gregoriana Rome).
Becker, A.H. and Reed, A.Y. (2003) *The Ways that Never Parted* (Mohr Siebeck Tübingen).
Bell, A.A. (1994) *A Guide to the New Testament World* (Herald Press, Pennsylvania).
Bellinger, A.R.; Brown, F.E.; Perkins, A. and Welles, C.B. (Ed.) (1956) *The Excavations at Dura-Europos* Vol. VIII part 1 Final Report (Yale University Press).
Belting, H. (1994) *Likeness and Presence A History of the Image before the Era of Art* (Univ. Chicago Press Chicago/London).
Benbassa, E. (1999) *The Jews of France* (Princeton University Press).
Besancon, A. (2000) *The Forbidden Image An Intellectual History of Iconoclasm* (University Chicago Press).
Beneševič, V. (1937) *Ioannis Scholastici Synagoga L Titulorum* t. I (Abh. Bayerischen Akademie für Wissenschaft, Philosophisch-Historische Abteilung Neue Folge Heft 14, Munich).

Bettenson, H. and Maunder, C. (1999) *Documents of the Christian Church*, 3rd edition (Oxford University Press).

Betz, H.D. (1986) The *Greek Magical Papyri in Translation* (University of Chicago Press).

Bevan, E. (1940) *Holy Images* (George Allen & Unwin Ltd. London).

Biarne, J. et al. (1986) *Provinces Ecclésiastique de Vienne et d'Arles* (Topographie Chrétienne des Cités de la Gaule, Ed. Boccard Paris).

Bij de Vaate, A.J. and van Henten, J.W. (1996) 'Jewish or Non-Jewish? Some Remarks on the Identification of Jewish Inscriptions from Asia Minor' in: *Bibliotheca Orientalis* 53, pp. 16–28.

Blaise, A. (1954) *Dictionnaire Latin-Français des Auteurs Chrétiens* (Ed. Brépols Turnhout).

Blázquez, J.M. (2002) 'Recientes aportaciones a la situación de los judíos en la Hispania Tardoantigua', in: Romero, E. (Ed.) *Judaísmo Hispano Estudios en memoria de José Luis Lacave Riaño* Vol. II (CSIC Madrid) pp. 409–425.

Blumenkranz, B. (1948) 'La parabole de l'enfant prodigue chez saint Augustin et saint Césaire d'Arles' in: *VC* 2, pp. 102–105.

Blumenkranz, B. (1960) *Juifs et Chrétiens dans le Monde Occidental* (Mouton et Co. Paris).

——. (1963) *Les auteurs Chrétiens Latins du Moyen Age sur les juifs et le judaïsme* (Mouton & Co. Paris).

——. (1969) 'Les premières implantations de Juifs en France: du 1er au début du Ve siècle' in: *Comptes Rendus de l'Academie des Inscriptions et Belles-Lettres* (Janvier-Mars) pp. 164–5.

——. (1972) *Histoire des Juifs en France* (Collection Franco-Judaica, Privat Toulouse).

——. (1977) '«Iudaeorum Conuiuia» à propos du Concile de Vannes (465), c. 12' in: *Juifs et Chrétiens Patristique et Moyen Age* (Variorum Reprints London) pp. 1055–1058.

Bokser, B.M. (1984) *The Origins of the Seder The Passover Rite and Rabbinic Judaism* (University of California Press Berkeley).

Boretius, A. (1883) *Capitularia Regum Francorum* (Monumenta Germaniae Historica part I Hannover).

Botte, B. (1984) *Hippolyte de Rome La Tradition Apostolique* (SC 11b, Edition du Cerf Paris).

Boudinhon, Abbé (1888) 'Note sur le concile de Laodicée' in: *Congrès Scientifique International des Catholiques* II, pp. 420–427.

Boulenger, F. (1908) *Discours Funèbres* (Librairie Alphonse Picard & Fils Paris).

Bowers, W.P. (1975) 'Jewish communities in Spain in the time of Paul the Apostle', in: *JThS* 26, pt. 2, pp. 395 f.

Bowersock, G.W. et al. (1999) *Late Antiquity* (Harvard University Press).

Boyarin, D. (2003) 'Semantic Differences; or, "Judaism/Christianity"', in: Becker/Reed (2003) pp. 65–85.

——. (2004) *Border Lines* (University of Pennsylvania Press).

Bradbury, S. (1996) *Severus of Minorca Letter on the Conversion of the Jews* (Clarendon Press Oxford).

Bradbury, S. (2006) 'The Jews of Spain, c. 235–638' in: Katz, S.T. (Ed.) *The Cambridge History of Judaism*, vol. IV (Cambridge University Press) pp. 508–516.

Bradley, K. (1998) 'The Roman Family at Dinner', in: Nielsen, I.; Nielsen, H.S. *Meals in a Social Context* (University Press Aarhus) pp. 36–55.

Bradshaw, P. (1981) *Daily Prayer in the Early Church* (Alcuin Club SPCK London).

Bradshaw, P.F. and Hoffman, L.A. (Ed.) (1999) *Passover and Easter* (Notre Dame Press Indiana).

Bradshaw, P. et al. (Ed.) (2002) *The Apostolic Tradition* (Minneapolis).

Brennan, B. (1985) 'The conversion of the Jews of Clermont in AD 576' in: *JTS* 36, pp. 321–337.

Brown, P. (1998) 'Christianization and religious conflict' in: *CAH* vol. XIII, pp. 632–664.

Buckler, W.H., Calder, W.M. and Cox, C.W.M. (1926) 'Monuments from Ancient Phrygia' in *JRS* 16, p. 53 f.

Burnett, A., Amandry, M. and Ripollès, P.P. (1992) *Roman Provincial Coinage* Vol. 1: *From the Death of Caesar to the Death of Vitellius (44 BC–AD 69)* (British Museum Press London).

Cameron, A. (1993) *The Later Roman Empire* (Fontana Press, London).

——. (Ed.) (1998) *The Cambridge Ancient History* vol. XIII (CUP).

Cameron, A. and Hall, S.G. (1999) *Eusebius Life of Constantine* (Clarendon Ancient History Series Oxford).

Cameron, A. (2005) 'The Reign of Constantine, AD 306–337' in: *CAH* XII, pp. 90–109.

Cantalamessa, R. (1981) *Ostern in der Alten Kirche* (Traditio Christiana IV, Peter Lang Berlin/Frankfurt am Main).

Cantera Burgos, F. (1984) *Sinagogas Españolas* (Instituto Benito Arias Madrid).

Cantera Burgos, F. and Millás, J.M. (1956) *Las Inscripciones Hebraicas de España* (Madrid).

Cantor, N. (1993) *The Civilization of the Middle Ages* (Harper Collins N.Y.).

Carson, D.A. (1982) *From Sabbath to Lord's day: a Biblical, Historical and Theological Investigation* (Zondervan Publ. Michigan).

Chadwick, O. (1976) *Priscillian of Avila* (Clarendon Press Oxford).

——. (1982) *The Early Church* (Penguin Books U.K.).

Chaniotis, A. (2002) 'The Jews of Aphrodisias: New Evidence and Old Problems' in: *Scripta Classica Israelica* 21, pp. 209–242.

Christern-Briesenick, B. and Borini, G. (2003) *Repertorium der Christlich-Antiken Sarkophage III Frankreich, Algerien, Tunesien* (Deutsches Archäologisches Institut, Verl. Philipp von Zabern, Mainz am Rhein).

Chupungco, A. (1977) *The Cosmic Elements of Christian Passover* (Ed. Anselmiana Rome).

Cohen, D. (1991) 'The Augustan law on adultery: the social and cultural context', in: Kertzer/Saller (1991) pp. 109–127.

Cohen, S.D. (Ed.) (1996) *Studies in the Cult of Yahweh* (Brill Leiden).

Cohen, S.J.D. (1999) *The Beginnings of Jewishness* (University of California Press).

Collins, R. (1995) *Early Medieval Spain Unity in Diversity 400–1000* (New Studies in Medieval History, 2nd Ed., Macmillan Hampshire/London).

Connolly, R.H. (1918) 'An ancient prayer in the mediaeval Euchologia' in: *JTS* 19, pp. 132–144.

Coquin, M. (1961) 'Le Sort des "Statuta Ecclesiae Antiqua" dans les collections canoniques' in: *Recherches de Théologie Ancienne et Médiévale* 28, p. 193 f.

Corwin, V. (1960) *St. Ignatius and Christianity in Antioch* (Yale Publications in Religion 1, Yale University Press).

Courreau, J. (1970) 'Saint Césaire et les Juifs' in: *Bulletin de Littérature Ecclésiastique* 71, pp. 92–112.

Crawford, J.S. (1999) 'Jews, Christians, and Polytheists in Late-Antique Sardis' in: Fine, S. (Ed.) *Jews, Christians and Polytheists in the Ancient Synagogue* (Routledge London/NY) pp. 190–200.

Cribiore, R. (2007) *The School of Libanius in late Antique Antioch* (Princeton University Press).

Crichton, J.D. (1992) 'A Theology of Worship' in: Jones, C. et al., *The Study of the Liturgy* (Oxford University Press).

Crouzel, H. (1971) *L'Eglise Primitive Face au Divorce Du Premier au Cinquième Siècle* (Théologie Historique no. 13, Beauchesne Paris).

Cumont, F. (1985) *Les Mystères de Mithra* (Var France).

Dale, A.W.W. (1882) *The Synod of Elvira and Christian Life in the Fourth Century* (Macmillan and Co. London).

Daly, W.M. (1970) 'Caesarius of Arles, a precursor of Medieval Christendom' in: *Traditio* 26, pp. 1–29.

Daniélou, J. (1958) *Théologie du Judéo-christianisme* (Desclee Tournai).

Daube, D. (1973) 'The Self-Understood in Legal History' in: *The Juridical Review* 18 (Law Journal of the Scottish Universities) pp. 126–134.

De Clercq, V.C. (1954) *Ossius of Cordoba* (Catholic University of America Press Washington DC).

Del Valle Rodríguez, C. (Ed.) (1998) *La Controversia Judeocristiana en España (Desde los orígenes hasta al siglo XIII) Homenaje a Domingo Muñoz León* (Consejo Superior de Investigaciones Científicas Madrid).

Des Gagniers, J. (1969) *Laodicée du Lycos Le Nymphée* (Boccard Paris).

Di Berardino, A. (2006) *Patrology The Eastern Fathers from the Council of Chalcedon to John of Damascus* (Christian Classics, Allen Texas).

Diamond, E. (2004) *Holy Men and Hunger Artists: Fasting and Asceticism in Rabbinic Culture* (Oxford University Press).

Döpp, S. and Geerlings, W. (1998) (Eds.) *Lexikon der Antiken Christlichen Literatur* (Herder Freiburg).

Douglas, M. (1973) *Natural Symbols* (Vintage Books New York).

Downey, G. (1961) *A History of Antioch in Syria* (Princeton University Press).

——. (1963) *Ancient Antioch* (Princeton University Press).

Drake, H.A. (2000) *Constantine and the Bishops The Politics of Intolerance* (Johns Hopkins University Press Baltimore/London).

Drews, W. (2006) *The Unknown Neighbour The Jew in the thought of Isidore of Seville* (The Medieval Mediterranean Peoples, Economies and Cultures 400–1500 vol. 59, Brill Leiden).

Dubois, J. (1990) *Martyrologes: d'Usuard au martyrologe Romain* (Imprimerie Paillart, Abbeville).

Dunlop Gibson, M. (1903) *The Didascalia Apostolorum in English Translated from the Syriac* (Horae Semiticae no. II, Clay and Sons London).

Duval, N., Maurin, L., Gauthier, N. (1995–1998) *Les Premiers Monuments Chrétiens de la France, I: Sud-Est et Corse, II: Sud-Ouest et Corse, III: Ouest, Nord et Est* (Atlas Archéologiques de France, Picard Paris).

Edwards, J.R. (1992) *Romans New International Biblical Commentary* (Hendrickson Massachusetts).

Effros, B. (2002) *Creating Community with Food and Drink in Merovingian Gaul* (The New Middle Ages Series, Palgrave Macmillan New York/Hampshire UK).

Elderlin, G.W. (Ed.) (1934) *Antioch-on-the-Orontes I The Excavations of 1932* (Published for The Committee for the Excavation of Antioch and its Vicinity, Princeton University Press).

Elliger, W. (1930) *Die Stellung der Alten Christen zu den Bildern in den Ersten vier Jahrhunderten* (Studien über Christliche Denkmäler, Diet. Verlag Leipzig).

Evans, C.A. (2000) 'Root causes of the Jewish-Christian Rift from Jesus tot Justin' in: Porter/Pearson (2000a) pp. 203–235.

Fabian, Cl. (1988) *Dogma und Dichtung Untersuchungen zu Prudentius' Apotheosis* (Europäische Hochschulschrifte R.XV Bd. 42, Peter Lang Frankfurt).

Feldman, L. (1993) *Jew and Gentile in the Ancient World* (Princeton University Press).

Ferguson, E. (1993) *Backgrounds of Early Christianity* (Eerdmans Publications Michigan).

——. (Ed.) (1993b) *Studies in Early Christianity* (Garland Publishers London/New York).

——. (Ed.) (1998) *Encyclopedia of Early Christianity* (Garland Publishing Inc. London/New York).

Fevrier, P.-A. (1978) 'Arles au IVe et Ve siècles Ville Impériale et capitale régionale' in: *Corsi di Cultura sull'Arte ravennate e bizantina* 25 (Università Bologna) pp. 127–158.

Fevrier, P.-A. and Barral I Altet, X. (1989) *Province Ecclésiastique de Narbonne* (Topographie Chrétienne des Cités de la Gaule, Ed. Boccard Paris).

Fiensy, D.A. (1985) *Prayers alleged to be Jewish An Examination of the Constitutiones Apostolorum* (Brown Judaic Studies 65: Scholars Press Chico California).

Finn, Th.M. (1997) *From Death to Rebirth Ritual and Conversion in Antiquity* (Paulist Press New York/New Jersey).

Flórez, H. (1904) *España Sagrada* vol. XII (Hispanic Society of America Madrid).

Floëri, F. and Nautin, P. (1957) *Homélies Pascales* III (Editions du Cerf Paris).

Fontaine, J. (1973) *L'Art Préroman Hispanique* vol. I (La Pierre-qui-Vire).

Fox, R.L. (1986) *Pagans and Christians* (Penguin Books, U.K./USA).

Franz, A. (1909) *Die Kirchlichen Benediktionen im Mittelalter* II (Herdersche Verlag Freiburg/Breisgau).

Fredriksen, P. (1996) 'Divine Justice and Human Freedom: Augustine on Jews and Judaism, 392–398' in: Cohen, J. (Ed.) *From Witness to Witchcraft Jew and Judaism in Medieval Christian Thought* (Wolfenbütteler Mittelalter-Studien Bd. 11, Harrassowitz Verlag Wiesbaden) pp. 29–54.

——. (2003) 'What parting of the ways?' in: Becker/Reed (2003) pp. 35–63.

Frend, W.H.C. (1982) *The Early Church* (SCM Press London).

——. (1984) *The Rise of Christianity* (Darton Longman Todd London).

Funk, F.X. (1883) 'Der Kanon 36' in: *Theologische Quartalschrift*, pp. 270–278.

Gager, J.G. (1972) *Moses in Greco-Roman Paganism* (Abingdon Press Nashville).

Gahbauer, F.R. (2001) 'Synode: I. Alte Kirche' in: *TRE* Bd. XXXII (Berlin/NewYork) pp. 559–566.

Gain, B. (1985) *L'Eglise de Cappadoce au IVe Siècle d'après la correspondance de Basile de Césarée (330–379)* (Pontifical Institute Orientale Rome).

García Iglesias, L. (1977) 'Los cánones del Concilio de Elbira y los judíos' in: *El Olivo*, pp. 3–4.

——. (1978) *Los Judios en la España Antigua* (Ed. Cristiandad Madrid).

García Moreno, L.A. (2005) 'El cristianismo en las Españas: Los orígenes' in: Sotomayor/Ubiña 2005, pp. 169–193.

——. (2005b) *Los Judíos de la España Antigua: Del primer encuentro al primer repudio* (Ediciones Rialp Madrid).

Garcia Villada, Z. (1929) *Historia Eclesiástica de España* I.1 (Compañía Ibero-Americana Madrid).

García Villoslada, R. (1979) *Historia de la Iglesia en España* I (Biblioteca de Autores Cristianos Madrid).

García y Bellido, A. (1967) *Les Religions Orientales dans l'Espagne Romaine* (Brill Leiden).

Gaudemet, J. (1963) 'Elvire' in: *DHGE*, col. 317–348.

——. (1957) *La Formation du Droit Séculier et du Droit de l'Eglise au IVe et Ve Siècles* (Inst. du Droit Romain de l'Université de Paris XV, Sirey).

——. (1958) *L'Eglise dans l'Empire Romain* t. III (Histoire du Droit et des Institutions de l'Eglise en Occident, G. le Bras Sirey Paris).

——. (1985) *Les Sources du Droit de l'Eglise en Occident du IIe au VIIe Siècle* (Ed. du Cerf, Paris).

——. (1989) *Les Canons des conciles Mérovingiens (VIe–VIIe siècles)* (SC 353 & 354, Editions du Cerf Paris).

——. (1994) *Église et Cité Histoire du Droit Canonique* (Editions du Cerf Paris).

Gavin, F. (1928) *The Jewish Antecedents of the Christian Sacraments* (SPCK London).

Geest, P. van, (2005) 'Gemeenschap, ontrouw, vergeving en onthouding. *De adulterinis coniugiis* en latere ontwikkelingen in Augustinus' spirtualiteit van het huwelijk' in: Geest, P. van and Oort, J. van (Ed.) *Augustiniana Neerlandica: aspecten van Augustinus' spiritualiteit en haar doorwerking* (Peeters Leuven) pp. 187–207.

Geisel, Chr. (1998) *Die Juden im Frankenreich Von der Merowingern bis zum Tode Ludwigs der Frommen* (Freiburger Beiträge zur Mittelalterichen Geschichte Bd. 10, Peter Lang Frankfurt).

Gelsi, G. (1978) *Kirche, Synagoge und Taufe in den Psalmenhomilien des Asterios Sophistes* (Dissertation University of Graz, Vienna).

George, J.W. (1992) *Venantius Fortunatus A Poet in Merovingian Gaul* (Clarendon Press Oxford).

Gerlach, K. (1998) *The Antenicene Pascha A Rhetorical History* (Liturgia Condenda 7, Peeters Louvain).

Gero, S. (1981) 'The true image of Christ: Eusebius' letter to Constantia' in: *JTS* NS 33 (1981) pp. 460–470.

Gibson, E. (1978) *The 'Christians for Christians' Inscriptions of Phrygia* (Scholars Press Montana).

Girard, P. (1986) *Pour le meilleur et pour le pire Vingt siècles d'histoire Juive en France* I (Ed. Bibliophane Paris).

Goffart, W. (1985) 'The conversions of Avitus of Clermont and similar passages in Gregory of Tours' in: Neusner/Frerichs (1985) pp. 473–497.

Goffart, W. (1988) *The Narrators of Barbarian History AD 550–800* (Princeton University Press).

Goldenberg, R. 'The Jewish Sabbath in the Roman World up to the Time of Constantine the Great' in: Temporini, H. and Haase, W. *Aufstieg und Niedergang der Römische Welt* II.19.1 (W. De Gruyter Berlin/New York) pp. 414–447.

Goldin, J. (1976) 'The magic of magic and superstition' in: Schüssler Fiorenza, E. *Aspects of Religious Propaganda in Judaism and Early Christianity* (University of Notre Dame Press London) pp. 132–138.

Goodenough, E.R. (1953) *Jewish Symbols in the Greco-Roman period Vol. 3 Illustrations* (Pantheon Books New York).

Goodman, M. (1994) *Mission and Conversion: proselytizing in the religious history of the Roman Empire* (Clarendon Press Oxford).

——. (2007) *Judaism in the Roman World* (Ancient Judaism and Early Christianity Vol. 66, Brill Leiden).

Gough, M. (1961) *The Early Christians* (Thames and Hudson London).

Graetz, H. (1909) *Geschichte der Juden von der ältesten Zeiten bis auf die Gegenwart* V (Oskar Leiner Leipzig).

Grayzel, S. (1970) 'The Beginnings of Exclusion' in: *JQR* 61, pp. 15–26.

Grégoire, H. (1933) 'Un patriarche Phrygien?' in: *Byzantion* 8, pp. 69–76.

Griffe, E. (1964) *La Gaule Chrétienne à l'Époque Romaine I Des Origines Chrétiennes à la fin du IVe Siècle* (Letouzey et Ané Paris).

Grigg, R. (1976) 'Aniconic worship and the Apologetic Tradition: A Note on Canon 36 of the Council of Elvira' in: *Church History* 45, pp. 428–433.

Grissom, F.A. (1978) *Chrysostom and the Jews: studies in Jewish-Christian Relations in Fourth-Century Antioch* (Southern Baptist Theological Seminary Kentucky USA, PhD Diss.).

Gross, H. (1878) 'Zur Geschichte der Juden in Arles' in: *Monatsschrift für Geschichte und Wissenschaft der Judentums*, pp. 64–65.

Gross, H. (1897) *Gallia Judaica* (Editions du Cerf, Paris).

Grubbs, J.E. (1995) *Law and Family in Late Antiquity* (Clarendon Press Oxford).

Gutmann, J. (1992) *The Dura-Europos Synagogue A Re-Evaluation (1932-1992)* (Scholars Press Atlanta).

Habicht, L. (1975) 'New Evidence on the Province of Asia' in: *JRS* 65, pp. 64-91.

Hahneman, G.M. (1992) *The Muratorian Fragment and the Development of the Canon* (Clarendon Press Oxford).

Handley, M. (2000) "'This stone shall be a witness' (Joshua 24.27): Jews, Christians and inscriptions in Early Medieval Gaul" in: Porter/ Pearson (2000) pp. 239-254.

Hanfmann, G.M.A. (1983) *Sardis From Prehistoric to Roman Times* (Harvard University Press).

Harkins, P.W. (1999) *Saint John Chrysostom Discourses against Judaizing Christians* (The Fathers of the Church A New Translation Catholic University of America Press, Washington DC).

Harmening, D. (1979) *Superstitio* (E. Schmidt Berlin).

Harnack, A. von, (1906) *Die Mission und Ausbreitung des Christentums in den Ersten Drei Jahrhunderten* (Hinrichs Buchhandlung Leipzig).

Harries, J.D. (1999) *Law and Empire in Late Antiquity* (Cambridge University Press).

——. (2001) 'Resolving Disputes: The Frontiers of Law in Late Antiquity' in: Mathisen, R.W. (Ed.) *Law, Society, and Authority in Late Antiquity* (Oxford University Press) pp. 68-82.

Hefele, C.J. and Leclercq, H. (1907) *Histoire des conciles d'après les documents originaux* (Letouzey et Ané Paris).

Heijmans, M. (2004) *Arles durant l'Antiquité Tardive de la Duplex Arelas à l'Urbs Genesii* (Collection de l'Ecole Française de Rome 324).

Herbst, J.G. (1823) 'Die Synode von Laodicea in Phrygien' in: *Theologische Quartalschrift* A.5, pp. 3-46.

Hess, H. (2002) *Early Development of Canon Law and the Council of Serdica* (Oxford Early Christian Studies, Oxford University Press).

Hill, R.C. (2005a) *Diodore of Tarsus: Commentary on Psalms 1-51* (Society of Biblical Literature n. 9, Brill Leiden).

——. (2005b) *Reading the Old Testament in Antioch* (Bible in Ancient Christianity series vol. 5, Brill Leiden).

Hoehner, H.W. (1972) *Herod Antipas* (Cambridge University Press).

Honoré, T. (1998) *Law in the Crisis of Empire 379-455 AD The Theodosian Code and its Quaestors* (Clarendon Press Oxford).

Horst, P. v.d. (1989) 'Jews and Christians in Aphrodisias in the light of their relations in other cities in Asia Minor' in: *Nederlands Theologisch Tijdschrift* 43, pp. 106-121.

Horst, P. v.d. (2000) 'Jews and Christians in Antioch at the End of the Fourth Century' in: Porter/Pearson (2000a) pp. 228-238.

Horst, P.W. v.d. and Newman, J.H. (2008) *Early Jewish Prayers in Greek* (Commentaries on Early Jewish Literature, W. de Gruyter Berlin/New York).

Hunt, D. (1998) 'The church as a public institution' in: Cameron, A. *CAH* vol. XIII (Cambridge University Press) pp. 238-276.

Immerzeel, M. (1994) 'Les Ateliers de Sarcophages Paléochrétiens en Gaule La Provence et les Pyrénées' in: *Antiquité Tardive* 2, pp. 233-249.

——. (1996) *De Sarcofaagindustrie rond 400. Het Westelijk Middellandse-Zeegebied* (Diss. Leiden).

James, E. (1982) *The Origins of France From Clovis to the Capetians, 500-1000* (New Studies in Medieval History, Macmillan Publ. Hampshire/London).

Jeffreys, E., Jeffreys, M. and Scott, R. (1986) *The Chronicle of John Malalas* (Australian Association for Byzantine Studies *Byzantina Australiensia* 4, Melbourne).

Jiménez Patón, L. (1998) 'Prudencio y la tradición *Adversus Iudaeos*' in: Del Valle (1998) pp. 24-27.

Joannou, P.-P. (1962) *Discipline Générale Antique (IVᵉ-IXᵉ s.)* vol. I. 2 *Les Canons des Synodes Particuliers* (Fonti Fasc. IX Pontificia Comissione per la Redazione del Codice di Diritto Canonico Orientale Grottaferrata/Rome).

Johnson, S.E. (1958) 'Early Christianity in Asia Minor' in: *JBL* 77, pp. 1–17.

——. (1975) 'Asia Minor and Early Christianity' in: Neusner (1975) pp. 77–145.

Jones, A.H.M. and Martindale, J.R. (1971) *The Prosopography of the Later Roman Empire* (Cambridge University Press).

Juster, J. (1913) 'La Condition Légale des Juifs sous les Rois Visigoths' in: *Études d'Histoire Juridique offertes à Paul Frédéric Girard*, vol. II (Librairie Paul Geuthner Paris) pp. 275–335.

Juster, J. (1914) *Les Juifs dans l'Empire Romain* II (Librairie Paul Geuthner Paris).

Katz, S. (1937) *The Jews in the Visigothic and Frankish Kingdoms of Spain and Gaul* (Cambridge Massachusetts).

Keely, A. (1997) 'Arians and Jews in the *Histories* of Gregory of Tours' in: *Journal of Medieval History* 23, pp. 103–115.

Kelly, J.N.D. (1995) *Golden Mouth The Story of John Chrysostom—ascetic, preacher, bishop* (Duckworth and Co. London).

Kertzer, D.I. and Saller, R.P. (Ed.) (1991) *The Family in Italy from Antiquity* (Yale University Press).

Kinzig W. (1990) *In Search of Asterius Studies on the Authorship of the Homilies on the Psalms* (Forschungen zur Kirchen- und Dogmengeschichte Bd. 47, Vandenhoeck & Ruprecht Göttingen).

——. '"Non-Separation": Closeness and Cooperation Between Jews and Christians in the Fourth Century' in: *VC* 45, pp. 27–53.

——. (2001) 'The Greek Christian Writers' in: Porter, S.E. *Handbook of Classical Rhetoric in the Hellenistic Period 330 BC–AD 400* (Brill Academic Publishers Boston/Leiden) pp. 633–670.

——. (2002) *Asterius Psalmenhomilien* (Bibliothek der griechischen Literatur 56, Hiersemann Stuttgart), 2 vols.

Klaassen, A.D. (1996) *Tien Preken van Caesarius van Arles (470–542) Een onderzoek naar de invloed van Augustinus in de prediking van Caesarius van Arles* (Diss. Leiden).

Klingshirn, W. (1994a) *Caesarius of Arles The Making of a Christian Community in late antique Gaul* (Cambridge University Press).

Klingshirn, W.E. (1994b) *Caesarius of Arles: Life, Testament, Letters* (Translated Texts for Historians vol. 19, Liverpool University Press).

Koch, H. (1917) *Die Altchristliche Bilderfrage* (Vandenhoed & Ruprecht Göttingen).

Kondoleon, Chr. (2000) *Antioch The Lost Ancient City* (Exhibition Worcester Art Museum, Princeton University Press/Worcester Art Museum).

Körtner, U.H.J. (1983) *Papias von Hierapolis* (Vandenhoeck Göttingen).

Kraabel, A.T. (1968) *Judaism in Western Asia Minor under the Roman Empire* (Harvard Theological Dissertation).

——. (1992) 'The Synagogue at Sardis: Jews and Christians' in: Overman J.A. and MacLennan, R.S. *Diaspora Jews and Judaism Essays in Honor of and in Dialogue with A.Thomas Kraabel* (Scholars Press Atlanta Georgia) pp. 225–236.

Kraeling, C.H. (1932) 'The Jewish Community at Antioch' in: *JBL* 51, p. 130–160.

Kraft, R.A. (1965) 'Some notes on Sabbath observance in early Christianity' in *Andrews University Seminary Studies* 3, pp. 23–32.

——. (2003) 'The Weighing of the Parts', in Becker/Reed (2003) pp. 87–94.

Krauss, S. (1902) 'Antioche' in: *REJ* 45, pp. 27–49.

Laeuchli, S. (1972) *Power and Sexuality The Emergence of Canon Law at the Synod of Elvira* (Philadelphia).

Lampe, G.W.H. (1961) *A Patristic Greek Lexicon* (Clarendon Press Oxford).

Langmuir, G.I. (1990) *History, Religion and Antisemitism* (University of California Press).

Le Blant, E. (1886) *Les Sarcophages Chrétiens de la Gaule* (Imprimerie Nationale, Paris).

Lecat, J.L. and Delhaye, Ph. (1966) 'Dimanche et Sabbat' in: *Mélanges de Science Religieuse* 23, no. 2, pp. 73–93.

Leclercq, H. (1906) *L'Espagne Chrétienne* (Lecoffre Paris).

Lenain, D. (1901) 'Le canon 36 du concile d'Elvire' in: *Revue d'Histoire et de Littérature Réligieuses* 6, pp. 458–460.

Leon, H.J. (1960) *The Jews of Ancient Rome* (Jewish Publishing Society of America Philadelphia).

Leonhard, C. (2006) *The Jewish Pesach and the Origins of the Christian Easter Open Questions in Current Research* (Studia Judaica Bd. XXXV, Walter de Gruyter Berlin/New York).

——. (2007) 'Blessing over wine and bread in Judaism and Christian Eucharistic prayers. Two independent traditions' in: Gerhards, A. and Leonhard, C. *Jewish and Christian Liturgy and Worship* (Jewish and Christian Perspectives Series, Brill Leiden) pp. 309–326.

Levi, D. (1947) *Antioch Mosaic Pavements* (Princeton University Press).

Lewis, N. and Reinhold, M. (1966) *Roman Civilization Sourcebook II: the Empire* (Harper New York).

Lewy, H. (1937) 'Imaginary journeys from Palestine to France', in: *Journal of the Warburg Institute* 1, pp. 251–3.

Leyerle, B. 'Meal customs in the Greco-Roman World' in: Bradshaw/Hoffman (1999) pp. 29–61.

Liebeschuetz, J.H.W.G. (1972) *Antioch City and Imperial Administration in the later Roman Empire* (Clarendon Press Oxford).

Liebs, D. (2000) 'Roman Law' in: Cameron, A. *CAH* vol. XIV (Cambridge University Press) pp. 244–252.

Lietzmann, H. (1903) *Die Drei Ältesten Martyrologen* (Marcus Verlag Bonn).

——. (1979) *Mass and the Lord's Supper* (Brill Leiden).

Lieu, J. (1996) *Image and Reality The Jews in the World of Christians in the Second Century* (T&T Clark Edinburgh).

Lieu, J.; North, J.; Rajak, T. (1992) *The Jews among Pagans and Christians in the Roman Empire* (Routledge London/New York).

Lieu, S.N.C. and Montserrat, D. (1998) *Constantine History, Historiography and Legend* (Routledge London/New York).

Limmer, J. (2004) *Konzilien und Synoden im Spätantiken Gallien von 314 bis 696 nach Christi Geburt* 2 vols. (Wissenschaft und Religion Bd. 10, Peter lang Frankfurt/Main).

Linder, A. (1987) *The Jews in Roman Imperial Legislation* (Israel Academy of Sciences and Humanities Jerusalem).

——. (1997) *The Jews in the Legal Sources of the Early Middle Ages* (Israel Academy of Sciences and Humanities Jerusalem).

——. (2006) 'The Legal Status of the Jews in the Roman Empire' in: Katz, S.T. *The Cambridge History of Judaism* vol. IV *The Late Roman-Rabbinic Period* (Cambridge University Press) pp. 128–173.

Lombardía, P. (1954) 'Los matrimonios mixtos en el concilio de Elvira (a. 303 ?)' in: *Anuario de Historia del derecho español* 24 (Madrid), pp. 543–558.

Loseby, S.T. (1996) 'Arles in Late Antiquity: *Gallula Roma Arelas* and *Urbs Genesii* in: Christie, N. & Loseby, S.T. (Ed.) *Towns in transition Evolution in Late Antiquity and the Early Middle Ages* (Ashgate Aldershot 1996) pp. 45–70.

Lotter, F. (1997) 'La crainte du prosélytisme et la peur du contact: les Juifs dans les actes des synodes mérovingiens' in: Rouche (1997) pp. 849–880.

Louth, A. (1999) 'Unity and diversity in the church of the fourth century' in: Ferguson, E. (Ed.) *Doctrinal Diversity* (Garland New York) pp. 1–18.

Lowrie, W. (1947) *Art in the Early Church* (Pantheon Books New York).

Maassen, F. (1956) *Geschichte der Quellen und der Literatur des Canonischen Rechts* I (Akademische Druk Graz).

MacMullen, R. (1984) *Christianizing the Roman Empire* (Yale University Press).

——. (1989) 'The Preacher's Audience' in *JTS* 40, pp. 503–511.

Magie, D. (1950) *Roman Rule in Asia Minor* I (Princeton University Press).

Mâle, E. (1950) *La Fin du Paganisme en Gaule et les plus anciennes basiliques chrétiennes* (Ed. Flammarion Paris).

Malnory, A. (1894) *Saint Césaire Evêque d'Arles 503–543* (Bibliothèque de l'École des Hautes Études Facs. 103, Librairie E. Bouillon Ed. Paris).

Mann, F. (2001) *Lexicon Gregorianum Wörterbuch zu den Schriften Gregors von Nyssa* (Brill Leiden).

Mansi, J.D. (1901) *Sacrorum Conciliorum Nova, et Amplissima Collectio* (Repr. by H. Welter Éd. Paris/Leipzig).

Maraval, P. (2001) *Le Christianisme* (Nouvelle Clio, Presses Universitaires de France Paris).

Marjanen, A. & Luomanen, P. (2005) *A Companion to Second-Century Christian 'Heretics'* (Suppl. to *Vigiliae Christianae* Vol. 76, Brill Leiden).

Markus, R. (1986) 'Chronicle and Theology: Prosper of Aquitaine' in: Holdsworth, C. & Wiseman, T.P. (Ed.) *The Inheritance of Historiography* (Exeter Studies in History no. 12 Exeter) pp. 31–45.

Martínez Díez, G. and Rodríguez, F. (1966–1984) (CCH) *La Colección Canónica Hispana*, four volumes (Monumenta Hispaniae Sacra Ser. Canónica, Madrid).

Mathison, R. (Ed.) (2001) *Law, Society and Authority in Late Antiquity* (Oxford University Press).

Maxwell, C. Mervyn (1966) *Chrysostom's Homilies Against The Jews An English Translation* (Diss. University of Chicago).

Maxwell, J.L. (2006) *Christianization and Communication in Late Antiquity John Chrysostom and his Congregation at Antioch* (Cambridge University Press).

Mayer, W. (1998) 'John Chrysostom: extraordinary preacher, ordinary audience' in: Cunningham, M.B. and Allen, P. *Preacher and Audience Studies in Early Christianity and Byzantine Homiletics* (A New History of the Sermon Vol. I, Brill Leiden) pp. 105–139.

Mayer, M. and Allen, P. (2000) *John Chrysostom* (The Early Church Fathers, Routledge London/New York).

McKay, H.A. (2001) *Sabbath and Synagogue The Question of Sabbath Worship in Ancient Judaism* (Brill Leiden).

McGowan, A. (1999) *Ascetic Eucharists* (Clarendon Press Oxford).

McLynn, N.B. (1994) *Ambrose of Milan* (University of California Press).

Meeks, W.A. and Wilken, R.L. (1978) *Jews and Christians in Antioch in the First Four Centuries of the Common Era* (Scholars Press Montana, Society for Biblical Literature n. 13).

Meer, F. v.d. and Bartelink, G. (1976) *Zestien Preken van Asterius, Bisschop van Amaseia* (Dekker en v.d. Vegt Nijmegen).

Meigne, M. (1975) 'Concile ou collection d'Elvire ?' in: *Revue d'Histoire Ecclésiastique* LXX, pp. 361–387.

Mellink, M.J. (1973) 'Archaeology in Asia Minor' in: *AJA* 77, pp. 186–187.

Messner, R. (1992) *Feiern der Umkehr und Versöhnung* (Gottesdienst der Kirche 7,2: Sakramentliche Feiern I/2, Verlag Friedrich Pastet Regenburg).

Metzger, M. (1985–7) *Les Constitutions Apostoliques* (3 vols. SC 320, 329, 336; Ed. du Cerf Paris).

Metzger, B. (1997) *The Canon of the New Testament* (Oxford).

Mikat, P. (1995) *Die Judengesetzgebung der Merowingisch-Fränkischen Konzilien* (Nordrhein-Westfälische Akademie der Wissenschaften Vortr. G 335, Westdeutscher Verlag Düsseldorf).

——. (1996) *Caesarius von Arles und die Juden* (Nordrhein-Westfälische Akademie der Wissenschaften Vorträge G 345, Düsseldorf).

Millar, F. (1986), Vermes, G. and Goodman, M. (Eds) *The Histroy of the Jewish People in the Age of Jesus Christ (175BC–AD 135)* by E. Schürer Vol. III.1 (T&T Clark Edinburgh).

Millar, F. (1992) 'The Jews of the Graeco-Roman Diaspora between paganism and Christianity, AD 312–438' in: Lieu/North/Rajak (1992) pp. 97–123.

——. (2004) 'Christian Emperors, Christian Church and the Jews of the Diaspora in the Greek East, CE 379–450' in: *Journal of Jewish Studies* 55, pp. 1–24.

Millgram, A.E. (1971) *Jewish Worship* (Philadelphia).

Mitchell, K. and Wood, I. (Ed.) (2002) *The World of Gregory of Tours* (Cultures, Beliefs and Traditions vol. 8, Brill Leiden).

Mitchell, S. (1993) *Anatolia: land, men and gods in Asia Minor* vol. II (Clarendon Press Oxford).

Moreschini, C. and Norelli, E. (2005) *Early Christian Greek and Latin Literature* vol. II (Hendrickson Massachusetts).

Morin, G. (1900) 'Deux Écrits de polémique antijuive' in: *Revue d'Histoire Ecclésiastique* 1, pp. 267–273.

——. 'Les *Statuta Ecclesiae Antiqua* sont-ils de S. Césaire d'Arles ?' in: *Revue Bénédictine* 30 (1913) pp. 334–342.

Muhlberger, S. (1990) *The Fifth-Century Chroniclers Prosper, Hydatius, and the Gallic Chronicler of 452* (ARCA Classical and Medieval Texts, Papers and Monographs no. 27, Francis Cairns Leeds).

Müller, G. (1952) *Lexicon Athanasianum* (W. de Gruyter & Co. Berlin).

Munier, Ch. (1960) *Les Statuta Ecclesiae Antiqua* (Presses Universitaires Paris).

——. (1987) 'Nouvelles Recherches sur les *Statuta Ecclesiae Antiqua*' in: Munier, Ch. *Vie Conciliaire et Collections Canoniques en Occident, IVᵉ–XIIᵉ s.* (Variorum Reprints London) pp. 170–180.

Muñoz, A.B. (1998) 'La Polemica Antijudia en los "Tractatus Origenis" de Gregorio de Elvira' in: Del Valle (1998) pp. 45–62.

Musurillo, H. (1972) *The Acts of the Christian Martyrs* (Clarendon Press Oxford).

Nathan, G.S. (2000) *The Family in Late Antiquity* (Routledge London/New York).

Neiman, D. (1963) 'Sefarad: The name of Spain' in: *Journal of Near Eastern Studies* 22, pp. 128–132.

Neusner, J. (1975) *Christianity, Judaism and Other Greco-Roman Cults* II Early Christianity (Brill Leiden).

——. (1981) *Judaism* (University of Chicago Press).

——. (1981b) *A History of the Mishnaic Law of Appointed Times* (Brill Leiden).

——. (1987) *Judaism in the Age of Constantine* (Chicago Studies in the History of Judaism, University of Chicago Press).

——. (1991) *Jews and Christians* (SCM Press London).

——. (1996) (Ed.) *Dictionary of Judaism in the Biblical Period, 450 BCE–600 CE* (Simon and Schuster/Macmillan).

——. (2004) *Making God's Word Work A Guide to the Mishnah* (Continuum New York/London).

Neusner, J. and Frerichs, E.S. (1985) *To see ourselves as others see us* (Scholars Press Chico California).

Nielsen, I. and Nielsen, H.S. (1998) *Meals in a Social Context* (University Press Aarhus).

Nilsson, M.P. (1961) *Geschichte der Griechischen Religion* (Bechse Verlag Münich).

Niquet, H. (2004) 'Jews in the Iberian Peninsula in Roman times' in: *Scripta Classica Israelica* vol. 23, pp. 159–182.

Nolte, H. (1877) 'Sur le canon 36' in: *Revue des Sciences Ecclésiastiques* Sér. 2, n.12, pp. 482–484.

Norris, F.W. (1991) *Faith gives Fullness to Reasoning The Five Theological Orations of Gregory Nazianzen* (Supplement to *Vigiliae Christianae* Vol. XIII, Brill Leiden).

Noy, D. (1993) *Jewish Inscriptions of Western Europe I Italy, Spain and Gaul* (Cambridge University Press).

Noy, D. and Bloedhorn, H. *Inscriptiones Judaicae Orientis Bd. III Syria and Cyprus* (Texts and Studies in Ancient Judaism 102, Mohr Siebeck).

O'Brien, P.T. (1982) *Word Biblical Commentary* Vol. 44, *Colossians, Philemon* (Word Books Texas).

O'Grady, D. (1991) *The Victory of the Cross* (Harper Collins London).

Olivier, J.-M. (1980) *Diodori Tarsensis Commentarii in Psalmos* (CCSG 6, Brepols Turnhout).

Orlandis, J. and Ramos-Lissón, D. (1981) *Die Synoden auf der Iberischen Halbinsel bis zum Einbruch des Islam (711)* (Paderborn).

Osiek, C. and Balch, D.L. (1997) *Families in the New Testament World* (John Knox Press Kentucky).

Pakter, W. (1985) 'Les esclaves chrétiens des Juifs Troisième concile d'Orléans (538)' in: *Archives Juives* 21, pp. 3–4.

——. (1988) *Medieval Canon Law and the Jews* (Verlag Rolf Gremer Ebelsbach).

——. (1992) 'Early Western Church Law and the Jews' in: Attridge/Hata (1992) pp. 714–735.

Palol, P. de (1967) *Arqueología Cristiana de la España Romana* vol. I Monumentos (España Cristiana Serie Monográfica Madrid/Valladolid).

——. (1969) *Arte Paleocristiano en España* (Poligrafa Barcelona).

Parenti, S. and Velkovska, E. (Ed.) (1995) *L'Eucologio Barberini gr. 336* (Bibliotheca "Ephemerides Liturgicae" 'Subsidia 80' (Ed. Liturgiche, Rome).

Parkes, J. (1964) 'Jews and Christians in the Constantinian Empire' in: Dudgmore, C.W. (Ed.) *Studies in Church History* I (Nelson London) pp. 69–79.

——. (1979) *The Conflict of the Church and the Synagogue* (Atheneum New York).

Patón, L.J. (1998) 'Prudencio y la tradicion Adversus Iudaeos' in: Del Valle (1998) pp. 23–41.

Paverd, F. van de (1981) 'Disciplinarian procedures in the early Church' in: *Augustinianum* 21, pp. 291–316.

Perchenet, A. (1988) *Histoire des Juifs de France* (Editions du Cerf Paris).

Peskowitz, M. (1993) ' 'Family/ies' in Antiquity: Evidence from Tannaitic literature and Roman Galilean Architecture', in: Cohen, S.J.D. *The Jewish Family in Antiquity* (Brown Judaic Studies n. 289, Scholars Press Atlanta) pp. 9–38.

Petit, P. (1957) *Les Étudiants de Libanius* (Nouvelles Éditions Latines Paris).

Pfuhl, E. and Möbius, H. (1979) *Die Ostgriechischen Grabreliefs* (Philipp von Zabern Mainz/Rhein).

Pharr, C. (1952) *The Theodosian Code and Novels and the Sirmondian Constitutions* (Princeton University Press).

Pietri, Ch. (1997) *Christiana respublica: Eléments d'une Enquête sur le Christianisme Antique* vol. I (École Française de Rome).

Plöchl, W.M. (1959) *Geschichte des Kirchenrechts I Das Recht des 1. Jahrtausend* (Verlag Herold Vienna).

Pontal, O. (1989) *Histoire des Conciles Mérovingiens* (Éd. du Cerf Paris).

Porter, S.E. and Pearson, B.W.R. (Ed.) (2000a) *Christian-Jewish Relations through the Centuries* (Sheffield Academic Press).

Porter, S.E. and Pearson, B.W.R. (2000b) 'Ancient understandings of the Christian-Jewish split' in: id. (Ed.) *Christian-Jewish Relations through the Centuries* (Sheffield Academic Press) pp. 36–51.

Prevot, F., Barral I Altet, X. (1989) *Province Ecclésiastique de Bourges* (Topographie Chrétien des Cités de la Gaule VI, Editions Boccard Paris).

Price, S. & Kearns, E. (2003) *The Oxford Dictionary of Classical Myth and Religion* (Oxford University Press).

Puertas Tricas, R. (1975) *Iglesias Hispanicas (Siglos IV al VIII) Testimonios Literarios* (Dirección General del Patrimonio artístico y cultural Ministerio de Educación y Ciencia Madrid).

Quasten, J. (1950) *Patrology* 4 volumes (Spectrum Utrecht/Brussels, Christian Classics Texas).

Quispel, G. (1950–1) 'De brief aan de Laodicensen een marcionitische vervalsing' in: *Nederlands Theologisch Tijdschrift* 5, pp. 43–46.

Rabello, A.M. (2000) 'L'observance des fêtes juives dans l'Empire romain' in: id. *The Jews in the Roman Empire: Legal Problems from Herod to Justinian* (Ashgate Variorum Aldershot) pt. VIII.

Rajak, T. (1999) 'The Synagogue within the Greco-Roman City' in: Fine, S. (Ed.) *Jews, Christians and Polytheists in the Ancient Synagogue* (Routledge London/NY) pp. 161–173.

Ramos-Lissón, D. (1980) '"Communio" y recepción de cánones conciliares de los sínodos hispánicos en los siglos IV y V', in: *Annuarium Historiae Conciliorum* 12, heft 1/2, pp. 26–37.

Ramsay, W.M. (1895) *The Cities and Bishoprics of Phrygia* I (Clarendon Press Oxford).

Régné, J. (1908) 'La Condition des Juifs du Narbonne' in: *REJ* 55, pp. 1–36.

Reichert, E. (1990) *Die canones der synode von Elvira* (Diss. Hamburg).

Reif, S. (1993) *Judaism and Hebrew Prayer* (Cambridge University Press).

Reynolds, J. and Tannenbaum, R. (1987) *Jews and Godfearers at Aphrodisias* (Cambridge Philological Society).

Richard, M. (1956) *Asterii Sophistae Commentariorum in Psalmos* (Symbolae Osloenses Fasc. Supplet. XVI, Oslo).

Richardson, P. 'Augustan-era synagogues in Rome' in: Donfried, K.P. and Richardson, P. (Eds.) (1998) *Judaism and Christianity in First-Century Rome* (Eerdmans Publ. Company Michigan) pp. 17–29.

Rivet, A.L.F. (1988) *Gallia Narbonensis Southern France in Roman Times* (BT Batsford Ltd. London).

Robert, L. (1994) *Le Martyre de Pionios Prêtre de Smyrne* (Dumbarton Oaks Research Library Washington DC).

Rordorf, W. (1962) *Der Sonntag* (Zwingli Verlag Zürich).

——. (1972) *Sabbat und Sonntag in der Alte Kirche* (TheologischeVerlag Zürich).

Rose, E.M. (2002) 'Gregory of Tours and the Conversion of the Jews of Clermont' in: Mitchell, K. & Wood, I. (Ed.) *The World of Gregory of Tours* (Cultures, Beliefs and Traditions Medieval and Early Modern Peoples Vol. 8, Brill Leiden) pp. 307–320.

Roth, N. (1994) *Jews, Visigoths and Muslims in Medieval Spain* (Medieval Iberian Peninsula Texts and Studies Vol. X, Brill Leiden).

Rouche, M. (1979) 'Les Baptêmes Forces de Juifs en Gaule Mérovingienne et dans l'Empire d'Orient' in: Nikiprowetsky, V. (Ed.) *De l'Antijudaïsme antique à l'Antisémitisme Contemporain* (Presses Universitaires de Lille) pp. 105–124.

——. (1997) (Ed.) *Clovis Histoire et Mémoire*, vol. I (Presses de l'Université de Paris-Sorbonne).

Rouquette, J.-M. (2000) 'Les Monuments Chrétiens d'Arles au Vie siècle' in: De Dreuille, Chr. (Ed.) *L'Eglise et la Mission au Vie Siècle* (Actes du Colloque d'Arles, Cerf Paris) pp. 201–212.

Rouwhorst, G.A.M. (1997) 'Jewish Liturgical traditions in Early Syriac Christianity' in: *VC* 51, pp. 72–93.

——. (2001) 'The reception of the Jewish Sabbath in early Christianity' in: Post, P., Rouwhorst, G., van Tongeren, L., and Scheer, A. *Christian Feast and Festival The*

Dynamics of Western Liturgy and Culture (Liturgia Condenda 12, Peeters Leuven) pp. 223–266.

——. (2002) 'The Reading of Scripture in Early Christian Liturgy' in: Rutgers, L.V. *What Athens has to do with Jerusalem Essays on Classical, Jewish, and Early Christian Art and Archaeology in Honor of Gideon Foerster* (Peeters Leuven) pp. 305–331.

——. (2004a) 'The cult of the seven Maccabee brothers and their mother in Christian tradition' in: Poorthuis, M. & Schwartz, J. *Saints and Role Models in Judaism and Christianity* (Jewish and Christian Perspective Series vol. VII, Brill Leiden) pp. 183–204.

——. (2004b) 'Liturgy on the Authority of the Apostles' in: Hilhorst, A. (Ed.) *The Apostolic Age in Patristic Thought* (Supplements to Vigiliae Christianae Vol. LXX, Brill Leiden) pp. 63–85.

——. (2006) 'Table Community in early Christianity' in: Poorthuis, M. and Schwartz, J. *A Holy People Jewish and Christian Perspectives on Religious Communal Identity* (Jewish and Christian Perspectives Series vol. 12, Brill Leiden/London) pp. 69–84.

Rutgers, L.V. (1995) 'Attitudes to Judaism in the Greco-Roman Period: Reflections on Feldman's *Jew and Gentile in the Ancient World*' in: *JQR* 85, pp. 361–395.

Rutgers, L. (1998) *The Hidden Heritage of Diaspora Judaism* (Contributions to Biblical Exegesis and Theology 20, Peeters Louvain).

Safrai, S. (1976) 'The Era of the Mishnah and the Talmud' in: Ben-Sasson, H.H. (Ed.) *A History of the Jewish People* (Harvard University Press) pp. 307–384.

Sandwell, I. (2007) *Religious Identity in Late Antiquity Greeks, Jews and Christians in Antioch* (Greek Culture in the Roman World Series, Cambridge University Press).

Schaff, P. and Wace, H. (1991) *A Select Library of Nicene and Post-Nicene Fathers* 2nd series (Eerdmans Michigan).

Schiffman, L.H. (1998) *From Text to Tradition. A History of Second Temple and Rabbinic Judaism* (Ktav New Jersey).

Schlunk, H. and Hauschild, Th. (1978) *Die Denkmäler der frühchristlichen und westgotischen Zeit* (Philipp von Zabern Mainz am Rhein).

Schlunk, H. (1988) *Die Mosaikkuppel von Centcelles: Text* (Madrider Beiträge Band 13, Philipp von Zabern Mainz am Rhein).

——. (1998) '*Omwille van de vrede*' *Verkenning van vroeg-rabbijnse uitspraken over de omgang met niet-joden* (MA Diss. Catholic Theological University Amsterdam).

Schönborn, C. (1976) *L'Icône du Christ* (Editions Université Fribourg).

Schreckenberg, H. (1973) 'Juden und Judentum in der altkirchlichen lateinischen Poesie' in: *Theokratia* III (Jahrbuch des Institutum Judaicum Delitzschianum) p. 104.

——. (1999) *Die Christlichen Adversus-Judaeos-Texte und ihr literarisches und historisches Umfeld* (Europäische Hochschulschriften Reihe XXIII, Theologie Bd. 172, Peter Lang Frankfurt).

Schultze, V. (1922) *Altchristliche Städte und Landschaften* (Bertelsmann Gütersloh).

Schümmer, J. (1933) *Die Altchristliche Fastenpraxis* (Liturgiegeschichtliche Quellen und Forschungen heft 27, Münster).

Schürer, E. (1986) *The History of the Jewish People in the Age of Jesus Christ (175 BC-135AD)* (Clark Ltd. Edinburgh).

Schwartz, S. (2001) *Imperialism and Jewish Society 200 BCE to 640 CE* (Princeton University Press).

Schwartzfuchs, S. (1973) 'Du nouveau sur la préhistoire des juifs de France?'in: *Revue des Etudes Juives* 132, pp. 579–585.

Scott, S.P. (1973) *Corpus Iuris Civilis The Civil Law* vol. XII (Central Trust Company Cincinnati).

Seager, A.R. (1972) 'The Building History of the Sardis Synagogue' in: *AJA* 76, pp. 425–435.

Seager, A. and Kraabel, A.Th. (1983) 'The Synagogue and the Jewish Community' in: Hanfmann, G.M.A. *Sardis From Prehistoric to Roman Times* (Harvard University Press) pp. 168–190.

Segal, A. (1986) *Rebecca's Children Judaism and Christianity in the Roman World* (Harvard University Press).

Sellès, J.-M. (1990) 'Péché Mortel et Discipline Juive de l'excommunication' in: De Clercq, P.-M. and Palazzo, E. *Rituels Mélanges offerts à Pierre-Marie Gy, o.p.* (Éd. Du Cerf Paris) pp. 455–464.

Shepherd, A.R.R. (1980–1) 'Pagan cults of angels in Roman Asia Minor' in: *Talanta Proceedings of the Dutch Archaeological and Historical Society* XII–XIII, pp. 77–101.

Shepardson, C.C. (2002) ' "Exchanging Reed for Reed" Mapping contemporary heretics onto Biblical Jews in Ephrem's *Hymns on Faith*' in: *Hugoye: Journal of Syrian Studies* Volume 5, no. 1. Internet edition: syrcom.cua.edu/Hugoye.

Siegert, F. (2001) 'Homily and Panegyrical Sermon' in: Porter, S.E. *Handbook of Classical Rhetoric in the Hellenistic Period 330 BC–AD 400* (Brill Academic Publishers Boston/Leiden) esp. pp. 441–443.

Simon, M. (1948) *Verus Israel* (Ed. de Boccard Paris. Repr. in English: Littman Library of Jewish Civilization, London 1996).

Simon, M. (1936) 'La Polémique anti-juive de S. Jean Chrysostome et le mouvement judaïsant d'Antioche' in: *Annuaire de l'Institut de Philologie et d'Histoire Orientales et Slaves* IV Mélanges F. Cumont, pp. 403–421.

Smeelik K.A.D. (1985) *De Anti-Joodse Prediking van Johannes Chrysostomus* (Serie Verkenning en Bezinning Uitg. Kok Kampen).

Smith, D.E. (2003) *From Symposium to Eucharist* (Fortress Press Minneapolis).

Sokolowski, F. (1960) 'Sur le culte d'*angelos* dans le paganisme grec et romain' in: *Harvard Theological Review* 53, p. 225 f.

Solá Solé, J.M. (1960) 'De Epigrafia. 3. Una marca hebraica'in: *Sefarad* 20, pp. 291–294.

Sotomayor, M. (1979) 'Antiguas tradiciones sobre los orígenes del cristianismo hispano' in: García Villoslada (1979) pp. 149–166.

——. (1979b) 'Los testimonios históricos más antiguos del cristianismo hispano' in: García Villoslada (1979) pp. 41–42.

——. (1979c) 'La iglesia en la España Romana' in: Garcia Villoslada (1979) pp. 372–400.

Sotomayor, M. and Ubiña, J.F. (2005) (Ed.) *El Concilio de Elvira y su Tiempo* (Ed. Univ. de Granada).

Souter, A. (1949) *A Glossary of Later Latin to 600 AD* (Clarendon Press Oxford).

Steimer, B. (1992) *Vertex Traditionis Die Gattung der altchristlichen Kirchenordnungen* (Beihefte zur Zeitschrift für die neutestamentliche Wissenschaft und die Kunde der älteren Kirche Bd. 63, Walter de Gruyter Berlin/New York).

Stemberger, G. (2000) *Jews and Christians in the Holy Land* (T&T Clark Edinburgh).

Stern, M. (1974) *Greek and Latin Authors on Jews and Judaism* 2 vols. (Israel Academy of Sciences Jerusalem).

Stern, P. (1991) *The Biblical Herem A Window on Israel's Religious Experience* (Brown Judaic Studies 211, Atlanta).

Stewart-Sykes, A. (1998) *The Lamb's High Feast Melito, Peri Pascha & the Quartodeciman Paschal Liturgy at Sardis* (Supplement to *Vigiliae Christianae* Vol. XLII, Brill Leiden).

Stillwell, R. (Ed.) (1938) *Antioch-on-the-Orontes II The Excavations 1933–1936* (Published For the Committee for the Excavation of Antioch and its Vicinity, Princeton University Press).

Stökl Ben Ezra, D. (2003) "Whose fast is it? The Ember Days of September and Yom Kippur", in: Becker/Reed (2003) pp. 259–282.

Strubbe, J.H.M. (1994) 'Curses against violation of the grave in Jewish Epitaphs of Asia Minor' in: Henten J.W. van, and Horst, P.W. v.d. (Ed.s) *Studies in Early Jewish Epigraphy* (Arbeiten zur Geschichte des Antiken Judentums und des Urchristentums Vol. 21, Brill Leiden) pp. 70–128.

Suntrup, A. (2001) *Studien zur Politischen Theologie im Frühmittelalterlichen Okzident Di AussageKonziliarer Texte des Gallischen und Iberischen Raumes* (Spanische Forschungen der Görresgesellschaft Bd. 36, Asschendorff Münster).

Tabbernee, W. (2007) *Fake Prophecy and Polluted Sacraments Ecclesiastical and Imperial Reactions to Montanism* (Suppl. Vigiliae Christianiae, Brill Leiden).

Taracena, B. and Huguet, P.B. et al. (1947) *Ars Hispaniae* II (Plus-Ultra Madrid).

Taylor, M. (1995) *Anti-Judaism and Early Christian Identity* (Brill Leiden).

Teja, R. (2002) *La Hispania del Siglo IV* (Edipuglia Bari).

——. (2005) ' "*Exterae gentes*": relaciones con paganos, judíos y herejes en los cánones de Elvira' in: Sotomayor/Ubiña (2005), pp. 197–228.

Trebilco, P.R. (1991) *Jewish Communities in Asia Minor* (Cambridge University Press).

Trebilco, P. (2004) 'The Jews in Asia Minor, 66–c. 235 CE' in: Katz, S. (Ed.) *The Cambridge History of Judaism vol. IV The Late Roman-Rabbinic Period* (Cambridge University Press) pp. 75–82.

Tremel, Y.-B. (1962) 'Du sabbat au jour du Seigneur' in: *Lumière et Vie* 11, pp. 29–49.

Trevett, Chr. (1996) *Montanism* (Cambridge University Press).

Tripolitis, A. (2002) *Religions of the Hellenistic Roman Age* (Eerdmans Michigan).

Turner, C.H. *Ecclesiae Occidentalis Monumenta Antiquissima* I Canones Apostolorum (Oxford 1899).

——. (1915) 'Notes on the Apostolic Constitutions II. The Apostolic Canons' in: *JTS* 16, pp. 523–538.

Ubiña, J.F. (2005) 'Mujer y matrionio en el concilio de Elvira' in: Sotomayor/Ubiña (2005) pp. 275–322.

Ubiña, J. Fernandez (2002) 'La Iglesia y la Formación de la Jerarquía Eclesiástica' in: Teja (2002) pp. 161–204.

Vallicrosa, J.M. (1957) 'Una nueva inscripción Judaica bilingüe en Tarragona', in: *Sefarad* 17, pp. 3–10.

——. (1958) 'Los plomos con inscripción hebraica de 'Ses Fontanelles' (Mallorca) in: *Sefarad* 18, pp. 3–9.

Van Dam, R. (1993) *Saints and their Miracles in late Antique Gaul* (Princeton University Press).

Vanneufville, E. (1996) 'L'Eglise en Provence du Ve au VIIIe siècles' in: *Mélanges de Sciences Religieuses*, pp. 60–81.

Vilella, J. (2002) 'Las Iglesias y las Cristiandades Hispanas: Panorama Prosopográfico' in: Teja (2002), pp. 117–160.

——. (2002b) 'Los cánones de la Hispana atribuidos a un concilio iberitano' in: *Studia Ephemeridis Augustinianum* 78, pp. 545–579.

Vööbus, A. (1979) *The Didascalia Apostolorum in Syriac* II (Corpus Scriptorum Christianorum Orientalium Vol. 407, Scriptores Syri 179, Louvain).

Vouaux, L. (transl.) (1922) *Les Actes de Pierre* (Letouzey et Ané Paris).

Waelkens, M. (1986) *Die Kleinasiatischen Türsteine* (Deutsche Arch. Inst., Philipp von Zabern Mainz am Rhein).

Wallace-Hadrill, D.S. (1982) *Christian Antioch A Study of Early Christian Thought in the East* (Cambridge University Press).

Waszink, J.H. and Winden, J.C.M. van *Tertullianus De Idolatria* (1987) (Supplement to Vigiliae Christianae 1, Brill Leiden).

White, L.M. (1998) 'Regulating fellowship in the communal meal: early Jewish and Christian evidence', in: Nielsen/Nielsen (1998) pp. 177–205.

Wiel, C. v.d. (1991) *History of Canon Law* (Louvain Theological and Pastoral Monographs 5, Peeters Louvain).

Wilken, R.L. (1976) 'Melito, the Jewish community at Sardis and the sacrifice of Isaac' in: *Theological Studies* 37, pp. 53–69.

——. (1983) *John Chrysostom and the Jews* (University of California Press Berkeley).

Woods, D. (1998) 'On the death of the empress Fausta' in: *Greece and Rome* 45, pp. 70–86.

Yarbrough, O.L. (1993) 'Parents and Children in the Jewish Family of antiquity', in: Cohen, S.J.D. *The Jewish Family in Antiquity* (Brown Judaic Studies n. 289, Scholars Press Atlanta) pp. 39–60.

Yuval, I.J. (2006) *Two Nations in your Womb Perceptions of Jews and Christians in Late Antiquity and the Middle Ages* (University of California Press).

Zerfasz, R. (1968) *Die Schriftlesung im Kathedraloffizium Jerusalems* (Liturgiewissensch. Quellen u. Forschungen 48, Aschendorffsche Verlagsbuchh. Münster).

Zetterholm, M. (2003) *The Formation of Christanity in Antioch A social-scientific approach to the separation between Judaism and Christianity* (Routledge London).

Zvi Werblowksy, R.J. and Wigoder, G. (Ed.) (1997) *The Oxford Dictionary of the Jewish Religion* (Oxford University Press).

INDEX

JEWISH AND CHRISTIAN
PERSPECTIVES

1. HOUTMAN, A., M.J.H.M. POORTHUIS and J. SCHWARTZ (eds.). *Sanctity of Time and Space in Tradition and Modernity*. 1998. ISBN 90 04 11233 2
2. POORTHUIS, M.J.H.M. and J. SCHWARTZ (eds.). *Purity and Holiness*. The Heritage of Leviticus. 1999. ISBN 90 04 11418 1
3. KOFSKY, A. *Eusebius of Caesarea against Paganism*. 2000. ISBN 90 04 11642 7
4. TEUGELS, L.M. *Aggadat Bereshit*. Translated from the Hebrew with an Introduction and Notes. 2001. ISBN 90 04 12173 0
5. ROKÉAH, D. *Justin Martyr and the Jews*. 2001. ISBN 90 04 12310 5
6. DEN HOLLANDER, A., U. SCHMID and W. SMELIK (eds.). *Paratext and Megatext as Channels of Jewish and Christian Traditions*. The Textual Markers of Contextualization. 2003. ISBN 90 04 12882 4
7. POORTHUIS, M.J.H.M. and J. SCHWARTZ (eds.). *Saints and Role Models in Judaism and Christianity*. 2004. ISBN 90 04 12614 7
8. FRISHMAN, J., W. OTTEN and G. ROUWHORST (eds.). *Religious Identity and the Problem of Historical Foundation*. The Foundational Character of Authoritative Sources in the History of Christianity and Judaism. 2004. ISBN 90 04 13021 7
9. NOTLEY, R.S. and Z. SAFRAI. *Eusebius, Onomasticon*. A Triglott Edition with Notes and Commentary. 2005. ISBN 0 391 04217 3
10. REULING H. *After Eden*. Church Fathers and Rabbis on Genesis 3:16-21. 2005. ISBN 90 04 14638 5
11. NOTLEY, R.S., M. TURNAGE and B. BECKER (eds.). *Jesus' Last Week*. Jerusalem Studies in the Synoptic Gospels — Volume One. 2006. ISBN 90 04 14790 X
12. POORTHUIS, M.J.H.M. and J. SCHWARTZ (eds.). *A Holy People*. Jewish and Christian Perspectives on Religious Communal Identity. 2006. ISBN 90 04 15052 8
13. RUZER, S. *Mapping the New Testament*. Early Christian Writings as a Witness for Jewish Biblical Exegesis. 2007. ISBN 978 90 04 15892 4
14. VAN ASSELT, W., P. VAN GEEST, D. MÜLLER and Th. SALEMINK (eds.). *Iconoclasm and Iconoclash*. Struggle for Religious Identity. 2007. ISBN 978 90 04 16195 5
15. GERHARDS, A. and L. CLEMENS (eds.). *Jewish and Christian Liturgy and Worship*. New Insights into its History and Interaction. 2007. ISBN 978 90 04 16201 3

16. JACKSON, B.S. *Essays on* Halakhah *in the New Testament.* 2007. ISBN 978 90 04 16273 0

17. POORTHUIS, M.J.H.M., J. SCHWARTZ and J. TURNER (eds). *Interaction between Judaism and Christianity in History, Religion, Art, and Literature.* 2008. ISBN 978 90 04 17150 3

18. GRYPEOU, E. and H. SPURLING (eds). *The Exegetical Encounter between Jews and Christians in Late Antiquity.* 2009. ISBN 978 90 04 17727 7

19. BODDENS HOSANG, F.J.E. *Establishing Boundaries.* Christian-Jewish Relations in Early Council Texts and the Writings of Church Fathers. 2010. ISBN 978 90 04 18255 4

ISSN 1388-2074